THE NEW
RUSSIAN
DIASPORA

Russian Minorities in the Former Soviet Republics

In the wake of the USSR's collapse, more than 25 million Russians found themselves living outside Russian territory. Just as uncertain as their citizenship status was the role they would play in the future—whether as homeless refugees in an unstable Russia or as a minority group of uncertain loyalty in other former Soviet republics.

This volume, prepared under the sponsorship of the Kennan Institute for Advanced Russian Studies, offers a comprehensive and amply documented examination of these questions.

THE NEW RUSSIAN DIASPORA

Russian Minorities in the Former Soviet Republics

Edited by
Vladimir Shlapentokh
Munir Sendich
and Emil Payin

M.E. Sharpe
Armonk, New York
London, England

Library of Congress Cataloging-in-Publication Data

The New Russian diaspora : Russian minorities in the
former Soviet republics / edited by Vladimir Shlapentokh,
Munir Sendich, and Emil Payin.
p.   cm.
Includes bibliographical references and index.
ISBN 1-56324-335-0 — ISBN 1-56324-336-9
1. Russians—Former Soviet republics.
2. Former Soviet republics—Emigration and immigration.
3. Immigrants—Russia (Federation).
I. Shlapentokh, Vladimir. II. Sendich, Munir. III. Payin, Emil.
DK35.5N48   1994
305.891′71047—dc20   94-727
CIP

Printed in the United States of America

The paper used in this publication meets the minimum requirements of
American National Standard for Information Sciences—
Permanence of Paper for Printed Library Materials,
ANSI Z 39.48-1984.

MV (c) 10   9   8   7   6   5   4   3   2   1
MV (p) 10   9   8   7   6   5   4   3   2   1

Contents

About the Editors and the Contributors

Vladimir Shlapentokh is professor of sociology at Michigan State University.

Munir Sendich is professor of literature at Michigan State University.

Emil Payin is director of the Department of Interethnic Relations under the president of the Russian Federation and is a member of the Presidential Council.

Ramazan Abdulatipov is vice chairman of the Federal Council of the Russian Federation.

Vladimir Bruter is director of the firm Agroinvest, Kishinev, Moldova.

Nikolai Churilov is president of the firm Sotsis-Gallup in Kiev, Ukraine.

Irina Dement'eva is a journalist with the newspaper *Izvestiia*.

Natalia Dinello is a graduate student in sociology at the University of Pittsburgh.

Leokadia Drobizheva is head of the department of the social psychology of interethnic relations at the Institute of Ethnology and Anthropology, Russian Academy of Sciences.

Vladis Gaidys is director of the Market and Opinion Research Center in Vilnius, Lithuania.

Evgenii Golovakha is head of the department of social psychology at the Institute of Sociology, Ukrainian Academy of Sciences.

Lev Gudkov is head of the department of methodology of public opinion research at the All-Russian Center for the Study of Public Opinion, Moscow.

Roman Levita is at the Central Economic–Mathematical Institute, Russian Academy of Sciences, Moscow.

Mikhail Loiberg is a professor at the Moscow Open University.

Tatiana Marchenko is a senior fellow in the Institute of Socioeconomic Problems of the Population, Russian Academy of Sciences.

Vladimir Mukomel is chief analyst in the Department of Interethnic Relations under the president of the Russian Federation.

Sergei Nikolaev is chairman of the department of sociology at Tashkent University in Uzbekistan.

Natalia Panina is head of the department of methodology of sociological research, Institute of Sociology, Ukrainian Academy of Sciences.

Galina Soldatova is a fellow of the Institute of Ethnology and Anthropology, Russian Academy of Sciences.

Vladimir Solonar is a deputy of the Moldova parliament and the head of the parliament's Committee on Human Rights and Ethnic Relations.

Aleksandr Susokolov is head of the department of ethnic demography and sociology at the Institute of Education, Moscow.

List of Tables

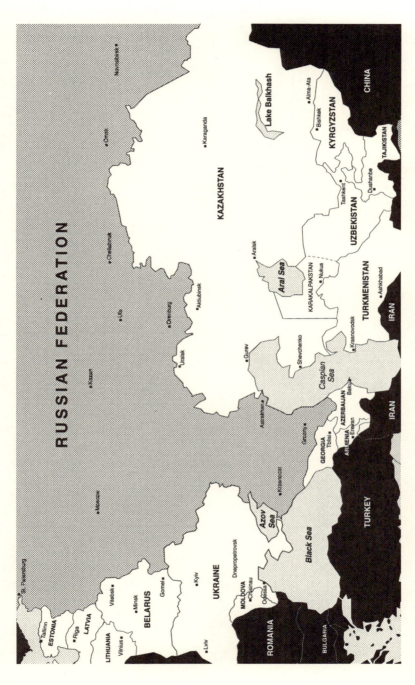

THE RUSSIAN FEDERATION AND THE NEWLY INDEPENDENT STATES

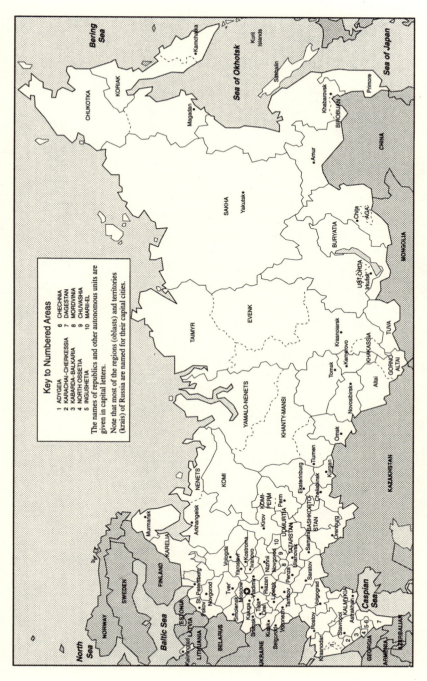

Key to Numbered Areas

1 ADYGEIA	6 CHECHNIA
2 KARACHAI-CHERKESSIA	7 DAGESTAN
3 KABARDA-BALKARIA	8 MORDOVINIA
4 NORTH OSSETIA	9 CHUVASHIA
5 INGUSHETIA	10 MARI-EL

The names of republics and other autonomous units are given in capital letters.

Note that most of the regions (oblasts) and territories (krais) of Russia are named for their capital cities.

THE RUSSIAN FEDERATION AND ITS INTERNAL DIVISIONS

xvii

Preface

It is clear that by 1989–90, Russian minorities in the republics had become one of the most crucial political agents in the process that ultimately led to the death of the Soviet empire and the turbulent events that ensued on the territory of the former Soviet Union.

Prior to 1987, Russian minorities within other national entities had not been much in evidence as independent political agents. In the 1970s, of course, in association with the growth of nationalist sentiments in certain organizations and the increasing autonomy of local officials, the Russians had already begun to experience the eclipse of their Big Brother role and even discern evidence of subtle discrimination. But serious efforts on the part of Ukrainian nationalists to strengthen their position (recall the arrests that took place in Kiev and Lvov, the Ivan Dziuba affair, the persecution of the poet Lina Kostenko, and other incidents) were ruthlessly crushed by Brezhnev.

At first Russian minorities reacted with surprise to the growth after 1985 of local nationalism which was, after all, unprecedented in Soviet history. Then came the realization that their lives in the far-flung regions where many of them had been born or had lived for decades would never be the same. New processes required of every Russian a reevaluation of fundamental conditions that most had never even questioned. This secondary ideologization of the Russian population (which took place in one form or another among all Soviet people, even the most politically naive) made the differentiation of this minority inevitable. This happened very differently in various regions, depending on specific conditions.

The idea of holding a conference on the fate of Russian minorities in the USSR was conceived in 1989. To those who realized as early as the 1987 events in Nagorno-Karabakh that the Soviet Union's ways were irreconcilable with democratic processes (one of the authors published an article on this subject at the beginning of 1987), it had already become clear that in many parts of the country the Russians' status would change from that of representatives of an imperial power to that of a minority facing discrimination, like so many other ethnic minorities in nondemocratic societies.

It was further evident that Russian minorities would soon constitute an urgent political, social, and economic problem not only in the USSR (at the time no one had counted on such a swift end to the Soviet empire) but worldwide. It seemed to us that a conference on the fate of these minorities would contribute to the search for humane solutions to this difficult problem and that the conference materials, presented herein, would prove useful to American as well as Soviet policy makers.

We were attracted to this topic not only by its practical significance but also by its theoretical potential as a case study of citizens of an imperial nation becoming a minority in its constituent provinces almost overnight. One need only recall the Roman or, more recently, the British and French empires to realize that the fate of Russians in the former Soviet national republics is not unprecedented in world history—consider the experience of the French in Algeria or the English in Rhodesia, to name only two recent instances. What could be more inviting to the sociologist or historian than such rich possibilities for comparative analysis?

There is yet another theoretical attraction in this subject—its link to the problem of mass movements, a topic that grew very popular in the West in the 1970s, chiefly under the influence of the left-wing movements of the preceding decade. A vast number of studies published since those years have examined the conditions under which oppressed minorities shift from passivity and reconciliation with the existing order to resistance and the establishment of organizations capable of directing the defense of their interests.

In this sense, Russian minorities present an outstanding opportunity for the examination of new aspects of this problem. Truly, nowhere else has the transition in status from ruling nation to discriminated-against minority been so nearly instantaneous as in the USSR in 1990–91. As late as 1989, Russians in any given republic controlled the KGB, the Communist Party, and the ideological apparatus—not to mention the military and the economy. Hostility toward Russians was one of the gravest crimes against the system and actually manifested itself quite rarely, especially in the social sphere. Then, before our very eyes, there took place a *saltomortale* comparable only to that which occurred at the time of the French Revolution of 1789–93 and the Russian Revolution of 1917, when members of formerly ruling classes became outcasts overnight.

How then will Russians living in the former Soviet republics react to the new situation into which they have been plunged? Will they try to fight to preserve their special status in the republics? Will they resist open discrimination? Will they form their own organizations, their own movements, for the defense of their rights?

It is patently obvious (and so we thought when we conceived this research) that Russians cannot comprise a homogeneous contingent. Among them will doubtless appear groups whose behavior will differentiate them sharply from one another. As was clear to us even then, at that point another most interesting theoretical issue arises—the differences among Russians living in various republics in various cultural environments.

The study of Russian minorities offers the chance to turn again and again to one of the most complex and fascinating problems in social science: man's adaptation to changing conditions of existence and the proportions and ways in which old cultural traditions and new environments intermix. What do Russians in the republics consider themselves to be—Russians above all, representatives of Great Russia, or citizens of new governmental constructs? Who has it right in this case—the culturologists or the Marxists? Which has the stronger influence on people, their mentality or their behavior—old cultural traditions or a way of life they are forced to adopt?

No matter what the answers to these questions, it is clear that the national environment in which Russian minorities have found themselves has had an effect on them. But then another question arises: in which republics is this influence lesser or greater? A comparison of Central Asia with the Baltic states seems particularly promising from this standpoint.

Another important theoretical research goal has been to study the mutual interaction among *democratic* (or panhuman, to use a term from the era of perestroika), *economic*, and *national* (cultural-historical and religious) values. The conflict among these values comprises the essence of many processes that have occurred and are occurring in the world. This means that within the framework of a national movement, forces that bring one of these three types of values to the fore are always at work. This conflict, without doubt, can be found in all national movements within the territory of the former USSR, as well as in the Russian diaspora. The conference was intended to shed light on this issue, if only to offer an approximate understanding of the influence of these values on the behavior of Russian minorities.

The research under consideration appears attractive for studying the roles of the above-mentioned three types of values for yet another reason. No less than a score of nationalist movements of significant strength existed in the USSR. Comparing them, however, like comparing various ethnic regions, is a most complex and laborious task. Indeed, direct comparison of different regions—for example, Estonia and Turkmenistan, Moldova and Georgia—could hardly be productive within the framework of a single research design, even a large-scale one. By contrast, the existence of one and the same minority group—Russians— in various ethnic regions of a single political and economic system in a state of radical transformation presents a unique opportunity to distinguish (only relatively, of course) the role of universal from cultural-historical variables and their effect on the intermixing of democratic and national values.

The use of Russian minorities as a unique general signifier allows for the establishment of a known comparability of all regions of the country with each other. Indeed, the relationship of national movements to local Russians reflects the role of purely national, economic, and democratic values in an ethnic region, degree of Westernization, degree of homogeneity of the national movement, intensity of opposition to the center, and much else. It was determined that the fundamental actors in the research would be:

(1) the national movement dominating a region in a given period and usually encompassing the chief nationalist organizations: as a rule such "national fronts" are characterized by a relative (as opposed to extreme) tolerance with respect to minorities and fundamentally oppose the use of violence in the struggle for independence;

(2) extremist nationalist movements which call for the expulsion of minorities and the use of any and all means in the struggle for independence;

(3) old legal and political structures (chiefly the party *apparat* and the officials of all-Union enterprises);

(4) illegal structures;

(5) the Russian minority, consisting of:

(a) long-time Russian residents of the region (chiefly those who were born there);

(b) Russians living in the region a comparatively short time;

(6) Russian political organizations;

(7) the army and officers' families.

It was on these actors that the authors of the conference program centered their attention.

At the same time, the authors of the study felt that the decisive role in determining the position of a Russian minority with respect to ongoing events was most likely played by variables describing:

(1) the demographic composition of the region;

(2) the economic situation;

(3) the degree of Westernization;

(4) interethnic relations;

(5) the nature of the national consciousness and the native population's nationalist movement;

(6) the nature of the Russian minority's nationalist movement.

Convinced of the considerable significance of the Russian minority question, we set to work planning the conference in 1990. First, one of the editors of this volume prepared a program for a survey of Russian and non-Russian regions of the USSR. This plan was presented to the Moscow-based All-Russian Center for the Study of Public Opinion for the implementation of joint research. We knew the center was also interested in this problem and had already completed several surveys that included questions pertinent to it.

Lev Gudkov proved to be the colleague from the center who would be heading the project from the Soviet side (a circumstance which was most gratifying to one of the present authors, who had known Lev back when he was a graduate student at the Institute of Sociology in the late sixties). Interest in the research on the part of Tat´iana Zaslavskaia, who was then director of the center, and Iurii Levada, head of the theoretical department—two sociologists who are highly respected internationally—could only increase the enthusiasm of those taking part in the project.

It happened that the survey took place in the middle of 1991; it was begun before the August putsch and completed afterward. This circumstance, needless to say, worked unfavorably against the correlative potential of the data, but it gave the research a unique value, for it "captured" the problem at a historic turning point—the fall of one of history's mightiest empires.

No doubt the survey is far from perfect for other reasons as well. The selection of respondents by nationality alone presents a most complex problem, but the sociologists' experience with this type of survey is more than modest. Certainly the center did everything it could, but this does not alleviate all concerns about the selection, although there is reason enough to be assured that it did not unduly influence the results of the analysis.

A greater concern has been raised as to the sincerity of the respondents. The survey was conducted at a time when Russians almost everywhere in the republics, even in Ukraine, were already feeling a real threat from growing local nationalism and were concerned about how their answers might influence their position. Therefore, the data in all likelihood downplay Russians' anxiety about their situation and exaggerate their loyalty to the republics and their authorities.

It must be kept in mind more generally that this book reflects the situation as it existed in 1991–92. Of course, many problems analyzed here, such as discrimination against Russians and the emigration of Russians from the former Soviet republics, are of no less significance now.

Another of these problems is the role of Russian minorities in the political arena and the impact of this factor on pro-imperial tendencies in Russian politics. In fact, in 1992 there arose a Russian irredentism—that is, a movement for the agglomeration of all Russians into a single state. In that year and the next, it became evident that Russia's relations with Ukraine, Moldova, Kazakhstan, and the Baltic states, with their huge Russian populations, as well as other new states, were far from settled, nor were the borders between them completely stabilized. Russian irredentism (some Moscow authors prefer to speak of a Russian variant of Zionism) has already exerted a palpable influence on events in Ukraine, the Baltic states, and Moldova. It is quite evident that the "Russian problem," which has already become an international one, will exert a considerable influence on events in the former Soviet Union and on political processes in Russia for many years into the future.

The research planners and the authors of these chapters also did not foresee the scale of destructive processes going on in the former republics—for example, in Tajikistan, where Russian emigration swelled to become a veritable flood of refugees. The authors have virtually ignored the process of regionalization which has since unfolded in the Russian Federation, and will materially affect the fate of Russians living in ethnic regions of Russia itself.

The reader should also bear in mind that there are great differences among the authors in their attitudes toward various issues relating to the role of the Russians in the Soviet Union and in the Russian Empire. In some cases the authors have chosen to use different statistics to describe the same phenomena. It is the hope of the editors that such pluralism of positions and methods will result not so much in confusion and contradiction as in fullness and three-dimensionality of the overall picture.

We hope that, in spite of prognostic gaps as well as other shortcomings, this book (which is also being published in Russia) will prove useful to Russian and American readers alike. Of course, we are very proud that this book is based on materials from the first conference, in Russia or the United States, dedicated to this crucial problem.

Vladimir Shlapentokh
and Munir Sendich

Acknowledgments

The editors would like to express their profound gratitude to the many individuals and institutions that helped to make this volume a reality. Their gratitude goes, first of all, to Michigan State University and to the Woodrow Wilson Center, Kennan Institute for Advanced Studies, in Washington, D.C. (Dr. Blair Ruble, director), for sponsoring the conference "Russian Minorities in the Former Soviet Union," which was held at Michigan State University on May 22–24, 1992. The editors are deeply indebted for conference support to the Soros Foundation, the MSU Foundation, and the following at Michigan State University: Dr. Gill Lym, Office of the Dean, International Studies and Programs; Office of the Dean, College of Social Science; Office of the Dean, College of Communication; Center for Advanced Study of International Development; James Madison College; Department of Sociology; Department of Community Health Science; and Department of Linguistics, Germanic, Slavic, Asian and African Languages; and to one private source, Mr. Edward Klein of New York.

Additional assistance in the conversion of the conference papers into this volume has been extended to the editors by the following colleagues at Michigan State University, without whose support this volume could not have been completed: Dr. Kenneth Corey, Dean of the College of Social Science; Dr. John W. Eadie, Dean of the College of Arts and Letters; and Dr. Norman Graham, Director of the Center for European and Russian Studies.

Finally, the editors would like to thank Ms. Tatiana Marchenko for the first draft of the English text and Mr. Lawrence Cosentino for his scrupulous proofreading of several drafts and his selfless efforts to prepare the texts for publication.

We would like to express our gratitude to Ms. Patricia Kolb for her support of this project. Her invaluable comments and suggestions greatly improved the quality of the manuscript. We would also like to thank Ms. Kathryn Szczepanska for her work as copyeditor. Her help is immensely appreciated.

I

Formation of a Diaspora

Problems of Russian-Speaking Minorities in
the Context of the Formation and Disintegration
of the Russian-Soviet Empire

1

The Empire and the Russians

Historical Aspects

Roman Levita and Mikhail Loiberg

1. The Formation and Colonization of the Russian Empire

Despite the fact that Russia lagged behind the countries of Western Europe both socially and economically, it entered upon the road of colonial seizures in step with such classic states of Western colonialism as Britain and Holland—that is to say, earlier than France and a bit later than the first colonial powers, Spain and Portugal. It was in the mid-sixteenth century that Russia seized the Kazan Khanate (1552) and the Astrakhan Khanate (1556)—the Tatar states on the Volga. So although the Russian Empire was not formally established until 1727, when Peter the Great was proclaimed emperor, its actual formation began much earlier, immediately after the setting up of the centralized Moscow state, in which Russians constituted the majority (6–7 million people).[1] During the Stalin era, the formation of the Russian colonial empire was considered a progressive phenomenon, hence the persistent efforts to prove that all the nations and nationalities constituting the empire joined voluntarily. After Stalin's death the approach to this question became more delicate: although the fact of annexation by force was recognized, it was also assumed that the progressive consequences of annexation compensated for the bloodshed. Special emphasis was laid on the assertion that as parts of the empire, these nations acquired an opportunity to enter with Russia upon a new, communist epoch in 1917.[2]

From Table 1.1 it is clear that the methods used to form the Russian colonial empire in no way differed from those used to form other empires. Within four centuries, five independent states (the Kazan, Astrakhan, Siberian, and Kokand khanates, and the Shamil Imamate) were seized by force, as were eight colonies and protectorates of other states (Latvia, Estonia, Karelia, the Crimea, Armenia, Azerbaijan, Bessarabia, and Finland). Moreover, territory of the sovereign Polish state was annexed, and the tsarist protectorate was forcibly established over two

Table 1.1

The Formation of the Russian Colonial Empire (stages and methods)

Century	Method of Annexation				
	Conquest of independent states	Forced annexation of independent states	Conquest of other countries' colonies and dependent states	Establishment of protectorates	Peaceful annexation
16th	Kazan, Astrakhan, and Siberian khanates				
17th					left-bank Ukraine
18th			Latvia, Estonia, Karelia, Crimean Khanate		Kazakhstan (except southern part)
19th	Kokand Khanate, Shamil Imamate	Kingdom of Poland (Congress of Vienna)	Armenia, Azerbaijan, Bessarabia, Finland	Bukhara, Khiva	Georgia

other states—Bukhara and Khiva. Only left-bank Ukraine, Kazakhstan, and Georgia were joined to Russia in a comparatively peaceful way.

A peculiar feature of the Russian Empire was not only its extreme ethnic and religious diversity, but also its variety of social, economic, and political structures. For centuries the mother country was an agrarian state. Even after serfdom was abolished, there remained in Russia such vestiges of feudalism as large landlords' estates and village communes, which were inimical to the economic independence of peasants, the development of the class structure, and so on.

Ukraine, the main European colony, which abolished serfdom simultaneously with Great Russia, was distinguished by a higher level of productivity in the countryside (thanks to higher soil fertility) and more advanced industrial development (the Donetsk and Krivoi Rog basins, Kharkov). Poland and especially the Baltic states and Finland retained well-pronounced features of the West European–type of civilization based on complete freedom of the producer.

Some parts of the Central Asian colonies were so-called river civilizations, where the predominant irrigated farming remained barely above the ancient level; others engaged in nomadic cattle breeding. The numerous peoples of the Far North and the Far East remained nomadic cattle breeders, hunters, and fishermen, as they had been for centuries.

The colonial policy of the tsars was based on three closely interwoven principles: unification, bureaucratization, and Russification. With rare exceptions (Finland, for example), the Russian Empire was administered from a unified center in accordance with common principles. It was divided into provinces (gubernias) or regions, which either were subordinated directly to St. Petersburg or were parts of the territories ruled by governors general or vicegerents. The core of the administration was made up of Russian officials, although the tsarist government did not insist on ethnic purity of the state apparatus, which included many Russified representatives of colonial peoples who earnestly served the autocracy. The state administration of all the regions of the empire was colonial not only in essence but also in form. The laws of the mother country were binding throughout the empire, and bookkeeping and court procedures were conducted only in Russian. However, the imperial system of administration was more flexible than could be surmised from its unitarian form. The mother country also sought the support of the local aristocracy, which enjoyed the same rights as the Russian nobility.

The policy toward the local clergy was also rather flexible. Although Christianity was the dominant religion in the Russian Empire, Islam and some other religious denominations were protected by the state, and their clergy had the rights of government officials.[3] As the local aristocracy and clergy were always held in high esteem by the native population, their inclusion in the system of imperial administration gave colonialism a degree of legitimacy.

Although all the Russian colonies were involved in the Russian market to some extent, they could easily do without the mother country. The vast natural resources of the empire had not even been properly surveyed, much less exploited. Thus the presence of the Russians in the colonies was not economically necessary. They were needed for the purpose of administering the Russian Empire, for only the Russian nation was large enough to serve as a pillar for tsarist power.

Niccolo Machiavelli described three methods of holding a conquered country: a sovereign could move there, as did the Turkish sultans who moved to conquered Byzantium; he could send large numbers of troops into the country; or he could "set up colonies in one or two places which would tie in the new lands with the conqueror-state."[4]

The Russian Empire, with its many possessions, was too big for the Russian sovereigns to visit, let alone dwell in. It is well known that the tsars never visited Turkestan and many other regions. However, the tsarist government managed rather adroitly to combine the methods of bringing in troops and organizing Russian settlements in national territories. The instrument was the Cossacks, who were both soldiers and land tillers.

Cossacks were a privileged military-agrarian estate, a unique Russian form of border defense. For their military service to the state (which lasted from 18 to 38 years of age, including four years of active service), each Cossack detachment was granted land, which it passed over to Cossack villages. The average plot of land of a Cossack family ranged from 9 to 23 desiatinas, while the average peasant's family plot was much less.[5]

Cossack troops provided those colonies that should, according to Machiavelli, tie the new lands with the conqueror-state. Eleven Cossack detachments—the Don, Kuban, Terek, Ural, Astrakhan, Orenburg, Semireche, Siberian, Baikal, Amur, and Ussuri Cossacks (4.4 million people at the beginning of the twentieth century)—were stationed in such a way as to be able to supervise, by force of arms, the Asian colonies inhabited by non-Slavic peoples. It seems that the present-day champions of the Russian Cossacks fail to realize that to revive them fully would imply restoring to them (at the very end of the twentieth century!) the privileges of a military class.

The economic colonization of these lands by the Russian people was achieved in several stages. First was the movement of peasants, which was especially active during the colonization of the Volga region, Bashkiriia, Siberia, and the Far East, a consequence of which was the native peoples' loss of part of their land. For instance, the Inspection Commission sent to the Turkestan Territory by the Senate noted that the Kazakhs and Kyrgyz had been banished from their lands en masse and their settlements and mosques razed.[6]

Adding to the flow of popular colonization was the movement to national territories of traders and handicraftsmen, which was especially pronounced in the Volga region in the nineteenth and early twentieth centuries.

A third element in this flow consisted of skilled Russian workers moving to colonies where formerly nonexistent industries began to be developed. For instance, in the late 1890s Russians constituted from 18 to 20 percent of the workforce in the Baku oil fields, primarily highly skilled repairmen and experienced machine operators. At the same time the unskilled labor force at the oil fields was made up not of the local Turkic population (their proportion did not exceed 12 to 13 percent), but of migrants—Iranians and Lezgins. In 1914, among the workers at the Turkestan plants and factories, 23 percent were Russians, 75 percent of whom were highly skilled machine operators and repairmen.[7] But the greatest number of Russian workers, especially from the overpopulated provinces of the central Black Soil region, moved to the European colonies, mainly to Ukraine and its Donetsk and Krivoi Rog regions. Such former Kursk residents as the locksmith Nikita Khrushchev and the metalworker Ilia Brezhnev (father of Leonid Brezhnev) were typical sights in the mines and the iron and steel shops of Ukraine. Russian migrants constituted the major portion of the workers employed in heavy and hazardous production. They actually colonized this territory, thus creating a serious problem for the future independent Ukraine (according to statistics, Russians constitute almost half the population of the Don basin).

A special flow was made up of Russian peasants who moved to the colonies (especially in the Caucasus) under pressure of religious persecution. These were Old Believers, Molokans, and representatives of other sects. They settled in compact groups, formed their own communities, and lived in seclusion.

Finally, many Russian intellectuals—doctors, teachers, and engineers—also moved to the colonies.

There were many reasons why Russians were not evenly distributed among the native population. At the beginning of the century the situation was summed up in this way: "Russian Bukhara, Russian Samarkand, Russian Tashkent, Russian Kokand, Russian Margilan side by side with native Samarkand, native Bokhara, native Margilan. . . . The ways of life of a Russian and an Asian are so unlike each other, are so difficult for those who are not accustomed to them, that the best way to live is, so to say, without interfering in each other's life."[8]

Very often Russian officials lived in genuine colonial settlements. A vivid example is the Turkestan town of Skobelev (now Fergana), which was built by Russians, and in which natives were not allowed. When they lived in accommodations rented from the local residents, Russian officials were in a state of "informal settlement."

Cossack villages were usually separated from the native settlements by a large river, the name of which was usually adopted by the Cossack troops. For example, Cossack villages were situated on the left bank of the Terek River; the Chechen auls were on the right bank. In the case of colonies whose populations were Slavic (Ukraine, Belarus, Poland) or non-Slavic but Christian (the Baltic states, Georgia, Armenia), the Russian migrants lived among the native population, but mostly in big cities.

The character of relations between Russian migrants and the native population depended mostly on the social status of the settlers from the mother country and the civilization type of the colonial region.

Russian peasants who moved to colonies because of persecution on religious grounds lived mostly in seclusion. Their contacts with the indigenous population were minimal.

The attitude of the Cossacks to the indigenous population was ambivalent: on the one hand, natives were seen as an enemy (at least potentially), and on the other, as partners in a peaceful economic life. The Cossacks, especially in the Caucasus, maintained rather close business relations with the natives. Leo Tolstoy, who lived for a long time among the Cossacks along the Terek River, wrote in his story "The Cossacks" that the best weapons were obtained from the Mountaineers (Chechens, Kabard, etc.) and the best horses bought or stolen from them. The Cossack respected a Mountaineer more than a Russian soldier or a Russian settler, but for him only a Cossack was a real man.

Russian urban dwellers—mostly artisans, handicraftsmen, petty traders, and so on —often had to reckon with local "native" competitors. That is why a hostile and arrogant attitude toward the indigenous population, especially non-Christians, was more widespread among these people than among peasant settlers.

Although Soviet social science labored persistently to create the myth of an idyllic "fraternal union" between Russian settlers and the indigenous populations of the colonies, in fact it was far from the truth, even in Ukraine, the colony closest to the Russians in ethnicity. One would expect that, having close everyday contacts with Ukrainians, the Russian workers would learn the Ukrainian language. Yet, Nikita Khrushchev, a former Kursk resident who lived and worked in Ukraine half his life, failed to learn to speak and write Ukrainian; the same was true of Leonid Brezhnev, who was born there.

Some of the Russian skilled workers in the colonies were under the strong influence of imperial ideology. It was at enterprises in Tiflis (now Tbilisi) and other cities of Transcaucasia that the first groups of the Union of the Russian People and similar Black Hundred organizations were formed. By contrast, those Russian workers who supported revolutionaries were opposed to colonialist policies.

Imperial rule in the colonies rested on officialdom, to which the Christian clergy also belonged. In Turkestan and other Muslim colonies, nonofficial relationships between Russian functionaries and the local population were practically nonexistent. In Ukraine, Transcaucasia, Poland, and even in the Baltic states, Russian officials had rather close relations with the local aristocracy and rich city dwellers. Mixed marriages were also common.

Naturally, the administration was the venue of the Petersburg-based policy of Russification of the colonies. Especially active in this respect were the two last Russian emperors. As George Fedotov justly remarked, as "pupils and victims of reactionary Slavophilism, they did much to hasten the future disintegration of their empire."[9]

The numerically weak democratically minded intellectuals in the colonies did their best not to identify themselves with government policy. The enlightened activities of these intellectuals (e.g., the setting up of national schools, hospitals, and first-aid stations) were analogous to the work of the missionaries in the colonies of West European states. It has long been stated that in the Russian Empire the Russians were not in fact an imperial people since, first, they gained nothing from their position as the ruling nation, and second, they did not share the imperial ambitions of the elite.

It should be noted that the living standards of the Russians living in the mother country and in the colonies were different. For instance, the standard of living of Russian peasants in the non–Black Soil zone was as a rule lower than that of the Estonian, Latvian, and Ukrainian peasants, while in Siberia the Russian settlers lived better. The living standards of the Cossacks were much higher than those of their Chuvash neighbors, and the land tiller in the not-so-rich non–Black Soil Russia was also richer than his Chuvash neighbor.

As for the issue of imperial ambition, it should be pointed out that although Russian people did not share the ambitions of the tsars and bureaucrats, they freely shed their own blood as well as the blood of other nations in fighting for these ambitions and conquering many other peoples and states on the tsar's behalf.

2. Political and Economic Forms of Russian-Soviet Colonial Expansion

The disintegration of the Russian Empire began after the February Revolution of 1917. Although the taking of power by the Bolsheviks accelerated this process, it was not the root cause. By 1917 the Russian Empire, which as a member of the Entente was technically undefeated in the world war, had in fact suffered defeat. In the course of military hostilities it had lost Poland and a significant part of the Baltic territory. Having overthrown the autocracy, the February Revolution of 1917 greatly weakened the imperial center, and the October coup dealt it a fresh blow.

In the period from 1917 to 1920, national independence was proclaimed by such countries as Poland, Finland, Estonia, Latvia, Lithuania, Ukraine, Belarus, Georgia, Armenia, Azerbaijan, and other colonies of the Russian Empire. Russia also lost real power over Turkestan. As a result, at the height of the Civil War the Soviet Republic incorporated only 25 provinces of Central Russia.

Nevertheless, by the end of the Civil War the Bolsheviks had managed to win back the majority of former colonies of the Russian Empire, with the exception of Poland, Lithuania, Latvia, Estonia, Finland, and Bessarabia. The actual preservation of the old empire (under new auspices) had become possible thanks to the effective nationalities policy of the Bolsheviks. The Bolsheviks proclaimed the "right of nations to self-determination," while the White movement fought under the despised slogan of "united and indivisible Russia." The right of nations to self-determination happened to be a very useful fiction for the Communists of

Russia, since the Communists in the former colonies were advocating unification with Russia. On the whole, these tactics were effective. It was much more difficult to structure the new empire. And here again the Bolsheviks resorted to fiction.

Poland, Finland, Lithuania, Latvia, Estonia, and Bessarabia having withdrawn, the following states (allegedly sovereign, but governed by the Bolsheviks from a single center) were formed: the Russian Soviet Federated Socialist Republic (RSFSR), the Ukrainian and Belorussian soviet socialist republics, and the Transcaucasian Soviet Federated Socialist Republic.

The Russian Federation incorporated the following autonomous republics: Bashkir, Tatar, Kazakh (called Kirgiz until 1925), Dagestan, Mountain, Crimean, and Turkestan. There were also autonomous regions, such as the Chuvash, Kalmyk, Mari, Komi, and others. The Transcaucasian Federation united Azerbaijan, Georgia, and Armenia, which had the status of autonomous republics.

Although Ukraine, Belarus, and the Transcaucasian Federation were legally independent, power in these republics rested solely with the Communist Party (Bolsheviks), whose members maintained strict obedience to the decisions and instructions of Moscow. Party unity was augmented by military unity, for the supposedly independent Soviet republics had no armed forces of their own.

In light of the above, the differences between Lenin and Stalin concerning the structure of the Union of Soviet Socialist Republics—much emphasized in the Soviet scientific literature since the time of Nikita Khrushchev—seem largely exaggerated. Stalin was of the opinion that Ukraine, Belarus, and the republics of Transcaucasia should enter the Russian Soviet Federated Socialist Republic as autonomous formations. His basic argument emphasized the need to ensure the unity of the state apparatus. Lenin was for the union of the Russian Federation with other republics along federal lines and at a higher level. He feared that in case of autonomization the Russian state apparatus would oppress the populations of the national republics.

Certainly, Lenin's model of a federative state was more flexible, but it differed very little from Stalin's in its unitarian essence. While Stalin's unitarianism was implemented through the hierarchy of the state officialdom, Lenin's relied on rigidly centralized party structures. Their contemporaries were more keenly aware of this than researchers of later periods. For instance, at the Twelfth Party Congress (1923), after the official victory of Lenin's approach, Filipp Makharadze, a prominent Georgian Bolshevik, stated: "Here there was much talk about independent Soviet republics. . . . Now everybody realizes what kind of independence it is. We have one party, one central body, whose decisions, in the final analysis, are binding on all the republics, even the smallest ones. Everything, up to the appointment of top officials, is the prerogative of this central body. So what kind of independence is this? The notion is absolutely unclear."[10]

Within the USSR, Russia did not formally play the role of mother country, with its attendant advantages. Still, the omnipotent center was objectively and correctly associated with Russia. The center was the arsenal of party cadres for all the national regions of the country. The decisive role in the party bodies—and consequently, in the state apparatus of the entire Soviet Union—was played by Russians and Russianized nationals who were not from among the indigenous population of the particular region.

Data made public at the Fifteenth Party Congress (1927) showed that the percentage of Russians in the administration of the national regions of the Russian Federation was extremely high (see Table 1.2), and the closer to the top, the higher.[11] Even in Ukraine and Azerbaijan, where the percentage of Russians in the administrative apparatus was lower than that of the indigenous nationality (by 3.5 and 1.5 times, respectively), Russian officials were numerically stronger in the capitals.

In the 1920s and 1930s the predominance of Russians was not the result of a discriminatory nationalities policy; it simply reflected the objective conditions of the formation of a Soviet government apparatus in the localities. With time the percentage of representatives of the indigenous population in the management apparatus of both union and autonomous republics grew. However, it would be wrong to assume that the decisive role of the Russians in the state and party apparatus both in the center and in the localities gradually weakened. Russians still held key party jobs in the national regions (by the end of the 1940s Jews, Latvians, and to a certain extent Armenians, who had once played a significant role, were removed from such posts). True, Russians acted mostly as "grey cardinals": the party first secretary was elected (actually, appointed by Moscow) from among the indigenous population, but all power was in the hands of the Moscow-appointed second secretary, who was Russian by nationality.

Maniacal great-power Russian chauvinism did not in fact become the official ideology until World War II. It is worth mentioning that in the new anthem of the Soviet Union adopted in 1944 there was nothing about the voluntary unification of independent republics. On the contrary, what was said was that the republics were eternally united into this Union by "great Rus." The true apotheosis of chauvinism was Stalin's toast at the reception on the occasion of the victory over Germany: "I would like, first and foremost, to drink to the health of the Russian people, for they are the most outstanding nation of all the nations comprising the Soviet Union. . . . I would like to drink to the health of the Russian people not only because they are the guiding force, but because they are distinguished by clear mind, staunch character, and patience."[12]

These words sent the unequivocal message that Russians were far superior to the other peoples inhabiting the Soviet Union. This speech resulted in a veritable explosion of chauvinism in the country. Later, in the period preceding Stalin's death, the mass media and "scientific" publications started to insist on the primacy of Russia and Russians throughout world history. All outstanding discoveries—from the law of the preservation of matter to the invention of aircraft—were attributed to Russians.

Table 1.2

National Composition of Employees of the Administrative Apparatus in the Autonomous Formations of the Russian Federation (1927)

	Nationality of administrators (in %)	
Republics	Russians	Indigenous nationality
Tatar Republic	65.8	25.5
including the capital	73.0	19.4
Crimean Republic	60.7	16.1
including the capital	57.6	12.1
Kazakh Republic	70.3	16.5
including the capital and provincial centers	72.5	13.5
Dagestan Republic	38.4	31.9
including the capital	58.9	18.0
Uzbek Republic	61.9	24.7
Karelian Republic	80.7	10.3
including the capital	86.5	4.8
Bashkir Republic	65.5	8.5
including the capital	77.2	4.2
Volga German Republic	37.0	48.9
including the capital	52.5	29.4
Buriat-Mongolian Republic	73.8	14.1
including the capital	81.2	4.3

In the 1940s, the declared internationalism used to disguise the imperial essence of the USSR was shunted to the background, if not discarded altogether. With the stroke of a pen, Stalin did away with national autonomous republics and regions without giving a thought to world opinion, to say nothing of the distorted public opinion at home. The Kalmyk, Checheno-Ingush, Kabardino-Balkar (only Kabardinian remained), and Volga German autonomous republics disappeared from the map. Union republics were threatened with the same fate. As part of a political calculus, in 1940 the Karelian Autonomous Republic was transformed into the Karelo-Finnish Union Republic; in 1956 it was again reduced to an autonomous republic within the Russian Federation. The year 1921 saw the appearance of the Tuva People's Republic. When in 1944 the puppet leadership of Tuva adopted a decision on voluntary unification with the USSR, this sovereign state received the hollow status of autonomous region. How naive and shallow would all the debates over autonomization and federation seem today!

The interests of the empire required that Russia be given economic priority. Even propagandistic Soviet official statistics testify that the widely advertised industrial upsurge of the national republics at the expense of Russia's interests is mostly a myth.

First, the major part of the USSR's industrial production was concentrated in

Russia. Second, a significant percentage of industrial enterprises located in the territory of the union republics were directly subordinated to USSR central ministries as so-called all-Union enterprises. In 1990, 81 percent of industrial fixed assets were Union-subordinated, with the worst situations in Turkmenistan and Azerbaijan, where, respectively, only 16 and 19 percent of the fixed assets were under republican jurisdiction. What is more, the enterprises that belonged to the Union were much superior from a technical point of view as compared with those administered by the republics. For instance, by the beginning of 1991 the capital–labor ratio at the Union-subordinated enterprises was 250 percent higher than at republic-subordinated enterprises. The respective figures for Azerbaijan and Turkmenistan are 330 and 1,120 percent.[13]

Third, the most important industries were concentrated in Russia. For instance, in 1990 Russia produced 90 percent of the Soviet Union's oil, 79 percent of gas, 63 percent of electric power, 57 percent of rolled stock, 81 percent of equipment for the oil industry, 64 percent of chemical industry equipment, 60 percent of agricultural machinery, 65 percent of forge-and-pressing equipment, 85 percent of paper, 70 percent of tires, and so forth.[14]

Fourth and most important, Russia was the main weaponry depot of the "Evil Empire." It contained the majority of the enterprises of the military-industrial complex with their superior equipment and highly skilled workers. The leading research and design institutes working directly or indirectly for military purposes were situated in Russia.

According to data from the Institute of Economics of the Russian Academy of Sciences, in 1990, Russia, with 51.3 percent of the country's population, accounted for 66.4 percent of Soviet industrial output. Only in Estonia was the per capita industrial output higher than in Russia—by 8 percent. If we assume that Russia's level in per capita industrial output was 100 percent, then the closest to it was Belarus (89 percent), with Lithuania far behind at 71 percent, followed by Latvia and Ukraine (69 percent each), Armenia (62 percent), Azerbaijan (52 percent), Georgia (49 percent), Kazakhstan (47 percent), and Moldova (41 percent). Turkmenistan and Kyrgyzstan each produced only a quarter of Russia's per capita industrial output (26 percent), Uzbekistan 19 percent, and Tajikistan only 17 percent.[15] This turned Russia into an industrial mother country with the decisive say in the Soviet empire.

3. The Evolution of the Settlement of Russians in the USSR and the Change in Their Situation

By the time of the Bolshevik victory in the Civil War, the major part of the former Russian diaspora—officials, businessmen, and intellectuals—had been exterminated or driven away from the Russian colonies. However, the famine that struck Russia in 1921 brought to the Caucasus and Turkmenistan many spontaneous Russian migrants.

Most Cossack settlements were included within the boundaries of national republics as repayment for fighting against Soviet rule, for the most part on the side of the White Guards. Thus, the Terek Cossacks were incorporated into the national formations of the North Caucasus, while the Semireche, and in part the Ural and Orenburg, Cossacks joined Kazakhstan.

Whereas in the early 1920s the migration of Russians into national regions was mostly spontaneous, later it began to assume an organized and purposeful character. Depending on the political situation in the country, the rate of migration of Russians into national territories was sometimes very high. There were several such periods in Soviet history.

The first wave (in the late 1920s–early 1930s) came with the industrialization campaign: the new industrial enterprises in the national republics and the autonomous units within the Russian Federation were built mostly by Russians. The second wave came in 1941, at the beginning of the war, when the Soviet Union was suffering major defeats. In the period from July to December 1941, over 300 large industrial enterprises—20 percent of the total—were moved east, mainly to Kazakhstan and Central Asia. After the war many Russians who had come with these enterprises stayed for good.

The mid-1940s witnessed the beginning of still another powerful wave of migration, this time to the Crimea and the Caucasus, from which some indigenous nations that had been declared politically unreliable during the war were deported—Chechens, Ingush, Balkars, Karachai, Kalmyks, Crimean Tatars, and others. When under Khrushchev some of the deported populations returned to their native lands, the Russian migrants stayed, becoming national minorities in the restored autonomous formations.

A new, powerful wave of migration was triggered by the campaign to develop the virgin lands in Kazakhstan. During the 1959–70 intercensus period the Russian population in this republic grew from 4 million to 5.5 million.

Many Russians migrated to Latvia and Estonia, and the percentage of Russians living there steadily grew. Whereas in 1959 Russians in Latvia constituted 25.5 percent of the population, in 1989 this figure had risen to 34 percent; the respective figures for Estonia were 20.1 percent and 30.4 percent. (For data on the change in the percentage of Russians living in national republics over the last three decades, see Table 1.3.)

Those Russians who moved to national regions found themselves not only among people speaking a different language, but also in an unfamiliar cultural environment. During the years of the Soviet regime, national lifestyles had not been completely homogenized. Centuries-old civilizations could not be eliminated quickly, even with the most intense exertion of despotic power. In the majority of cases the change was external only, assuming a form and color that was satisfactory to the rulers but without deep internal transformation.

For instance, the communal-irrigation system of land tilling in Uzbekistan acquired the outward form of collective and state farms spread by the Commu-

Table 1.3

Dynamics of the National Structure of the Republics Comprising the Soviet Union

	Percentage of indigenous population				Percentage of Russians			
	1959	1970	1979	1989	1959	1970	1979	1989
Ukraine	76.8	74.9	73.6	72.7	16.9	19.4	21.1	22.1
Belarus	81.0	81.0	79.4	77.8	8.2	10.4	11.9	13.2
Moldova	65.4	64.6	63.9	64.5	10.2	11.6	12.8	13.0
Georgia	64.3	66.8	68.8	70.1	10.1	8.5	7.4	6.3
Azerbaijan	67.5	73.8	78.1	83.3	13.6	10.0	7.9	5.0
Armenia	88.0	88.6	89.7	93.3	3.2	2.7	2.3	1.6
Kazakhstan	30.0	32.6	36.0	39.7	42.7	42.4	40.4	40.8
Uzbekistan	62.2	65.5	68.7	71.4	13.5	12.5	10.8	8.3
Kyrgyzstan	40.5	43.8	47.9	52.4	30.2	29.2	25.9	21.5
Tajikistan	53.1	56.2	58.8	62.3	13.3	11.9	10.4	7.6
Latvia	62.0	56.8	53.7	52.0	26.6	29.8	32.8	34.0
Lithuania	79.3	80.1	80.0	79.6	8.5	8.6	8.9	9.4
Estonia	74.6	68.2	64.7	61.5	20.1	24.7	27.9	30.4

Sources: Narodnoe khoziaistvo SSSR v 1960, Statisticheskii ezhegodnik (Moscow, 1961), pp. 17–20; *Narodnoe khoziaistvo SSSR, 1922–1972 Iubileinyi statisticheskii ezhegodnik,* pp. 499–681; *Naselenie SSSR* (Moscow, 1983), pp. 185–89; and *Natsional'nyi sostav naseleniia SSSR, Po dannym Vsesoiuznoi perepisi naseleniia 1989* (Moscow, 1990), pp. 9–19.

nists, but the basic type of civilization remained the same. The majority of the native population regarded the modern industry created by Russian migrants as something alien and useless. Hence, while the agrarian regions were overpopulated, urban industry always experienced a shortage of labor.

The Europeanized economies of Latvia and Estonia, characterized by a high culture of labor, personal initiative, enterprise, and individualism, also changed in character (the percentage of Communists among the indigenous population in Estonia was the highest among the republics). Still, Russians were as alien to this civilization type in their culture, traditions, and customs as they were in Uzbekistan, although in a somewhat different way.

Most of the Russian migrants to Central Asia were more or less skilled workers, technicians, and engineers. Initially, Kazakhstan, with its nomadic and seminomadic population, attracted mostly industrial, albeit semiskilled or even unskilled, workers. These were yesterday's peasants, who relied only on their physical strength and endurance and who were prepared to do heavy labor and hazardous jobs. Those sent to Kazakhstan to develop virgin lands were mostly rural machine operators (often low-skilled ones), urban lumpen, and low-paid employees who had few if any skills and hoped by acquiring a new trade to change their lives for the better.

In Latvia and Estonia as well, migrants tended to do heavy and nonprestigious jobs (in mines or at construction sites). Forced to leave their impoverished Russian villages, the majority were from the Pskov region. As a rule they were far below the local population in their educational and general cultural level.

Admittedly, the lower the cultural and technical level of migrants, the more difficult it is to get accustomed to a more developed social environment and greater is the desire to isolate themselves and to form close communities. This behavior, while in fact a manifestation of an inferiority complex, easily assumes the guise of national superiority, especially if the migrants are representatives of the nation that is declared the leading force in the country by the official propaganda machine. That was exactly the case with most Russian settlers in the Baltic region.

There were other smaller, but nonetheless significant, flows in the history of the resettlement of Russians throughout the territory of the Soviet Union.

First, party functionaries, leading officials of planning and financial bodies, administrative workers in industrial, construction, supply and services departments, organizations, and enterprises, as well as workers from the security services and legislative bodies were sent to work in national regions. Second, stationed in all the national regions were detachments of the Soviet Army, whose officers were mostly Russians who settled there with their families. Third, intellectual workers, who had completed college or postgraduate courses were often sent to these regions and sometimes even voluntarily moved there. They played a prominent part in the resurgence (more exactly, Europeanization) of the culture and science of the Asian republics and helped to create national cadres of doctors, teachers, and scientists. For a very long period Russians played a dominant part in the intellectual life of these regions. For instance, in 1967 there were 20,000 researchers in Uzbekistan, although there were only 9,000 researchers of Uzbek or Karakalpak nationality in the entire Soviet Union. Among 22,000 scientific workers in Kazakhstan, less than 6,000 were Kazakhs.[16]

In recent years it has become commonplace in Russia to assert that although Russians constituted the majority in the Soviet empire, they were not an imperial nation. This thesis is substantiated differently depending on the political orientation of the author. According to democrats, the Soviet Union was a hitherto unknown type of empire in which an imperial party (or to be more precise, the apparatus of this party) was substituted for an imperial nation. The chauvinistic-minded publicists explain everything in terms of the dominance of Jews and Masons. But democrats and chauvinists alike insist that Russians were virtually the most deprived group in the USSR and for this reason alone cannot be considered an imperial nation. These emotional statements are not supported by any kind of systematized data.

Let us try to make up for this deficiency and objectively assess the position of Russians compared with the standard of living in other nations of the Soviet

Table 1.4

Average Monetary Wage of Workers and Employees in Soviet Republics
(as percentage of Russia's average)

	1940	1960	1970	1980	1985	1990
Russia	100.0	100.0	100.0	100.0	100.0	100.0
Ukraine	95.0	94.2	91.4	87.3	86.3	83.7
Belarus	84.3	76.0	84.4	84.4	86.2	89.1
Moldova	78.8	81.1	81.5	77.8	78.3	78.5
Armenia	101.2	91.3	97.5	91.8	89.5	81.3
Azerbaijan	104.4	93.0	86.9	83.5	80.7	65.6
Georgia	98.2	90.0	84.1	81.7	83.2	72.1
Kazakhstan	87.9	98.0	98.1	94.0	92.6	89.4
Uzbekistan	87.6	84.4	91.0	87.5	81.5	72.6
Tajikistan	107.7	94.2	93.3	81.9	78.4	69.7
Kyrgyzstan	89.1	90.1	89.3	93.3	81.9	78.4
Turkmenistan	103.8	102.2	103.1	99.2	94.9	82.1
Lithuania	89.7	87.1	94.8	93.5	94.3	95.4
Latvia	92.6	94.5	99.6	96.4	97.3	98.0
Estonia	95.0	98.6	107.3	106.2	106.8	114.8
USSR avg.	97.6	96.9	96.6	94.8	94.1	91.9

Sources: Narodnoe khoziaistvo SSSR za 70 let, Iubileinyi statisticheskii ezhegodnik (Moscow, 1987), p. 434; *Narodnoe khoziaistvo SSSR v 1990*, p. 38.

Union that have now taken the road of independent statehood. The available statistical data are extremely meager and the methods of assessing many indicators are unreliable. However, a certain analysis can be made.

First of all, as regards the economic level of the Russian people, statistics indicate that for the last fifty years the average wage in the Russian Federation has been higher than in the majority of union republics (see Table 1.4). Certainly it would be better to consider wages of people of different nationalities, but no such data are available. It should be stated in all fairness that comparing by republic rather than by nationality leads to certain distortions in the overall picture not unfavorable to Russians. Naturally, the average wage of Russian industrial workers in Turkmenistan is higher than the average wage earned by Turkmen workers, because of the Russians' higher skills. Over time the gap in the remuneration for labor grew in Russia's favor: in 1940 the average monthly wage of workers and employees in Russia was 2.4 percent higher than the country's average; in 1950, 3.1 percent higher; in 1980, 5.2 percent higher; and in 1990, 8.1 percent higher. In 1940 four republics were ahead of Russia in this indicator; from the mid-1970s on, only Estonia was ahead of the Russian Federation.

The more rapid growth of wages in Russia cannot be explained by higher growth rates of labor productivity. For instance, in the period from 1970 to 1986, labor productivity in Russia increased by 93 percent; in Georgia, by 104 percent;

and in Azerbaijan, by 115 percent. Still, the national republics' lag behind Russia in average wages did not decrease; in fact, it increased—in Georgia from 16 to 18 percent and in Azerbaijan from 13 to 22 percent.[17]

The same trend could be observed in the wages of state farm workers and the cash remuneration of collective farmers. In 1970 Russia was fourth in the level of average monthly wages of state farm workers among the Soviet republics; in 1955, third; and in 1990, second. As for the cash remuneration of collective farmers, Russia moved from eleventh place in 1970 to sixth place in 1985 and fourth place in 1990. Moreover, the growth rate of wages in collective and state farms of the Russian Federation was higher than the average for the Soviet Union.[18]

This should not be viewed as direct wage discrimination against other nations. The tendency toward higher wages in Russia is a secondary phenomenon, the result of imperial economic policy. The military-industrial complex developed at a higher rate in Russia, and the wage level in that sector greatly exceeded that of civilian industries. The faster growth of wages in agriculture can be explained by the preference given to Russia's collective and state farms when allocating money from the budget and giving credits, the major part of which was spent not on the development of production but on higher wages.

Although average wage is an important indicator, it fails to characterize fully people's living standards. Per capita gross income is a more precise indicator in this respect. It must be kept in mind that when citing the data for the republics, we understate the incomes of Russians compared with Muslim nations, which as a rule have many children in a family. Table 1.5 shows the results of a survey of family budgets. The survey demonstrated that the percentage of people with the lowest per capita income (less than 100 rubles) is much lower in Russia than in all other republics, with the exception of the Baltic republics and Belarus. The percentage of people with the lowest income in Tajikistan is 5.9 times higher than in Russia; it is 5 times higher in Uzbekistan, 4.3 times higher in Azerbaijan and Turkmenistan, and 4 times higher in Kyrgyzstan. On the other hand, in terms of the percentage of people with per capita gross income exceeding 200 rubles, Russia is inferior—and barely so—only to the Baltic republics and Belarus.

Obviously, money is only the manifestation of solvent demand. For many years the population of Russia was faced with empty or half-empty counters, queues, and the need to travel to the capital or large cities, which were a little bit better supplied with basic goods and foodstuffs. In the past the great majority of Russians were firmly convinced that the constant shortage of goods was caused by a drain of foodstuffs and industrial consumer goods from Russia to other republics of the Soviet Union. The fact that the data on Russia's exports and imports were kept secret helped maintain this impression. However, this is just another myth among the many that were promulgated in this country of socialism. In 1990 Russia was seventh in per capita production of consumer goods

Table 1.5

Distribution of Population According to Per Capita Gross Income
(1990; as percentage of entire population)

	Up to 100 rubles	100–200 rubles	200–300 rubles	Over 300 rubles
Russia	11.4	53.2	26.9	8.5
Ukraine	11.5	59.2	24.1	5.4
Belarus	7.4	55.9	29.1	7.6
Moldova	18.6	57.4	19.4	4.6
Georgia	17.7	51.8	22.7	7.8
Azerbaijan	49.4	39.8	8.7	2.1
Armenia	16.7	56.2	21.4	5.7
Kazakhstan	24.4	52.6	17.9	5.1
Uzbekistan	57.1	36.9	5.1	0.9
Kyrgyzstan	46.5	44.5	7.6	1.4
Tajikistan	67.8	28.4	3.3	0.5
Turkmenistan	49.2	42.3	7.1	1.4
Lithuania	5.7	46.7	33.8	13.8
Latvia	4.7	45.6	35.2	14.5
Estonia	3.3	39.0	37.9	19.8
Total in USSR	18.3	52.0	22.9	6.8

Source: Narodnoe khoziaistvo SSSR za 70 let, p. 115.

among the Soviet republics and eighth in light industry products. According to 1989 data, the import of consumer goods into Russia exceeded exports by 26,000 million rubles. The figure for foodstuffs was 14,000 million rubles.[19]

It is also worth noting that the miserable way of life of Russians so vividly shown in Govorukhin's "That's Not the Way to Live" is not solely the result of low incomes. The appearance of people and their dwellings and tastes in entertainment depend greatly on traditions and customs, including pernicious ones. For instance, Russia ranks first in the number of cases of alcoholism and related traumas per 100,000 population. On the other hand, it lags behind many other republics in the number of tuberculosis cases, although tuberculosis is considered a disease of the poor.[20]

Russia was also given preference as far as the social services sphere is concerned. For instance, in the period from 1976 to 1990 almost 65 percent of all capital investments in housing construction were made in Russia. Russia is ahead of all the republics except Latvia in per capita number of hospital beds and trails only Georgia in the number of outpatient clinics per 100,000 population.[21]

The leading role of Russia in the sphere of science and education is indisputable. During Brezhnev's rule the old Marxist slogan of the "merging" of nations was revived, and the first step toward its realization was the official declaration of Russian as the language of the entire Soviet population. This banner of merging actually was used to cover the process of Russification.

True, it had all started long before Brezhnev. The unification of national alphabets, which were nearly all transferred to the Cyrillic alphabet in the 1930s and 1940s, served the same purpose. Even the ancient Romanian language (a direct descendant of Latin) of the native population of Moldova was transferred to the Russian alphabet. Only the Latin alphabets of the Baltic peoples and those of Georgia and Armenia survived. Not a single colonial episode in world history bears comparison.

There is no need to speak of such well-known things as the preference given to Russians in appointments to diplomatic jobs, state security agencies, top posts in military districts and the army, and so on.

No one ever formally rejected the traditional communist appeals for internationalism. They existed side by side with Great Power chauvinistic propaganda and practice, forming a kind of a perverted hybrid. In general, life in the Soviet Union can be aptly described by the phrase from George Orwell's *Animal Farm* to the effect that all animals are equal, only some are more equal than others.

Notes

1. Ia. E. Volodarskii, *Naselenie Rossii za 400 let (XVI–nachalo XX vv.)* (Moscow, 1973), p. 27.

2. See, for instance, "Materialy ob"edinennoi nauchnoi sessii, posviashchennoi progressivnomu znacheniiu prisoedineniia Srednei Azii k Rossii" (Tashkent, 1959). Similar publications appeared in other republics as well.

3. I. Ermeshev, *Istoriko-sotsial'noe issledovanie kul'tury Uzbekistana* (Tashkent, 1985), p. 26.

4. Niccolo Machiavelli, *Principe* (Moscow, 1990), p. 7.

5. See M. Khorosikhin, *Kozachii voiska* (St. Petersburg, 1881).

6. *Otchet po revizii Turkestanskogo kraia, proizvedennyi po vysochaishchemu poveleniiu senatorom Palenom* (St. Petersburg, 1909–10), p. 109.

7. P.I. Liashchenko, *Istoriia narodnogo khoziaistva SSSR,* vol. II, *Kapitalizm* (Moscow, 1950), pp. 550, 565.

8. E. Markov, *Rossiia i Sredniaia Aziia* (St. Petersburg, 1901), p. 525.

9. G. Fedotov, "Sud'ba Imperii," *Znamia,* 1992, nos. 3–4, p. 196.

10. *XVII s"ezd RKP(b), Stenograficheskii otchet* (Moscow, 1967), p. 51.

11. See *XV s"ezd Vsesoiuznoi Kommunisticheskoi partii (bolshevikov), Stenograficheskii otchet* (Moscow–Leningrad, 1928), pp. 399–401.

12. I.V. Stalin, *O Velikoi Otechestvennoi voine Sovetskogo Soiuza* (Moscow, 1952), p. 196.

13. Ibid., p. 35.

14. Calculated according to data in *Ekonomika suverennykh respublik v preddverii rynka. Statisticheskie tablitsy (Moscow, 1992), p. 9.*

15. Ibid.

16. *Narodnoe khoziaistvo SSSR v 1967* (Moscow, 1968), pp. 811–12.

17. *Narodnoe khoziaistvo SSSR za 70 let* (Moscow, 1987), pp. 142, 434.

18. Ibid., pp. 434–35; *Narodnoe khoziaistvo SSSR v 1990,* pp. 38–39.

19. *Ekonomika suverennykh respublik v preddverii rynka,* pp. 14, 15, 17.

20. *Narodnoe khoziaistvo SSSR v 1990,* pp. 249–51.

21. Ibid., pp. 187, 256, 258; *Narodnoe khoziaistvo USSR v 1989,* p. 164.

2

The Disintegration of the Empire and the Fate of the "Imperial Minority"

Emil Payin

1. On the Definition of "Imperial Minority"

It is not by chance that the term national (or ethnic) minority is usually associated with internal conflicts. The problem of ethnic and ethnoreligious minorities is becoming more acute even in the traditionally democratic European states, with their smoothly operating mechanisms guaranteeing the observance of human rights (e.g., the problem of Basques in Spain, Irish Catholics in Ulster, or Corsicans in France). The problem, however, may turn out to be even more perilous and painful in post-Communist countries, which have timidly embarked upon the road leading to democratic and civilized forms of interethnic community (consider, for example, the case of Hungarians in Romania or Turks in Bulgaria).[1] One can easily imagine both the scope and the urgency of the problem of Russian minorities in the republics of the former USSR if one takes into consideration the size of that group,[2] the imperial type of the Soviet state, and its citizens' sense of justice as distorted by decades of totalitarian rule.

Since World War II the world community has done much to protect the rights of minorities. Several legislative acts dealing with human rights and minority rights have been adopted.[3] However, in 1992 the United Nations did not adopt the Declaration on Rights of Minorities, on which a special UN group had worked for more than twelve years.[4]

Thus, up until now there has been no international document recognized at the highest levels that provides for appraisal of the lawfulness of national governments' acts concerning minorities or the legitimacy of the minorities' demands. This can be attributed mainly to political motives, that is, the counteraction of some states concerned by the fact that the recognition of minorities' rights might lead to instability in society.[5]

As for the problem of Russian minorities in the newly independent states, the inadequate attention paid by international organizations can be explained, to the author's mind, by ideological reasons: Russians continue to be perceived as bearers of communist ideology and defenders of imperial power. Besides, both politicians and the public at large lack relevant information due to lack of proper study. Most important, there are no strict criteria to evaluate the conditions of Russian minorities. One of the main tasks of this work will be to reveal typologically important peculiarities of the Russian diaspora (Russian minorities) in the post-Soviet period.

This analysis is based on information from literary sources, sociological studies carried out in the period from 1987 to 1988 by the Institute of Ethnology and Anthropology of the USSR Academy of Sciences and by several other scientific institutions in the early 1990s, monthly bulletins and analytical reviews of the Center for Ethnic and Political Research, and articles published by the author in *Nezavisimaia gazeta* in the column "Nations" from March 1991 until August 1992.

By making the problem of the "imperial minority" the subject of his research, the author has put himself in a difficult position both theoretically and psychologically.

Theoretical difficulties stem first of all from the fact that even international law documents provide no universally recognized definition of an ethnic minority. In 1987 the UN Secretariat issued a collection of official proposals made in the past forty years in an attempt to define the term.[6] Today the most widely accepted definition is the one proposed by Francesco Capotorti. He defines ethnic minorities as groups of people who: (a) form a numerical minority in a given state; (b) do not dominate politically; (c) differ from the main population by their ethnic, linguistic, or religious characteristics; and (d) express a feeling of intragroup solidarity in preserving their own culture, traditions, and language.[7] If these four points are applied to the Russians who live in the former Soviet republics, the term "minority" is inadequate for defining their status. They used to live in a state where they formed the ethnic majority, and they regarded the republics of their residence merely as provinces of a single power. A poll conducted in Georgia, Moldova, Uzbekistan, and Estonia by the Institute of Ethnography of the USSR Academy of Sciences in the early 1980s shows that, regardless of their place of residence, Russians in most cases (70 percent or more) named the Soviet Union as their homeland, while most members of the titular nations referred to their republics as their homeland.[8] In December 1990 the All-Russian Center for the Study of Public Opinion carried out a survey in eighteen cities of ten republics and found that, despite the proclaimed sovereignty of many republics, the majority of Russians (70–80 percent) continued to consider themselves first and foremost to be citizens of the USSR, which means that they preserved their state (all-Union) consciousness.[9]

Furthermore, the Russians in the Soviet republics could not be called a group not dominating politically. Despite the existence of certain features of statehood in the union republics, their real leaders, the secretaries of the republican communist parties, were in fact appointed by the Politburo of the CPSU Central Committee. In the last Politburo itself, eight out of its ten members were Russians; among the secretaries of the Central Committee, ten out of eleven members were Russians; on the CPSU Central Committee, Russians accounted for more than 75 percent of the members; and the Communist Party as a whole, according to 1990 data, was 59.8 percent Russian.[10] Besides, the post of second secretary of a republican central committee was traditionally occupied by a Russian. Russians usually headed republican state security committees, ministries of the interior, and military garrisons stationed in the republics.

The feeling of intragroup solidarity in preserving their specific culture and historical traditions was weak among the Russians in the republics. The above-mentioned poll indicates that interest in books about the history of their people occupied first or second place among Georgians, Moldovans, and Estonians, while it occupied fourth or fifth place among Russians, who gave preference to books on the history of World War II, as they wanted to learn more about the glorious past of the Soviet Union as a whole, and to books on the topical political events in the USSR.[11] Russian national-cultural movements and societies did not exist in any of the republics prior to 1985, but as soon as those republics proclaimed their independence such organizations began to mushroom. This is an indication of the fact that once the republics seceded from the USSR, Russians in these republics became a minority and their actions became typical of a minority: they rallied for the sake of their ethnic and cultural self-preservation.

Only two of the above-mentioned four criteria for minority status can be applied to the Russians in the former Soviet republics: they constitute the minority of the population and they differ from the titular nations in their ethnocultural, and particularly their linguistic, characteristics (see Table 2.1). According to data from the 1989 All-Union Census, 99.4 percent of Russians in the republics named the Russian language as their native tongue.[12] No other ethnic community has ever demonstrated such a strong adherence to its own language, especially outside its own republic. Command of the language of the titular nation is very poor among the Russians: only 19 percent of Russians know the local language. The lowest figure (0.9 percent) of those who speak the second language is among Russians in Kazakhstan. The best record is in Lithuania—33.4 percent. This "Russian phenomenon" is unique indeed. According to the well-known ethnosociologist Iurii Arutiunian, all ethnic communities of the former USSR residing outside their republics (except the Russian) are bilingual, or even recognize the language of another ethnic community as their native tongue.[13] We can concur with this statement if it is stipulated that the term "Russians" in this case includes all Russian-speaking people in the republics, irrespective of the nationality specified in their documents—Russian, Ukrainian, Belarusian, Jewish, and so forth. They all had every opportunity not only to live and work in the republics of the former Soviet Union but also to rise in social status without knowing

Table 2.1

Russians and the Languages of the Republics (in %)

Republic	Russian population in republic	Consider language of titular nationality their mother tongue	Fluent in titular national language	Are bilingual
Ukraine	22.1	1.6	32.8	77.2
Belarus	13.2	2.3	24.5	7.1
Uzbekistan	8.4	0.1	4.5	1.5
Kazakhstan	37.8	0.0	0.9	1.1
Georgia	6.3	1.3	22.5	1.6
Azerbaijan	5.6	0.2	14.3	1.1
Lithuania	9.4	4.4	33.4	2.6
Moldova	13.0	0.9	11.2	1.3
Latvia	34.0	1.2	21.1	4.0
Kyrgyzstan	21.5	0.1	1.2	0.2
Tajikistan	7.6	0.1	3.5	0.3
Armenia	1.6	1.6	32.2	0.4
Turkmenistan	9.5	0.1	2.5	0.2
Estonia	30.3	1.4	13.7	1.4

Source: 1989 data of the USSR State Committee for Statistics.

the language of the titular nation. Meanwhile, people of other nationalities were deprived of that opportunity, not only outside their own republics but also at home. It is noteworthy that the Soviet state not only granted advantages to those who could speak Russian but also obliged all peoples to know this de facto official language without binding the Russians in the republics to master the language of the people among whom they lived.[14]

Thus, the Russians who constituted a numerical minority in the Soviet republics and differed from the majority of the population in their language and culture were not, in fact, a typical ethnic minority according to the canons of international law and the criteria on typological peculiarities of the way of life of ethnic minorities. As an "unusual" minority, the Russians in the republics could reproduce on a large scale and preserve their power consciousness as well as their monolingualism only due to the support of the imperial state, which provided certain privileges, at least in the ethnic and cultural spheres.

To the author's mind, this explains the meaning and determines the limits of "imperial minority." This term designates the following features of the Russian diaspora in the republics of the USSR prior to its disintegration:

(1) the genesis of Russian colonization of the former Soviet republics, now independent states. In most cases this colonization was organized by the state. In the pre-Soviet period, it was the colonization of lands that were annexed by the

Russian Empire or that joined it voluntarily. In the Soviet period, the colonization followed the annexation of territories after World War II, the deportation of many peoples to the eastern regions of the USSR in 1937–44 and their replacement with Russians, the development of virgin lands, and the industrialization and urbanization of the outlying regions;

(2) Russians as (usually unwilling or even forced) bearers of imperial policy in the republics, primarily as a kind of "cementing element" of power;

(3) imperial consciousness as the predominant type of mass psychology of the Russians in the republics;

(4) the indigenous population's perception of the Russians as representatives of the empire.

2. Russians Become a Minority:
Factors Aggravating the Problem of Russian Minorities

Since the collapse of the USSR, Russians in the republics have been gradually turning from an imperial minority to an ordinary one. Only now do many of them perceive themselves as a minority. This is an extremely painful and complicated process accompanied by general historical factors continually emerging in the specific historical period called postimperial or postcolonial. The collapse of an empire is as a rule accompanied by: (1) the development of local nationalism and the emergence of national movements; (2) the division of the "colonial legacy," first of all through territorial redivision; and (3) the striving of national movements to restore former ethnodemographic proportions and ultimately a monoethnic state.

Each of the above-mentioned features of the process of disintegration aggravates the problems of ethnic minorities in some way.

Under the conditions of politically rarefied space and immature civil institutions typical of postimperial states, nationalism and its political manifestation, national movements, are a natural and accessible form for engaging the broad masses in political life. It is not accidental that the first political movements and parties in Bohemia after the disintegration of Austria-Hungary were nationalistic.[15] Similarly, as soon as the political climate in the USSR grew a bit warmer during Khrushchev's "thaw," the first signs of national movements appeared.

The same phenomenon arose during another political thaw, Gorbachev's "perestroika," when the first non-Communist mass movements emerged in 1987–88: Sajudis in Lithuania, Rukh in Ukraine, the Karabakh Committee (which was later transformed into the Armenian National Movement), and others.

National movements are characterized by their total and fundamental opposition. National movements can be called associations whose motto is "against."

In the imperial states, especially in their outlying regions, the naturally oppositional character of the national movements generally leads them into the camp of antitotalitarian forces. But antitotalitarianism is not yet democracy, because the latter presupposes readiness to protect the rights not only of one's own nation but also of other nations and of each individual. That is why the defeat of an external imperial enemy leads inevitably to the transformation of democratic movements into national movements. Many of these movements are discarding their democratic veil and degenerating into movements whose oppositional stand is aimed against ethnic minorities. No wonder legislative acts in those republics of the former USSR where national movements have come to power often restrict the rights of minorities even more than the imperial center restricted the rights of the republics. This is what happened in Georgia when Zviad Gamsakhurdia was in power, in the Baltic republics, in Moldova, and so forth. Naturally, the policy of nationalism pursued by the majority did not go unheeded: outbursts of internal interethnic conflict between the ethnic majority and the minorities take place in virtually all postimperial societies.

It is noteworthy that local national leaders had been pursuing a policy of discrimination toward minorities in the republics even before the USSR's disintegration. Thus, for example, in Uzbekistan a policy of "Uzbekization" of Tajiks (especially in Samarkand and the adjacent areas where Tajiks were forced to register as Uzbeks in official documents), was carried out throughout the postwar period. In Azerbaijan, the Talysh suffered from forced assimilation, and the same policy was pursued in tolerant Latvia toward the Livonians.[16] It was only after the former union republics proclaimed their independence that the policy of national discrimination affected the Russian minority.

In all the former union republics language laws adopted the only official language of a republic designated as the language of the nationality for which the republic is named.[17] This norm is far from standard for polyethnic states. For instance, the constitutions of the Republic of Finland, the Kingdom of Belgium, the Swiss Confederation, and even the Grand Duchy of Luxembourg provide for the use of from two to four state languages.[18] In these states, and in some other countries as well, the second (and other) state languages are recognized especially for ethnic minorities—for the 6.3 percent of Swedes living in Finland, the 10 percent of French-speaking people living in Switzerland, the small category of people (comprising less than 1 percent of the population) speaking the Luxembourg dialect (actually the residents of several settlements in Luxembourg)—and so on.[19] At the same time, the percentage of Russians in all the union republics (except in the Transcaucasus) is much greater than that of Swedes in Finland; and in Estonia, Latvia, and Kazakhstan, Russians comprise almost half of the population.

Of course, the fact is that ethnic communities living in compact settlements usually use only their own language or dialect in everyday life, no matter how strict the demands concerning use of the state language. Probably for this reason, in many states—for instance in Spain—in compact settlements of ethnic minorities the use of the language of small ethnic communities alongside the state language has been made legal. Spain has conferred official status not only on the

Basque language but also on dialects of Spanish—Castilian, Andalusian, and Catalonian, among others. All of them have the status of regional languages.[20]

A similar provision is included in the language law of the Kazakh Republic, which provides for the right of local governments in regions of compact settlement of national groups on the territory of the republic to give the language of this group the status of a local official language to be used alongside the state language (Kazakh) and the language of interethnic communication—Russian.[21]

The laws of Estonia, Tajikistan, Kyrgyzstan, Uzbekistan, Ukraine, and Turkmenistan include provisions for local governmental bodies to use as a working language the language of the population that constitutes a majority in a certain locality. Meanwhile, the laws of Latvia, where Russians constitute over a third of the population, and Lithuania, where in Snieckus 95 percent of the population is Russian, do not permit the use of local languages even for working purposes. This means that in a compact settlement of an ethnic minority, a mayor who is Russian by nationality should give orders to a policeman, also a Russian, or a fireman, only in the state language (Lithuanian in Snieckus). In all the republics, with the exception of Kazakhstan, Belarus, and Uzbekistan, it is mandated by law to use the state language in bookkeeping at all enterprises and establishments. The following terms have been set for the transfer of bookkeeping to the state language: in Lithuania, two years; in Latvia, three years; in Estonia, four years; in the Ukraine, five years; in Moldova, seven years; in Turkmenistan and Tajikistan, eight years; and in Kyrgyzstan, ten years. Counting from the adoption of this law (1988–90),[22] the term of transfer of bookkeeping to the state language expired in the Baltic republics by 1992. Meanwhile, in these republics, just as in all others, there are no material prerequisites for learning the language of the indigenous population; there is a shortage of textbooks, teachers, and schools.

The rigid rules governing the introduction of the state language into the production sphere not only aggravate interethnic relations in the republics, but also have a negative effect on the economy, since the percentage of Russians in the production sphere of the economy is significantly higher than that of the entire population. This may account for the great flexibility of some of the republican laws on language. For instance, in Ukraine and Moldova the laws provide for prolonging the linguistic transition in production as well as use of the language of ethnic minorities within compact settlements. In Belarus and Uzbekistan the laws allow for the use of both the state and the Russian language in bookkeeping. In Kazakhstan no regulations have been imposed on language use in bookkeeping.

Thus, it is the legislation of the Baltic republics that to a great extent limits the conditions for the free ethnic and cultural development of Russians. The same is true of the laws of these republics on citizenship. Measures have been adopted in all the republics (in the period from 1989 to 1992), and the majority of them have been based on the so-called "zero principle," according to which all people permanently residing within their territory at the moment of the enactment of the law can become citizens.[23]

In some of the republics, such as Azerbaijan, Kazakhstan, and Kyrgyzstan, the zero option has been adopted without any additional conditions, an application for citizenship being sufficient.[24] In other republics certain additional limitations are imposed: (1) a residency requirement for those who arrived in the republic after the introduction of the law; in Ukraine and Belarus the requirement is five years, and in Moldova and the Baltic republics, from ten to sixteen years; (2) a language requirement specifying "knowledge of the state language within the limits necessary for communication"—in all the republics with the exception of Azerbaijan, Kazakhstan, and Kyrgyzstan; and (3) a "moral requirement"—an oath of allegiance to the republic—in Moldova and the Baltic republics. In addition, Moldova's law on citizenship contains a vague legal provision on "the need to prove with one's behavior and attitude loyalty to the state and people of the Republic of Moldova." The vagueness of the requirement to prove loyalty allows for arbitrary rule on the part of the state with respect to the individual.

Many analysts consider improper certain provisions in the laws of Moldova and the Baltic republics that confer naturalization privileges upon people (and their descendants) of the indigenous nationality who left the republic before 1940.[25]

Modern humanitarian consciousness cannot reconcile itself with the differentiation of rights according to ethnicity, especially when privileges are extended to descendants on the merits or sufferings of their forebears. This provision resembles more closely the "communal law" of the tribal epoch than the norms of modern society.

There is also no precedent in modern legislative practice for including in laws on citizenship provisions such as those now existing in Estonia and Latvia regarding the residency requirement for persons permanently residing in the republic prior to the adoption of the laws.

This opinion is shared, for instance, by Jeri Laber, executive director of Helsinki Watch, which monitors the observance of human rights. She addressed special messages to the leaders of Estonia and Latvia, one of which conveyed the request that, although Latvia as a sovereign state has an unquestionable right to establish new norms in the field of naturalization and citizenship, the Latvian leadership should not let this law limit the rights of people who settled in Latvia prior to its independence—law-abiding citizens who could not have foreseen the circumstances that were to change their legal status.[26] In her opinion, the residency requirements in the laws of both Latvia and Estonia give equal rights to those who move to these republics after the adoption of the law on citizenship, and consequently voluntarily agree to change their status, and those who have their status changed forcibly.

UN experts pointed out that Latvia and Estonia should be careful not to violate Article 15 of the Universal Declaration on Human Rights, which asserts that each person has the right to citizenship and that no one can be arbitrarily deprived of citizenship or the right to change one's citizenship.[27]

In the opinion of UN experts, the question of citizenship in Latvia and

Estonia should be resolved in accordance with Article 10, Part 2, of the 1961 Covenant (on the reduction of the number of people without citizenship), which says that the state to which a territory is transferred or which acquires a territory by some other means should grant citizenship to such people who otherwise as a result of such a transfer or acquisition would become people without citizenship.[28] The covenant asks for the same rights for those who are born on the territory of this state in Article 1, which declares that the state grant citizenship to a person born on its territory who would otherwise not be a citizen.[29]

This article has many points in common with a similar article in the Covenant on the Rights of the Child. Latvia, Lithuania, and Estonia joined in this pact after they gained independence; since September 1, 1992, however, birth certificates of a new type issued in Latvia to the children of Russians use the phrase "citizenship not established."[30]

The lack of citizenship rights is a great hardship for a person in any country, but only in post-Soviet societies does the lack of these rights make it virtually impossible for a person to find housing and earn a living. For instance, the laws of Latvia and Estonia deprive persons without citizenship—the majority of Russians belong to this category—of the following rights: land ownership, choice of place of residence within the state, the right to hold state jobs (the majority of jobs are still in the public sector of the economy), the right to join political parties, to carry weapons, and so forth. Only the citizens of Latvia and Estonia have the right freely to enter the country or to leave it; others can only depart.

The life of Russian minorities without citizenship in some of the states of the former Soviet Union is further aggravated by much more rigid regulations, or so-called pieces of subordinate legislation, issued by executive governmental agencies. For instance, registration of residence, which is now considered unconstitutional, has not only been preserved in Latvia but has acquired a special significance since it remains the only legal confirmation that a person not registered as a citizen has some relation to Latvia. The resolution adopted in 1992 by the Council of Ministers on the termination of registration of residence of immigrants has, in practice, deprived many people of even such confirmation.[31]

So the laws on citizenship, as well as subordinate legislation, infringe to a great extent upon the rights of minorities, especially Russians. They are the product of nationalistic ideology in its worst manifestation, promoting the legal inequality of the people of one country but of "different blood."

As has already been mentioned, both a nationalistic ideology and its legal consequences are historically inevitable in postimperial societies. At the same time, in the opinion of the author, this historical inevitability does not free states from responsibility when they adopt laws that contradict norms of international law, primarily principles of human rights and rights of minorities.

The division of colonial inheritance (territorial redivision) is a process that always accompanies the collapse of an empire, since ethnic boundaries inside a former empire are as a rule vague and unfixed. Moreover, an imperial state usually consciously strives not to allow the strict administrative assignment of ethnic boundaries.

Even in Western Europe, with its centuries-old experience with coexistence of many national states, the political boundaries do not meet any rational criteria—ethnic, historical, economic, or geographical. As a rule, these boundaries are established as a result of seizure by military force or through signed conventions—that is, in the course of diplomatic negotiations—and thus there are always grounds for dispute. On other continents in this postcolonial world, the situation is even more complicated. Thus, out of fifty-seven African states, a little over a dozen have their own historical tradition of statehood and can start there when determining their national-administrative boundaries. The remainder of the states are former colonies, "artificial" products of colonial expansion, and territorial disputes among them are the rule rather than the exception.[32]

The Soviet empire's entire history was a nearly continuous process of recarving administrative boundaries, especially the Caucasian and Central Asian republics' boundaries. It is only natural that today they are the venue of acute territorial disputes that also affect the Russian population: the majority of Russian refugees come from areas of territorial conflicts (Armenian-Azerbaijani, Georgian-Ossetian, Georgian-Abkhazian, Uzbek-Tajik, Uzbek-Kyrgyz, Ossetian-Ingush, and others). The boundaries of settlement of ethnic communities were significantly affected by the deportation of many nations in the period from 1937 to 1943 from the territory of the Caucasus, the Volga region, and the Soviet Far East, and in the period from 1946 to 1948 from the territory of Moldova, western Ukraine, and the Baltic region. As the repatriation of the deportees has not yet been completed, it affects the fate of Russian minorities in the Crimea, the North Caucasus, and the Baltic states.

One can judge the potential for territorial conflicts on the territory of the former USSR, and consequently the ensuing problems for Russian minorities living in the conflict zones, from research done by Professor George Demko. In the 1980s he and his staff began to generalize and mark all territorial claims of members of various national movements in the Soviet Union. It turned out that all the boundaries between the republics were considered disputable to some degree, as were some of the boundaries deep inside the republics.[33]

So far we have discussed the effect of territorial conflicts on the fate of Russian minorities, but there are cases when the fate of the minorities themselves becomes the focus of a territorial dispute. It is possible to distinguish at least two types of causes for these conflicts: first, when the territory of a compact settlement of the minority is claimed by neighboring republics (for instance, certain members of Russia's political circles of various ideological hues repeatedly laid claims to the territories of Russians' compact settlements in other republics: to the Crimea and to Novorossiia in the Ukrainian Republic, to the northeastern regions of Estonia, and to some regions of northern Kazakhstan); second, when the minorities themselves put forth separatist demands (to proclaim their enclave territory an independent state) or irredentist demands (to join their territory to another republic).

Irredentist demands have been put forth by only a small part of the Russian minorities in the North Caucasus, northern Kazakhstan, and the Crimea. By contrast, Russian separatism is not simply proclaimed but has been effected by Russians and Russian-speaking people in the Dniester region and by the Terek and Kuban Cossacks in the North Caucasus.

The Cossacks, more than any other ethnographic group of Russians, constitute the "imperial minority." They took shape at the boundaries of the empire, performing important military-frontier and military-police functions. Since they personified the conquerors, they were hated by the native population, were the first to be killed during national uprisings on the outskirts of the empire in 1917–18, and were persecuted as a class enemy (loyal to the autocracy) by Bolshevik rulers. Nevertheless, even today approximately three million descendants of the Cossacks still live in the traditionally Cossack regions, having preserved specifics of language, everyday life, customs, and mentality, as well as —most amazingly—group cohesion based on the epic "military glory" as the defenders of the motherland. Political organizations of Cossacks are the most consistent and active advocates of Russian national-sovereign ideology, do not recognize the disbanding of the Soviet Union, and at the same time have proclaimed the formation of several Cossack republics in the Northern Caucasus.

But nothing could more aggravate the problem of minorities than separatism and irredentism: the bloodiest of recent conflicts have emerged over these issues—Nagorno-Karabakh, South Ossetia, the Dniester, Abkhazia, and so forth. Nationalism is the driving force of the so-called "historical memory" of the nation, and ethnic territory is its most important symbol. Thus, any encroachment on one's territory is considered by the peoples of the postimperial world as an encroachment on their most sacred possession.

The effort to restore a violated ethnodemographic structure, as well as nationalism and the struggle for territory, is the response of national movements to imperial colonialism.

Russian colonization was accompanied by the ouster of indigenous people from their native territory, sometimes even by their physical extermination, and almost always by a change in the ratio between the indigenous people and migrants in favor of the latter. When speaking of the physical extermination of peoples in the Soviet period, it is first of all necessary to recall the tragic fate of those who were deported. One can judge the depth of this tragedy by considering that within only four years (1944–48), 16 to 18 percent of those exiled to the so-called "special settlements" in Central Asia died.[34] Twenty percent of the deported Crimean Tatars, Greeks, and Bulgarians also died.[35] Inhabitants of some of the settlements who put up resistance to the authorities were completely exterminated.[36]

During the years of Soviet government, the number of Russians living beyond

Table 2.2

Changes in the Percentage of Russians Comprising the Population of the Union Republics, 1959–89 (in %)

Republic	Russian population (%)				Net change	
	1959	1970	1979	1989	1959–79	1979–89
Ukraine	16.9	19.4	21.1	22.1	+2.5	+1.0
Belarus	8.2	10.4	11.9	13.2	+2.2	+1.3
Uzbekistan	13.5	12.5	10.8	8.4	−1.0	−2.4
Kazakhstan	13.5	12.5	10.8	8.4	−1.0	−2.4
Georgia	10.1	8.5	7.4	6.3	−1.6	−1.3
Azerbaijan	13.6	10.0	7.9	5.6	−3.6	−2.3
Lithuania	8.5	8.6	8.9	9.4	+0.1	+0.5
Moldova	10.2	11.6	12.8	13.0	+1.4	+0.2
Latvia	26.6	29.8	32.8	34.0	+2.6	+1.2
Kyrgyzstan	30.2	29.2	25.9	21.5	−1.0	−4.4
Tajikistan	13.3	11.9	10.4	7.6	−1.4	−2.8
Armenia	3.2	2.7	2.3	1.6	−0.5	−0.7
Turkmenistan	17.3	14.5	12.6	9.5	−2.8	−3.1
Estonia	20.1	24.7	27.9	30.3	+4.6	+2.4

Source: Russkie (etnosotsiologicheskie ocherki) (Moscow: Nauka, 1992), p. 21.

the boundaries of Russia proper grew from 6.7 to 17.4 percent.[37] Nonetheless, the growth in the percentage of Russians was not a characteristic feature of all union republics (see Table 2.2). The 1960s witnessed the appearance of a "western" tendency in Russian expansion: in the period from 1959 to 1979 the number of Russians in the European republics grew rapidly, while their numbers in the Transcaucasian and Central Asian republics decreased. The regional differences in the character and scale of the growth of the percentage of Russians can be explained not only by the direction of migration flows but also by ethnic differences in the natural growth of the population. For instance, the percentage of Russians in the Baltic republics grew, thanks to the arrival of new members of this nationality and a birth rate higher than that of the titular nations.

In any case, the ethnodemographic ratio between Latvians, Lithuanians, and Estonians on the one hand, and Russians on the other, changed in favor of the latter. Moreover, in certain regions of the Baltic states, such as northeast Estonia and the Latvian capital, Russians became the ethnic majority. This fact explains why national movements, especially in the Baltic republics, which were born in the depth of the empire, usually put forth programs of demographic self-preservation, and after winning power as independent states adopted laws limiting immigration, as did the Estonian Republic. However, the idea of restoring the ethnodemographic ratio begins to assume huge proportions in independent states and often becomes extremist. For instance, practically all the political parties in Estonia have formed along ethnic lines, and among the pure Estonian parties, the overwhelming majority demand the mass ouster of Russians.[38] Since only a small part of the Russian population (not more than 10 percent, according to surveys conducted by Estonian sociologists) wish to depart from Estonia, the implementation of this policy would inevitably mean their forced removal.[39] Roughly the same political tendencies prevail among Latvian political parties and movements.

In the opinion of the author, these ideas are exceptionally dangerous for the Baltic states themselves, for they are pregnant with great economic and political losses. As for the Russian minorities, the idea of re-emigration signifies a further curtailment of their civil rights.

While in the Baltic region political actions aimed at limiting in-migration and even at ousting Russians can be explained by the titular nations' fear of losing their status as ethnic majority in their historical motherland, in the states of Central Asia similar ideas are put forth by nationalistic forces for quite another reason—mainly because of ethnosocial competition.

The development of a national intelligentsia is always accompanied by the growth of national self-awareness and simultaneously by the international delimitation of peoples. The Soviet Union was no exception in this respect. Under socialism this process meant that those social strata that would have been capable of ensuring a relatively conflict-free development of the national culture (the so-called "bourgeois" intelligentsia) were ruthlessly exterminated. Simultaneously, the so-called workers' faculties—the universities of "Red professors" and later, general educational establishments, which had very relaxed admission and graduation rules—began rapidly to educate the new "people's intelligentsia."

Thus, in the republics of Transcaucasia and Central Asia and in Kazakhstan, as well as in Lithuania and Estonia, the percentage of members of the indigenous population in higher-level schools exceeded their percentage of the total population.[40] In the Kyrgyz SSR in 1974, the share of Kyrgyz in the Agricultural Institute was 85 percent, and in the university's economic department, 100 percent. In 1985, 86 Yakuts constituted 79.5 percent of the student body at Yakut State University, while their share of the population of this autonomous republic was 31.1 percent.[41] These gigantic disproportions can hardly be explained by the greater zeal and industriousness of local boys and girls as compared to other nationalities. The members of the indigenous population were not faced with the notorious Item No. 5 (the question about nationality in any application form). On the contrary, they were given preference in accordance with the policy of making members of the indigenous nationality top officials, which prevailed from Stalin's times to perestroika. That is why the greatest disproportions occur in these strata of the intelligentsia. For instance, in 1974 in Kazakhstan among doctors and candidates of science, 43 and 39 percent, respectively, were Kazakhs, although Kazakhs constituted only 16.5 percent of the gainfully employed urban population. The same is true of Kyrgyzstan: with only 18.9 percent of the urban population Kyrgyz, their share of the candidates and doctors of science was 43.1 and

39.1 percent, respectively.[42] One naturally asks how this practice was combined with a policy of Russification? The fact is, the Union government's policy was far from promoting the cultural level of the entire population of the republics of Central Asia, or doing away with its chronic shortage of industrial workers—which, by the way, was compensated for through the recruitment of labor in Slavic regions. To secure the support of the local national elite, the Union government cultivated this elite as a kind of comprador class. Prestigious institutes, unions of creative workers, and academies of sciences were established in each republic. The heads of these institutions were usually members of the central committee of the republic's Communist Party and were the obedient servants of the Kremlin for the time being.

In all of these postcolonial states the "new" national intelligentsia is inclined toward interethnic confrontation. As has already been mentioned, this predisposition stems from the very necessity to make a career in conditions of competition. Moreover, the Soviet policy described above was conducive to the emergence of an especially conflict-prone generation which demanded its place at the intellectual and political top solely by virtue of social or national origin. Hence the increased toughness of political demands on the minorities advanced by the national elite.

Besides rational (or seemingly rational) grounds for the national movements' efforts to displace Russians from their rung on the social ladder, or even from the republics, there are also irrational grounds, such as a tendency to direct hatred of the empire itself and of its totalitarian system against Russians. According to ethnic and sociological surveys conducted in different countries of the world, this is a rather universal phenomenon. Almost everywhere the members of the "imperial minority" remain victims of sharply negative attitudes for decades, even a century after the nation in question has acquired independence. For instance, according to surveys conducted in 1989–90 in Czechoslovakia, 20 percent of Czechs do not very much like Germans (Austrians), who in the imperial period constituted the second largest group of the population in Prague and the majority in some other regions. These Germans now have been almost completely ousted or assimilated.[43] In Bulgaria, 39 percent of the respondents admitted that they are hostile to Turks, and 21 percent to Muslim Bulgarians.[44] Both these groups are numerically small, speak Bulgarian, and do not present any competition to the Bulgarians. Their only "sin" lies in the fact that they are descendants of the former elite, which was driven from Bulgaria a century ago.

It is very likely that the anti-Russian tendencies in former union republics and the rise of such current stereotypes as "migrant-occupiers," "rolling stones," and so forth, can be explained by similar reasons.

Thus, the process of transformation from "imperial minority" to simple "minority" is not unique. It happened to Turks in Bulgaria, Cyprus, and Egypt, to Frenchmen in Algeria, to Englishmen in India and Zimbabwe, and to many other peoples on different continents. However, no state has ever disintegrated with the speed at which the Soviet Union broke apart. Even if we assume that the process of turning Russians into a minority began not in the autumn of 1991 (when the treaty on the formation of the USSR was officially denounced) but in 1987–89, history still gave 25 million Russians too little time to adapt to new realities.

Unlike the Austro-Hungarian or the Ottoman empires, the USSR collapsed not in wartime, which could have been blamed for the hardships that befell the population, but in peacetime, with no outside interference. This makes the process of the overall collapse of a once powerful state completely incomprehensible to the man in the street and makes it even more difficult for Russian minorities to adapt to the idea that their life in a foreign ethnic milieu will never be the same. Some Russians still entertain the hope that some wonderful day everything will be back as it was and the single state will reappear.

Finally, never before has the collapse of a multinational state been accompanied by such a sharp and rapid decline in people's living standards as in the former USSR. The economic crisis only further aggravates the position of Russians in the newly independent states as the most vulnerable of ethnic minorities.

Notes

1. The actions of the Romanian and Bulgarian governments concerning minorities were condemned by the European parliament, which adopted a special resolution on this point (Resolution No. 927, 1989).

2. In 1989, 25.3 million Russians lived outside the Russian Federation. See *Soiuz*, 1990, no. 32.

3. *Convention on the Prevention and Punishment of the Crime of Genocide* (United Nations, 1948); *Covenant on Civil and Political Rights* (United Nations, 1965); *Convention on the Rights of Indigenous Peoples and Those Leading a Tribal Way of Life in Independent States* (no. 169, International Labor Organization, 1982); and others.

4. See Alfredson Gudmundur, *Prava menshinstv: ravenstvo i nediskriminatsiia. Leningradskaia konferentsiia po pravam menshinstv (doklady i soobshcheniia)* (Leningrad, 1991), p. 12.

5. See Tore Lindholm, "Zakonny li i osushchestvimy li 'kollektivnye prava cheloveka' dlia menshinstv," Leningrad (conference), pp. 93–96.

6. Gudmundur, *Prava menshinstv*, p. 34.

7. Minority Rights Group, *World Directory of Minorities* (Harlow, Essex: Longman Group UK Ltd., 1991), p. xiv.

8. L. Drobizheva, "Kto zavoiuet russkoe bol'shinstvo," *Nezavisimaia gazeta*, June 16, 1991.

9. *Nezavisimaia gazeta*, February 18, 1991.

10. Iu.V. Arutiunian, chief editor, *Russkie: etnosotsiologicheskie ocherki* (Moscow: Nauka, 1992), p. 414.

11. *Nezavisimaia gazeta*, June 15, 1991.

12. Based on 1989 population census data from the State Committee of the USSR for Statistics.

13. Iu.V. Arutiunian, *K voprosu o razvitii natsii v "svoei" i inoiazychnoi srede. Etnosy v svoei i inonatsional'noi srede. Materialy sovetsko-amerikanskogo simpoziuma* (Erevan, 1987), p. 10.

14. Universal military service (taking into consideration the fact that the Russian language is the only means of communication in the army) and compulsory secondary

education (with Russian language and literature as required subjects) served as instruments of administrative coercion for learning the Russian language. Opportunities for social promotion were also connected with knowledge of what amounted to the official language of the Soviet Union. This was especially noticeable in the field of science, because theses for scientific degrees had to be written and presented only in Russian. That was the strongest indirect motive of people of different nationalities of the USSR for learning the Russian language.

15. See Miroslav Khrots, *Staryi natsionalizm ili novye natsional'nye dvizheniia v Tsentral'noi i Vostochnoi Evrope. Neopublikovannye doklady na konferentsii po pravam menshinstv i pravam cheloveka v novoi Evrope* (Oslo, January 30–February 3, 1991).

16. A. Kuznetsov, *O nashykh mezhnatsional'nykh otnosheniiakh,* Part 1 (Tallinn, 1991), p. 6.

17. A.V. Aklaev, *Iazykovoe zakonodatel'stvo soiuznykh respublik i natsional'noe samosoznanie* (Moscow: INION, 1992).

18. *Strany mira (politiko-economicheskii spravochnik)* (Moscow: Politizdat, 1988).

19. Ibid., pp. 71, 98, 111.

20. Ibid., p. 63.

21. Zakon Kazakhskoi SSR "O iazykakh Kazakhskoi SSR," *Vedomosti Verkhovnogo soveta Kazakhskoi SSR* (Alma-Ata, 1989), st. 4.

22. A.V. Aklaev, *Iazykovoe zakonodatel'stvo,* pp. 211–12.

23. The term "zero principle" (option) means that there is no residency requirement (it equals zero) for permanent residents of the republic. The term appeared in the course of the discussion on the introduction of this requirement in the Baltic republics.

24. "Zakony o grazhdanstve v respublikakh" (Dos'e "NG"), *Nezavisimaia gazeta,* December 3, 1991.

25. See N. Aleksandrov, "Latysh tretei kategorii," *Soiuz,* 1991, no. 49, p. 16.

26. Ibid.

27. Quoted from Irina Litvinova, "Russkii vopros v Latvii: Narushenie prav cheloveka," *Izvestiia,* September 28, 1992.

28. Ibid.

29. Ibid.

30. Ibid.

31. Ibid.

32. Algis Prazauskas, "SNG kak postkolonial'noe prostranstvo," *Nezavisimaia gazeta,* January 7, 1992.

33. George Demko, "Nachnem c tipologii," *Nezavisimaia gazeta,* July 25, 1991.

34. *Materialy 1-go s"ezda Konferentsii repressirovannykh narodov RSFSR* (Moscow, 1991).

35. Ibid.

36. Ibid.

37. *Russkie (etnosotsiologicheskie ocherki),* p. 18.

38. Helen Krag and Nikolai Vakhtin, *O politicheskoi situatsii v Estonskoi respublike, v sviazi s polozheniem natsional'nykh grup* (Report of St. Petersburg Group on the Rights of Minorities) (St. Petersburg, GPM, 1992).

39. Ibid.

40. Iu. Bromlei, *Narody i kul'tury: Razvitie i vzaimodeistvie* (Moscow: Nauka, 1989), p. 102.

41. Ibid., p. 103.

42. Ibid.

43. "Kto kogo nenavidit?" *Nezavisimaia gazeta,* January 11, 1992.

44. Ibid.

3

Russian Minorities
The Political Dimension

Ramazan Abdulatipov

Throughout its long history, Russia has undergone upheavals that have shaken not only peoples historically sharing one territory and destiny, but the entire world. The nations located on the unstable fault line of Russian history are the peoples of the former republics of the USSR that are now part of the Commonwealth of Independent States (CIS), as well as the Baltic states. The Russians, owing to their large numbers (145 million people, according to the 1989 census) and scale of settlement, are the one nation that has interacted intensively with all the other peoples inhabiting the territory of the former USSR on an ethnic as well as political-economic level.

Indeed, until recently these areas encompassed more than 25 million Russians, or 17 percent of the entire Russian population of the former Soviet Union and 18 percent of the total population of the non-Russian republics.[1] After August 1991, these Russians found themselves to be residents of new, independent states.

The political, economic, historical, and cultural implications of this phenomenon have not been adequately studied or conceptualized, even though these changes will markedly affect world development by the end of the twentieth century. The statistics characterizing the settlement of Russians are pertinent if we are to understand the essence of current political and cultural processes which all too often take the form of conflicts. The Russians living in the following areas are mostly urban residents: 95–97 percent in Turkmenistan; Azerbaijan, and Uzbekistan; 85–86 percent in Georgia, Moldova, and Latvia; 51 percent in Kazakhstan; 41 percent in Latvia; 40 percent in Kyrgyzstan; 39 percent in Estonia; 29 percent in Ukraine; 24 percent in Moldova.[2]

It is important to note that most of the Russians permanently living outside the Russian Federation were born in these (non-Russian) regions. Sixty-seven percent of the Russians registered by a census conducted in Kazakhstan were born in towns or villages. Sixty-six percent of the Russians permanently residing in Azerbaijan were born on its territory. In Kyrgyzstan, Ukraine, Uzbekistan, Latvia, Moldova, and Turkmenistan over 50 percent of the Russian population consider these republics to be their native land. The figure is 49.7 percent for Lithuania and 42–48 percent for Tajikistan, Georgia, Estonia, and Belarus. Only in Armenia is the percentage of Russians born on its territory a relatively low 26 percent.[3]

These statistics contrast with phenomena that until recently seemed of minor importance, but have today assumed historical, cultural, and political significance, even causing political clashes and human tragedy. Much of the problem lies in the fact that the proportion of Russians with a good command of the language of the indigenous (or "titular") nationality of their republic is extremely low, even among those born and raised on the territory of the former Union republics. Less than 1 percent of Russian residents of Kazakhstan are fluent in the Kazakh language, although they constitute 40 percent of the population. In Kyrgyzstan the figure is 1.2 percent, in Turkmenistan 2.5 percent, in Tajikistan 3.5 percent, Uzbekistan 4.6 percent, Moldova 12 percent, Azerbaijan 14 percent, Estonia 15 percent, Latvia 22 percent, Georgia 24 percent, and Belarus 26 percent. Only in Lithuania, Armenia, and Ukraine do more than a third of the Russians living there (37 percent, 34 percent, and 34 percent, respectively)[4] know the national language well.

It goes without saying that this is due to circumstances that did not encourage Russians to study the languages of other peoples, such as the settlement of Russians in multiethnic districts mostly in towns where they constituted the bulk of the population, as well as widespread knowledge of Russian on the part of non-Russians. Other contributing factors were the great number of schools, higher-education establishments, and other institutions in which classes were taught in Russian and the established network of Russian-language mass media and cultural institutions.

The situation has not changed much since the adoption of state language laws in the republics of the former Soviet Union. The trouble is not that, as some believe, Russians do not want to study these languages. Unfortunately, the creation of conditions conducive to mastering the language of the indigenous population by Russians and other "nonindigenous" nationalities did not follow the proclamations of a particular language as the state language. Neither did the economic plight of the republics of the former Soviet Union help the situation.

In light of these problems, we deem it important to extensively investigate the phenomenon of Russian populations fluent in two or more languages, as well as Russian ethnolinguistic adaptation in other ethnic mediums in terms of their historical dynamics and perspective. This implies studying the attitude of Russians in the republics toward the law on the state language and its consequences. It is also necessary to determine the conditions affecting use of the Russian language in the republics, and the degree of satisfaction of Russian and other Russian-speaking populations with these conditions.

Clearly, infringement on the right of the Russian people to develop their native tongue and speak it is bound to cause interethnic tensions (to say nothing of contradicting international human rights). A case in point is the negative experience with the language policies in the Baltic area and Moldova, which led to, among other things, mass migration of the Russian and Russian-speaking populations.

The economic impact of the employment situation of Russians is central to the overall role played by the Russian minorities in the former union republics and their strained relations with the indigenous majority of these republics. First of all, Russians generally are engaged primarily in industry. For instance, 44 percent of the Russians living in Estonia work in industry (against 25 percent of Estonians). In Ukraine the corresponding figures are 39 percent and 31 percent, in Latvia 37 percent and 25 percent, in Lithuania 36 percent and 28 percent, in Moldova 35 percent and 17 percent, in Azerbaijan 34 percent and 18 percent, and so on.[5]

The proportion of Russian specialists with a higher or specialized secondary education employed in their national economies by far and everywhere exceeds the Russians' share in the total population in the former union republics. For example, in Tajikistan Russians constitute roughly 7 percent of the total population but 21 percent (2.7 times more) of the working specialists having such an education; in Turkmenistan the figures are 9.5 percent and 22 percent, respectively (2.4 times more); in Uzbekistan 8.3 percent and 17 percent (2.1 times more). The ratio is 1.7–1.3 times more in favor of the Russians in Azerbaijan, Moldova, Belarus, Kyrgyzstan, Armenia, Lithuania, and Ukraine.

As for agriculture, the proportion of Russians engaged in farming is not great, ranging from 2.3 percent in Turkmenistan (the lowest figure) to 10 percent in Kazakhstan (the highest figure).[6]

The number of Russians in the former union republics and their employment distribution in the national economies make it clear why relations between town and country—including the problem of nonequivalent exchange between them—inflame interethnic conflicts. This, among other things, has been borne out by events in Dushanbe and the Fergana Valley.

These statistics lead to the conclusion that, in ethnic terms, the Russians were the one people that united all republics and regions in the Union. One further important factor is that the Russians' vital economic and cultural activity, perhaps more than that of any other Soviet people, proceeded on the scale of the entire Soviet Union. This objective fact, affirmed and proclaimed by the mass media, could not help but have an effect on the Russian people's self-awareness.

Characteristically, in the course of large-scale ethnosociological investigations conducted in Russia and other union republics in the 1970s and 1980s, Russians, more often than members of other nationalities, named the USSR as a whole as their native land, rather than Russia or the republic of their residence. No wonder they experienced a sociopsychological shock upon the disintegration of the USSR. No wonder there is such concern—especially in the context of the activization of extremist, nationalistic forces—over their human, socioeconomic, and national-cultural interests. After all, the destinies of 25 million people are at stake.

The new status of the former union republics, their establishment and development as independent states, the upsurge of national awareness among their peoples, the reorientation of their economies, and above all the predominance of heavy industry in the employment of the local Russian population all have contributed to the unique position of Russians living outside Russia. Historically, their socioeconomic, political, national, and cultural interests have been connected not so much with the republics or with the new Russia as with the integrated Union state. This leads the governments of the sovereign republics and their indigenous populations to look upon Russians living in their republics as advocates and representatives of the now-compromised former state system, and therefore as potential opponents of new and independent development. In the common consciousness of indigenous nationalities, local Russians are frequently branded as occupiers, unwanted migrants, and so forth.

While the position of Russians and Russian-speaking populations in the republics differs from region to region, Russians everywhere are to some extent in favor of new relations with the new Russia. As we see it, these relations can and must be diversified and multifaceted, providing for the defense of political, property, and other rights, assistance in meeting national-cultural needs (education and information in the Russian language, development of national culture, and so on), help in returning to Russia, and other needs.

This kind of aid could be given primarily by incorporating appropriate provisions in interstate political, economic, and other agreements, since what is being done is, in the view of the Russian people living outside Russia, not adequate. The question of dual citizenship, favored by many Russian residents in the former union republics, should be given serious attention. Capable Russian missions and other services are also needed to effectively assist Russian cultural movements, societies, and centers (such activities are not allowed everywhere). These and similar steps on the part of Russia are vitally needed by the Russian population in the former union republics. Moreover, they would tangibly augment Russia's prestige in these republics and the world. Why indeed could Russia not follow the example of Germany in its relations with the ethnic Germans of the diaspora, or of Israel in its relations with Jews living outside that country?

Such steps with regard to Russians living in the former union republics are essential from the sociopsychological point of view as well. It is no secret that the sweeping "sovereignization" of former union and autonomous republics, the dramatic rise of the indigenous peoples' national awareness, the drastic expansion of the communicative role of their national languages, and a concomitant diminution in the function of the Russian language have resulted in a considerable change in status for Russians in the sovereign republics. As a result, person-to-person interethnic relations are not improving. All of the above gives rise to insecurity among the Russian and Russian-speaking populations, propelling them to become a potential multimillion-strong army of refugees.

According to the Center for the Study of Public Opinion, at the beginning of last year about a third of the Russians in the Baltic region and Transcaucasia replied in a survey that they would like to emigrate in the near future, most of them to Russia. In the Central Asian republics the figure stood at 70–80 percent. In Central Asia, from 50 to 75 percent of Russians feared that possible interethnic conflicts in the area might lead to bloodshed. Between 13 and 34 percent of the Russians in the Baltic states and Transcaucasia held that opinion.

At present there are no reliable statistics on Russians and Russian refugees, but the main migration tendencies are clear and distinct. In 1990–1991, an average of 470,000 people arrived in Russia each year—70,000 more than in 1989. Migration of Russians to regions other than Russia over the same period decreased by 60,000 (17 percent).[7]

If the situation persists for some time in the future, one may expect a much greater influx of migrants of Russian and other Russian-speaking nationalities. The Russian Ministry of Labor and Employment projects at least a tripling of migration annually.

Given the present economic dislocation, most migrants will face accommodations in substandard housing or in camps, as well as unemployment. Such conditions present are a favorable environment for extremist sentiments and movements. This may pose fresh problems for Russia's political life and endanger its fledgling democracy.

It is in the political and economic interests of Russia and the other sovereign states of the former Soviet Union to stabilize the situation, since massive and uncontrolled migration of Russians to Russia is sure to aggravate socioeconomic and political problems in Russia as well as in the CIS member-countries and the Baltic states.

These factors make it imperative to study the status of Russians outside Russia, the dynamics of and prospects for their resettlement in former union republics, the demographic structure of the Russian population, problems with their social and economic development, and ways for satisfying their national-cultural requirements, including the development of national culture through the formation of a Russian cultural autonomy. It is also necessary to investigate the problem of introducing the republics' Russian populations to the language and culture of the indigenous nationality.

The national awareness of the aforementioned groups of the Russian population and their relationships with other nationalities (primarily with the republics' titular nationalities) should figure prominently in the research. It is important to study the Russians' involvement in the political life of the CIS and Baltic countries —especially their representation in the power structures and public and cultural movements and organizations—cornerstones of stable social and political status in a sovereign republic or state.

The latter circumstance is of particular importance, since in the opinion of many Russian specialists on ethnic politics an analysis of the trends of development in the Baltic states, Transcaucasia, Moldova, and other republics (and currently in the south of Russia as well) reveals that the success of the nationalistic forces does nothing but exacerbate contradictions between the indigenous nations, on the one hand, and the so-called "Russian-speaking population," on the other.

It would be naive to believe that after the formation of the Commonwealth of Independent States these conflicts and contradictions would recede into the past. When possibilities are inadequately explored and reliable mechanisms for adjustment are left undeveloped, the alternatives are either assimilation or a forcible rejection of the alien national element. The inexorable logic of political struggle and the practice of "postsocialist nationalism" are pushing ruling circles in some republics toward the idea of a mononational state, which implies substantial alterations in the national structure of the population in the former Union republics. The negative consequences of monoethnicization are easy to predict, but it is already obvious that it affects chiefly the interests of the Russian nation.

Hence, the spontaneous rise of all sorts of parties, leagues, associations, clubs, and movements concerned with the defense of the national interests of Russians residing both inside and outside Russia. To date the number of such organizations runs into the dozens. For all the differences in their programs and actions, they share one goal—to consolidate the Russian nation and revive its power and culture.

What can be said of the swiftly changing Russian national-patriotic political spectrum? It is made up of the following major players: (1) traditional right-wing Orthodox monarchists (the Pre-Council Conference, Vladimir Osipov's League "Christian Revival"); (2) the New Right, or the Rightists who have renounced monarchism and the fundamental principles of traditional right-wing Orthodoxy (Vladimir Zhirinovskii's Liberal Democratic Party or, under a proposed name change, the Liberal Patriotic Party, Valery Skurlatov's Russian National Front, Sergei Baburin's Russian People's League, Alexander Barkashov's Russian National Unity, and the Slavic Council); (3) the Cossacks (Alexander Martynov's Cossack League and numerous regional Cossack armies, communities, and organizations); (4) national democratic organizations that regard democracy as a fundamental value and ideological pillar (Nikolai Travkin's Democratic Party of Russia, Mikhail Astaf'ev's Constitutional Democratic Party–The Party of the People's Freedom, Victor Aksiuchits's Russian Christian Democratic Movement); (5) National Bolsheviks seeking to synthesize the Soviet Bolshevik version of Marxism with Russian national values (the party of the United Workers' Front, Aleksandr Romanenko's League of Russia's Revival).

Some specialists hold that national democrats oriented toward the Western neoconservative model (the "National Accord" bloc uniting the Democratic Party of Russia, the Christian Democratic Party, and the Russian Christian Democratic Movement) constitute a formidable political force.

If we look upon the "Russian question" as a mass ethnosocial movement, then the Cossacks, especially the Don and Kuban Cossacks, are its more united and organized detachment. They can be said to control the political situation in Russia's south, which is turning into a bulwark of Russian unity. Yet despite their avowed adherence to pan-Russian rallying cries ("one and indivisible Russia"), the Don and Kuban Cossacks will hardly be able to unite and lead the Russian national movement on a nationwide scale. This is due to the following factors: (a) the subethnocentrist character of the present-day Cossack movement (they are concerned primarily with the rehabilitation and revival of the Cossacks as a separate people), (b) its localization within a single region, and (c) their forced orientation toward neutralization of "outbursts of national energy" from the North Caucasus, which are directly or indirectly anti-Cossack.

Given the propitious circumstances, the so-called New Right ideology is likely to become active. First, it relies on a broadly understood tradition, on qualities organic and inherent in the Russian land, unlike Orthodoxy, monarchy, or Bolshevism alone. This makes the New Right ideologically open and attractive to like-minded people. Second, since social justice and social protection are the key principles of the New Right, the movement is able to unite not only right-wing forces, but also those on the left political flank.

At the same time, it should be stressed that the term "New Right" bears a generalizing character, and among its more influential members are such divergent political forces as Zhirinovskii's Liberal Democratic Party and Baburin's Russian People's League. The former, preaching imperial nationalism and economic liberalism coupled with runaway populism, is deliberately imitating the fascist model and might enlist all kinds of motley right-wing radical groups. The League is a moderate right-wing movement that formally espouses leftist catchwords and seeks support among nationalist-minded pragmatists and political centrists.

The Russian movement has great appeal. First, due to the poor development of liberal democratic ideas, it is the key integrating and consolidating force that Russian society needs to extricate itself from its current crisis and to bring about large-scale modernization. Second, the patently atavistic thrust of the Russian movement has a special appeal in this period of considerably weakening and disintegrating power structures, mounting chaos, and sharply increasing crime. Third, while Russian or any other brand of nationalism undermined the Soviet Union's political stability, for which Marxist ideology served as the legitimizing factor, it greatly contributes to political stability within the framework of a national state. Indeed, the Russian Federation, where Russians constitute 81.5 percent of the total population, is one of the most monoethnic republics in the former USSR, second only to Armenia.

The degree of self-realization of the Russian movement, its forms, methods and political prospects depend on a number of internal factors (the ability to offer clear-cut and attractive programs; the availability of leaders, nationally oriented intellectuals, and material and financial resources; and access to the mass media, with their power to consolidate heterogeneous groups) as well as external factors (the scope of the political, social, and economic crises; the dimension and nature of the migration, verging on exodus, of Russian populations from former union republics to Russia; the pitch of interethnic tension in Russia proper; and the relationship of Russia's political leadership, army, and law enforcement bodies to Russian nationalists).

There are serious grounds to conclude that the Russian movement has every right to claim if not full political power in Russia, then at least a level of participation commensurate with the historical role played by this great nation. The crucial question is what character this movement will assume and which of its trends will prove to be the most mass-based, influential, and patriotic.

Notes

1. *Chislennost' naseleniia i nekotorye sotsial'no-demograficheskie kharakteristiki natsional'nostei i narodov RSFSR, Osnovnye pokazateli sotsial'no-ekonomicheskogo razvitiia natsional'no-gosudarstvennykh obrazovanii RSFSR* (Moscow: RSFSR Goskomstat, 1991).

2. *Materialy Vsesoiuznoi perepisi naseleniia 1979* (Moscow: USSR Goskomstat, 1990).

3. Ibid.

4. Ibid.

5. Ibid.

6. Ibid.

7. Computed on the basis of the data cited in the scientific paper "Migratsia russkogo naseleniia v Rossii" (Moscow: Institute of Sociology, Russian Academy of Sciences, 1992).

4

Processes of Disintegration in the Russian Federation and the Problem of Russians

Leokadia Drobizheva

From the moment the status of former autonomous formations of the Russian Federation became subject to negotiations, and especially after these states proclaimed their sovereignty in the summer and autumn of 1990, the Russian Federation has been undergoing a test of the strength of its unity and territorial integrity.

Will Russia repeat the path traveled by the Soviet Union? This is what now worries not only the Russian public but also politicians throughout the world, for on this depends the future shape of Russia and of the geopolitical space it currently occupies.

The process of disintegration is greatly affected by the presence of Russians in the republics, their social status there, and their political orientation.

In this chapter the author would like to concentrate on two points: (1) an examination of how this process is affected by changes in the social status of Russians compared to the members of the titular nationalities of other republics of the Russian Federation, along with the demographic and ethnocultural factors determining their situation and interethnic relations; and (2) an analysis of the situation in the former Soviet Union and Russia from the point of view of the relationship between the republics and Moscow and how the Russians might act if these relations become strained.

At present Russia is comprised of twenty-one republics. There are also ten national areas, of which the Yamalo-Nenets, Koriak, Nenets, and Chukchi areas have declared themselves either republics or autonomous republics; Evenkia has declared itself an autonomous region. As yet the Supreme Soviet has not adopted any decision on their status, and they are still considered national-administrative or autonomous formations just like the Jewish Autonomous Region.

In these republics, autonomous regions, and areas live 11.8 million Russians. The greatest number of Russians live in Tatarstan and Bashkortostan (over 1.5

million in each). About 1 million Russians live in Udmurtia, 0.7 million in Buriatia, 0.50 million in the Komi Republic, 0.50 million in the Sakha Republic (Yakutia), 0.58 million in Mordvinia, and 0.58 million in Karelia.[1]

However, most important are not the raw numbers (11.8 million Russians versus 17.7 million non-Russians of the titular nations having their own national-state formations),[2] but the ratio between the Russian population and that of a republic's titular nation.

In eight republics—Dagestan, North Ossetia, Chechnia, Ingushetia, Kabardino-Balkaria, Chuvashia, Kalmykia, and Tuva—Russians constitute the minority (9 percent in Dagestan and 23–37 percent in the other republics). In Tatarstan, Russians constitute 43.3 percent of the population and coexist with Tatars (48.5 percent) and other largely non-Slavic nationalities, so here too they constitute a minority. Bashkortostan has a 39.1 percent Russian population, which makes them the largest national group. Together with the Ukrainians and Belarusians their number reaches 41.6 percent, still not a majority; 22 percent of the population are Bashkirs and 28 percent Tatars and other peoples of the Volga. In Mari Russians comprise 47.5 percent (and with the Ukrainians and Belarusians, 48.6 percent) of the population. Although the Mari are a minority of the population (43.3 percent), together with other Volga peoples they constitute a majority.

In the Sakha Republic (Yakutia), Russians constitute half of the population (with the Ukrainians and Belarusians, 58 percent), and in eight republics—Mordvinia, Udmurtia, Karachai-Cherkessia, Gorno-Altai, Karelia, Buriatia, Adygeia, and Khakassia—they range from over 50 percent to 79 percent.[3]

So, if demographic criteria alone are considered, Russians constitute the numerical minority in eleven republics of Russia and in one (the Sakha Republic), half the population (58 percent together with the Ukrainians and Belarusians), while in the remaining nine republics they constitute the majority. So the question of the applicability of the term "ethnic minority" to Russians in the republics is open to discussion.

"Ethnic minority" is not a purely demographic term. It defines the people belonging to an ethnic group whose name is not included in the name of their state or republic. Psychologically, the state is mainly perceived as the state of the titular nation. As is known, the republics of Russia have proclaimed sovereignty. The majority of the presidents or chairmen of the supreme soviets of the republics are either members of the titular nation or Russians who know the language of the titular nation, which is a precondition for their election. Supreme soviets of the republics have adopted special resolutions on this matter.

It should also be borne in mind that the intragroup solidarity of Russians in the republics of Russia makes them acutely sensitive to the fate of their compatriots in the states of the former Soviet Union, and this greatly promotes their intergroup solidarity. Considering that they live in Russia (where they constitute the overwhelming majority of the population), that they can count on support, and that they now feel their national unity threatened, it should be expected that this solidarity of Russians living among peoples of other nationalities will grow steadily. Among the important objective factors affecting Russians' attitudes and behavior will be their changing role in the republics.

Up until the 1960s the social status of Russians differed greatly from that of the non-Russians among whom they lived. Twice as many Russian workers were nonmanual workers or specialists with a higher education than were members of the native population. At times the gap was quite considerable. During the 1970s and the 1980s the educational level and professional skills of members of all the nationalities grew considerably, sometimes by 100 percent and more, as was the case with the Buriats, Bashkirs, Tatars, Yakuts, Ossetians, and Chechens. So the situation in the republics of Russia had changed quite a bit by the early 1990s.

As of the 1970 census in Buriatia, the educational level of Buriats was already higher than that of Russians, a gap especially pronounced among the employed.[4] Since the 1970s there have been twice as many specialists with a higher education among Buriats as among Russians living in the republic.[5] The same is true for the Lak in Dagestan and Adygei in Adygeia. In the Sakha-Yakutian, North Ossetian, Karachai-Cherkessian, Khakass, and Kabardino-Balkar (among Balkars) republics, the percentage of specialists with a higher education who were members of the titular nation was approximately equal to that of the resident Russians, while in Tatarstan, Bashkortostan, and Mordvinia their number differed only slightly (by 20–30 percent).

In other republics and autonomous formations the members of the titular nations lag significantly behind Russians in this indicator (in Tuva, Karelia, Chechnia, Ingushetia, Chuvashia, and the Mari Republic by almost 50 percent).[6] On the whole, social mobility among the majority of the non-Russian peoples is high. According to the data of ethnosociological studies conducted by scientists of the Institute of Ethnology and Anthropology of the USSR Academy of Sciences from 1972 through 1989 in Tatarstan, Udmurtia, Chuvashia, and the Mari Republic, over 65 percent of the gainfully employed population had raised their social status in one way or another compared with their parents.[7] The same tendencies have been observed in other republics and autonomous formations as well.

The state of interethnic communication is influenced by at least two major social circumstances. First of all, in the republics the greater percentage of the people belonging to the titular ethnos live in the countryside (58 percent among Bashkirs, 70 percent among Tuvinians, 74 percent among Yakuts, etc.),[8] while Russians live mostly in towns and cities. Only in the capitals of the North Caucasian republics and Chuvashia do Russians constitute less than half the population (in Dagestan 21 percent, in the rest 34–44 percent). In all the other republics they constitute the majority of the population in the capitals (in Buriatia, Mordvinia, Karelia, and Udmurtia as much as 70 percent or more).

Second, as a rule, Russians are employed in advanced branches of production in all the republics and autonomous formations (except in Tatarstan and Bashkortostan). They more often hold prestigious posts, and more of them work in the sciences as well as the arts. Naturally, they feel they are the main creators of modern material values, yet their representation is inadequate among most elite groups. For instance, although only 35 percent of scientists in Tatarstan are Tatar (56 percent are Russians), their percentage of doctors and candidates of science is 42 and 45 percent, respectively. In Bashkortostan, Bashkirs constitute 17.2 percent of all scientists, 34 percent of candidates of science, and 30 percent of doctors of science.[9]

Meanwhile, the criteria of social differentiation are undergoing changes. Among them property, material well-being, and access to power are gradually becoming basic needs. In the power bodies the percentage of members of the titular nations is greater than their share of the population. Quite recently in many republics secretaries of the regional party committees and chairmen of the executive committees were mostly Russians. Now the situation has changed radically. Chairmen of the supreme soviets who are Russian by nationality are a rare exception—and they must know the language of the titular nation (as in Buriatia, for instance). The number of members of the indigenous population elected to the soviets of people's deputies is also growing: in the Supreme Soviet of Tatarstan in 1990 there were 57.6 percent Tatars, as compared with 49 percent in the Supreme Soviet of the previous convocation. The respective figures for Yakutia are 51 percent and 48.5 percent. In these republics the figures for the deputies to the regional and city soviets were 64.7 and 65 percent, compared with 50.2 and 57.7 percent, respectively. These changes are all the more significant since these nationalities do not constitute the proportional majority of the population. Moreover, today representatives of titular nations hold a larger number of prominent posts in the leadership of the soviets and the government. In Tatarstan and Yakutia, for instance, 75 percent of the chairmen of the soviets at all levels are Tatars and Yakuts. In Yakutia, 70 percent of ministers are Yakut by nationality.

Naturally, the competition between ethnoses that began in the late 1970s has now become more acute, and this tendency continues to grow.

There is another circumstance that has an impact on interethnic competition—members of titular nations of the republics of Russia seldom migrate to other regions outside their territory. The most mobile people concentrate in the capitals, which is also bound to increase competition. The Russians feel it more acutely, since their role and status in the republics are subject to change. Some adapt, but others cannot reconcile themselves to the new situation.

This process is accompanied by migration flows. Up until the late 1980s, population growth in the republics of Russia was due both to natural reproduction and to the fact that more people were entering than leaving the republics. But Russians have been leaving the Komi and Buriat republics and the Nenets and Chukchi areas since the mid-1980s. In 1990 this process embraced the Sakha (Yakutian) Republic and the Yamalo-Nenets and Khant-Mansi areas. In the wake of interethnic conflict in Tuva in 1990, over ten thousand people left.[10]

Russians living among people of other nationalities are more acutely aware of the sharp awakening of national self-consciousness that we are witnessing in Tatarstan, the Sakha Republic, Komi, Karelia, North Ossetia, Chechnia, Ingushetia, Kabardino-Balkaria, and other republics. The sharp increase in the awareness of ethnic identity has objective reasons. What has been happening in the former autonomous formations of Russia since the late 1980s (although among some intellectuals the process started a little bit earlier) is quite similar to what took place in the late 1960s and early 1970s in the polyethnic states of the West (French Canadians vs. British Canadians, the Walloon-Flemish conflict in Belgium, and others) and what in the late 1970s and early 1980s began to develop in the republics of the Soviet Union. Change in the status of the nations in contact became the source of new ambition for the non-Russian peoples and a cause of anxiety for the Russians.

Since the late 1980s, those subject to the most tension have been Russians living in Tuva, Checheno-Ingushetia, Yakutia, Tataria, and Bashkiria. In these republics the ethnopolitical conflict between the republic and Russian center was exacerbated by the intrarepublic, intergroup ethnic conflict.

Since the situation in the North Caucasus is dealt with in chapter 9, I shall analyze the situation in other republics.

According to data from surveys conducted under our supervision in Tuva by E. Anaiban in 1990, surveys we conducted in Tataria in 1989–90 with Damir Iskhakov and Rosa Musina, and expert surveys conducted in Bashkiria in 1990–91 that were made available to us, Russians have reacted primarily to the new ethnopolitical situation in the republics and to the decline in their material standard of living. In Tuva, 35 percent of the Russian respondents cited disrespectful statements about Russians, while another 43 percent said that they came across such cases very rarely. By the way, the percentage of Russians and Tuvinians who perceived such infringements on their national interests was roughly the same. Still, Russians mentioned acts of hooliganism perpetrated by young people on ethnic grounds twice as often as Tuvinians did, keeping in mind that open interethnic clashes have taken place in Tuva.

Naturally, there are several reasons for interethnic tension. One of the most important is expanding social competition. Between the population census of 1979 and that of 1989, the percentage of nonmanual workers among Tuvinians increased by seven points, while among Russians the increase was four points.[11] If in the early 1980s there were twice as many specialists with a higher education among Russians as among Tuvinians, in the late 1980s the share of specialists with a higher education among Russians (15 years of age and older) was 10.3 percent, while the respective figure for Tuvinians was 6.1 percent, so the gap was not as great. Moreover, the number of graduating students on the verge of receiving their diplomas was approximately the same among Russians and Tuvinians.[12]

Almost 75 percent of Russian respondents said that it was difficult to find a job. Very few of them said that they were satisfied with their jobs (about 25 percent). This too has a negative effect on interethnic relations.

The survey data also show that Russians more often than Tuvinians were faced with ethnic discrimination when seeking high posts, which they experienced as an insult to their personal dignity. At the same time, a study of ethnic stereotypes shows that Russians' self-esteem is significantly higher than Tuvinians'.

Conflicts also arise on demographic grounds. The birthrate among Tuvinians in Tuva is twice as high as that of Russians living there. Thus Tuvinians have larger families, so even if their wages are equal to Russians', their per capita income is much smaller. This arouses hostility toward Russians, which in turn provokes a defensive reaction among the latter. Moreover, since a large number of the Tuvinians now living in towns and cities only recently moved there from the countryside, their housing conditions are inadequate. This, too, aggravates the conflict situation. Russians are also blamed for the ever-worsening environment. Tuvinians wish to solve their own economic problems and take over the management of their own natural resources.

As tension mounts, the Russians' attitude toward interethnic contacts is unfavorable. No more than 35 percent are prepared to work in an ethnically mixed collective (the Tuvinians' attitude is roughly the same).

The attitude of the respondents toward family contacts better reflects the general interethnic situation than everyday practice, for although more than half of the Russian respondents opposed mixed marriages, their number increased by 30 percent in the period between the last two population censuses.[13] Unofficial friendly contacts have been preserved: 84 percent of the Russians have friends among people of other nationalities.

One might judge the prospects for Russians in Tuva by the fact that, although at least half of the Russian respondents said they wanted to leave the republic, no less than 40 percent said they wanted their children to learn the Tuvinian language, which means they wanted to stay where they were.

The situation in another republic, Tatarstan, is also undergoing rapid changes. Here, earlier than in other republics of Russia, statements were made, both in power structures and public organizations such as the Tatar Public Center and the Party of National Independence, about independence and the adoption of a new constitution. This tendency was most pronounced among Tatar elite groups, both in the republic and in Moscow. Under ordinary conditions, however, in everyday life Tatars display rather stable tolerance in their contacts with Russians. Although compared to the 1970s and 1980s, the Russians' interethnic attitudes have deteriorated, the percentage of people who have experienced difficulties in interethnic relationships at their places of work still did not exceed 20–25 percent among different social groups.

In 1990 no less than 65 percent of the Russians living in the towns and cities of Tatarstan were happy to have interethnic contacts at work. Naturally, the atmosphere in large cities such as Kazan, Naberezhnye Chelny, and Almetevsk differed from that in small towns such as Menzelinsk, where the situation is much more strained.

The loyalty of the Russian population is higher than that of the members of the titular nation (there are rather few shared negative attitudes in various spheres), although in general their attitudes do not differ much.

Interethnic tension in the business world stems from the fact that the social status of the two main competing ethnoses has been leveled out very quickly in Tatarstan.

In recent years the number of locals in new cities such as Almetevsk and Naberezhnye Chelny, including people from the surrounding countryside, has mushroomed rapidly. Now they constitute a significant part (in some cities up to 50 percent) of Tatarstan's main population. They are less skilled than Russian or Ukrainian migrants and consequently earn less. At the same time, Tatar families are larger than Russian families, and they need housing (75 percent still lack adequate housing), and the need for social services in response to urban conditions continues to grow. These factors stimulate social competitiveness and a readiness to defend one's interests (in early 1990 over half of city residents, mostly Tatars, supported the idea of broadening the rights of the republic).

In this context Russians had a narrow choice: either consider the advantages of broadening rights or engage in confrontation. The Russians in Tatarstan were not ready to make such a choice. Although residing in Tatarstan, the majority of Russians seemed to believe that they were living in their native Russia.

The national idea has united the Tatars of Tatarstan, both radical democrats and party functionaries, and together they are pursuing the course of independence. The World Congress of Tatars held in Kazan in 1992 strengthened their resolve.

Russians in towns and cities united in the organizations of the Democratic Party (Travkin's party) and around the Tatarstan branch of the Movement for Democratic Reforms. In May 1992 the Christian-Democratic Party was founded. There is some hope for reaching a political consensus among ethnic communities, especially if their loyalty under ordinary circumstances is taken into consideration. In Tatarstan there are as yet no mass political organizations of Russians.

The national idea among the non-Russian peoples of Russia gained further power from their confrontation with Moscow. The democrats in the capital did little to ameliorate this confrontation, inasmuch as they postponed the signing of the Federation Treaty and favored adoption of a constitution in which regions and areas are given the same status as republics—which, in the view of the proponents of this concept, should eliminate ethnic nationalism from the Russian state structure.

Meanwhile, Russians in the republics found themselves to a considerable degree in a marginal state. Economic hardship prompted them to support the idea of independence in hopes of improving their standard of living. At the same time they were frightened by growing ethnic nationalism. They did not wish to take the blame for all the unresolved economic and political problems that were due first to the Union and then to the Russian government. The attitude of Russians toward conflict situations differs in various republics. In areas of open conflict and military clashes, they prefer to move, as, for instance, in Tuva and the North Caucasus. However, in the majority of the republics their behavior depends on the relationships between Moscow and the republics, and on the situation within the latter.

It seems that Russia is in danger of repeating the fate of the Union in its inability to settle upon a consistent form of relations with the republics.

Non-Russian nations understand national interests as embracing not only culture and language but also independence in economic policies and in public and political life. Virtually all the republics have proclaimed their sovereignty, while Chechnia and Tatarstan have declared themselves to be independent states. Although the chairman of the Tuva Republic Supreme Soviet, Kaadyr-ool Bicheldei, announced that he was ready to set aside the slogan of independence for the time being, he added that "it is quite realistic to restore the Tuva Republic to the status it enjoyed up until 1944."[14] He announced that he was ready to implement his ideas within the scope of the law, without conflicts with other nationalities, relying on the support of the young people and intellectuals of Tuva.

The independence of Chechnia has not been recognized by the Russian parliament. However, the attempts of the Russian leadership to resort to a "policy of strength" there have failed.

The leaders of the republics that have signed the Federation Treaty emphasize that the very title of the treaty means that it has been concluded by the bodies of state power of the Russian Federation and the bodies of state power of sovereign republics within the Russian Federation. Moreover, Article 111 of the treaty says that the republics (states) enjoy all state power except those functions that have been delegated to the federal bodies.

The Protocols to the Federation Treaty concerning territories, regions, autonomous regions, and areas vary. In addition, different economic agreements are concluded with different republics. This confirms that the building of a soft, or rather flexible, federation is under way, but the process is extremely painful, and the agreements are not always observed. Popular among many new Russian leaders and democrats is the idea of realizing national interests through cultural autonomy and the realization of self-government through regional structures "capable of reducing the exclusiveness of the status of 'national republics.' "[15]

Meanwhile a struggle is being waged for leadership in the effort to make Russia a powerful world state—a struggle in which such organizations as the Civic Union Association (the so-called Volskii party, including the People's Party of Free Russia, the Democratic Party of Russia, and the Revival Party), the national patriots, and other forces are involved.

There is a danger that in the course of this endeavor the Russian government, as well as Russia's scientists, political analysts and politicians, might not wish to admit that the processes taking place first in the union republics and now in the Russian republics depend not only upon the "good or bad" policies of Moscow (although this is an important factor), but also on how the nations' development unfolds.

For good or ill, the backdrop for competition between ethnic communities in the republics, as well as between the central government of Russia and the republics, has already taken shape. The most important considerations here are the following:

(1) The social status of the various nationalities is changing, and the titular nations are demanding change in social and political roles, engendering fear among Russians.

(2) The nations have intellectuals of their own, a factor that stimulates the growth of national self-consciousness. Moreover, among the intellectuals of the former autonomous formations the percentage of production and scientific-technical intelligentsia is rather small, while that of managerial personnel and representatives of the mass humanistic professions, whose professional interests are especially closely interwoven with national interests, is high.

(3) The entire ideology of ethnic identity has already been elaborated. The underlying ideas are basically the same as in the case of peoples of new states. These are, as a rule, the determination that damage was done to culture and language in the years of the totalitarian regime; the guarantee of environmental protection and demographic reproduction of the ethnic nation; the restoration to the people's historical memory of their former statehood; and finally, the realization that the national interest demands not only ethnic and cultural but also economic and political independence. The example of the former union republics seems attractive for the ethnic elite of the former autonomous formations, who are afraid to miss their chance.

From 1990 until the autumn of 1991 the Union center relied on former autonomous formations in its struggle with the Russia of Boris Yeltsin. By that time the autonomous formations had already been recognized as subjects of the Union. Gorbachev was prepared to consider them as equal partners when signing the Union Treaty, for they supported its policy. That is why, immediately after the events of August 1991, the new leadership of Russia attempted to remove the Gorbachev-oriented leaders in the republics from their posts, but did not succeed in doing so everywhere.

Thus, in many respects the present situation in Russia is a repetition of the situation in the Union:

1. The status of the Russians in the majority of the republics was reduced in the 1980s to, at best, "equal partnership" with the titular nations, just as it was in the Soviet Union.

2. Like the union republics, the republics of Russia have no powerful mass political parties capable of uniting the majority of the population. Thus, political leaders can win in the struggle for power only by rallying the majority with the

help of national slogans. That is why in the case of interethnic conflicts the prospects for dialogue are uncertain.

There are also many common features between Russia and the former Union from the point of view of the relationships between the center and the republics.

1. The Union center failed to articulate the principles of its nationalities policy. The Russian government has also failed to do this.

2. In its policy toward the republics, the Russian leadership, just as the Union had in its time, vacillates between a policy of strength and one of concession. Each attempted show of strength does great harm to the position of Russians in the republics.

3. Russian leaders, just like Union leaders, underestimate the significance of psychological factors in relations with former autonomous formations and their peoples. (For instance, there were no republican flags in the House of Nationalities.)

However, there are also distinct differences between the present situation in Russia and that in the Union.

1. In the majority of the union republics, the movement for independence was perceived by the titular nations not only as a public but also as a personal achievement. There are no such mass movements in the republics of Russia.

2. There have been virtually no precedents for the taking of power by national democratic leaders. As a rule, the leaders in the republics are the former top officials who have assimilated national ideas and slogans.

3. The majority of the titular nations of the republics of Russia profess non-Christian religions. Thus, it may be expected that with the growing influence of Islam, the role of religion in interethnic relations will increase in the republics of the Russian Federation.

4. The basic feature that distinguishes the situation in Russia from that in the Union is that the majority of its republics have no outside borders (the exceptions are Karelia, Yakutia, Tuva, Buriatia, and the republics of the North Caucasus).

5. In contrast to the union republics, the majority of the titular nations of the republics of the Russian Federation historically had no statehood of their own (the exceptions being the peoples of Dagestan, Chechnia, Tuva, and Tatarstan).

6. Finally, in nine Russian republics Russians comprise the numerically dominant ethnic community.

Thus, as has already been mentioned, Russia will follow the course traversed by the Soviet Union in that it will not be able to maintain only one type of relationship with all of the republics. However, it should not repeat this path where the integrity of the Federation—and, let us hope, the forms and methods of the settlement of interethnic conflicts—are concerned.

Notes

1. *Chislennost' naseleniia i nekotorye sotsial'no-demograficheskie kharakteristiki natsional'nostei i narodov RSFSR (statisticheskii spravochnik)* (Moscow, 1991), pp. 27–39.

2. Ibid., p. 5.

3. Ibid., pp. 27–35.

4. *Itogi Vsesoiuznoi perepisi naseleniia, 1989 g., Raspredelenie vsego zaniatogo naseleniia otdelnykh natsional'nostei po vozrastu i urovniu obrazovaniia* (Moscow, 1990), p. 3.

5. *Osnovnye pokazateli sotsialno-ekonomicheskogo razvitiia natsional'no-gosudarstvennykh obrazovanii RSFSR* (Moscow, 1991), p. 41.

6. Ibid., pp. 41–42.

7. Ibid., p. 35.

8. *Osnovnye pokazateli sotsial'no-ekonomiceskogo razvitiia,* pp. 8–9.

9. *Sovremennye mezhnatsional'nye protsessy v TSSR* (Kazan, 1991), p. 45.

10. *Etnopoliticheskie protsessy v Bashkortostane* (Moscow, 1992), p. 12.

11. V. A. Tishkov, "Etnichnost' i vlast' v SSSR," *Sovetskaia etnografiia*, 1991, no. 3, pp. 4–7.

12. Chislennost', pp. 102–3.

13. Ibid., pp. 42–44.

14. Ibid., p. 43.

15. Ibid., p. 55.

II

Life in Diaspora

The Social Status, Attitudes, and Social Behavior of the Russian Population in the Former Union Republics

5

Russians in Ukraine

*Evgenii Golovakha, Natalia Panina,
and Nikolai Churilov*

For millions of Russians, the collapse of the Soviet Union has meant their transformation into a Russian diaspora, a national minority whose language, culture, and sociopolitical status are being shifted toward the periphery of national and state interests.

As far as Russians now residing in independent Ukraine are concerned, their new role is most unusual because in most regions of Ukraine they felt ethnically and culturally quite at home. This was due to the common roots of the Russian and Ukrainian nations and to a long imperial history which did not end with the advent of the communist era, when a policy of "de-Ukrainization" was conducted under the slogan of "proletarian internationalism."

The situation of Russians in Ukraine is also peculiar given the different policies of Russia and Ukraine concerning the rate and scale of social transformations. Taking into account the fact that out of more than eleven million Russians residing in Ukraine, some three-quarters are concentrated in five industrially developed regions (Donetsk, Dnepropetrovsk, Zaporozhe, Lugansk, and Kharkov), where they account for over a third of the population, and in the Crimea, where they are in the majority, it is easy to see that the position of the Russian population in those regions may be of great significance for political stability in Ukraine, Russia, and the Commonwealth as a whole.

In the southern regions of Ukraine (Nikolaev, Odessa, Kherson) the share of Russians is also large—almost one-fourth of the total population. Bearing this in mind, certain political circles in Russia consider the Crimea and the eastern regions of Ukraine as the subject of territorial claims; in the southern regions advocates of the imperial idea place their hopes upon the restoration of Novorossiia (New Russia) within the borders that existed before the October 1917 revolution.

The situation is quite different in the northern, central, and western regions, where the Russians' share is from 3 to 8 percent of the population and where the roots of Ukrainian culture are particularly deep. The position of Russians is especially uncomfortable in Galicia (Ivano-Frankovsk, Lvov, and Ternopol regions), where the Ukrainian population is characterized by strong anti-imperial sentiment often verging on radical nonacceptance of the "Moscow influence" in Ukraine. In these regions, unlike in other parts of Ukraine, Russians experienced negative attitudes toward them even in the period of the "final solution of the nationalities problem" in the USSR.

These peculiarities of the situation of Russians in Ukraine influence greatly their attitude toward the social processes upon which Ukraine's future depends. Therefore, of great interest are research data characterizing the views and feelings of the Russian population in Ukraine as a whole and in several of its regions in particular. However, in order to assess adequately the results of this research, one should take into account the general sociopolitical and psychological atmosphere in Ukraine, special features of its formation as a new state, and its relations with Russia.

1. The Sociopolitical Situation in Ukraine and Russian-Ukrainian Relations

The basic contradiction in Russian-Ukrainian relations certainly does not lie in the dispute concerning the Black Sea Naval Fleet, nor in the personal ambitions of Boris Yeltsin and Leonid Kravchuk, who were in agreement throughout the talks that confirmed the independence of former union republics. The chief obstacle to further cooperation between the two countries was the unwillingness of the Ukrainian leadership to support Russia's course toward radical economic reforms.

The Ukrainian leaders had good reason to pursue such a policy, since real power in Ukraine belonged to forces for whom the rate and scope of Russian reforms were unacceptable, while a large part of the population regarded any resolute actions in the economic sphere with mistrust and skepticism. The irresponsible economic experiments of the Russian government not only doomed it to utter failure, but also largely discredited the very idea of a fundamental renewal of society. Against that background, the conservatism of the Ukrainian authorities even managed to acquire a somewhat attractive air of political wisdom.

"Democratic" opposition leaders who advocated national and state revival through laws on citizenship and ethnic minorities failed to convince the people that democracy would help prevent the aggravation of interethnic relations, conflict with Russia, and the emergence of centrifugal forces capable of shattering the independent Ukraine following the collapse of the Soviet Union.

These factors to a great extent determined the outcome of the presidential elections and also the main task of national and state development: strengthening and preserving what is probably the main asset of Ukraine at the present time—a high level of tolerance between Ukrainians and Russians residing in Ukraine. In the course of our research we were impressed by the fact that, according to a "social distance scale," Ukrainians perceive their fellow citizens of Russian descent as people who are much closer to them than Ukrainians living abroad. In other words, closeness between people in Ukraine, their desire to strengthen contacts (kindred, friendly, neighborly, etc.), is explained not so much by the "voice of blood" as by their common concerns and a wish to build a common home.[1] The same tendency is seen in the attitude of Russians in Ukraine to their Ukrainian neighbors.

Of course, sentiments that place the highest value on one's own national interests are also in evidence. However, such sentiments are supported by a small segment of the population and not by the public at large, nor are they adopted by significant political and national-cultural movements. It is not accidental that the openly nationalistic slogans of the National Ukrainian Assembly are shared by less than 1 percent of the population, while organizations like the "International Movements" in the Baltic states or the Russian "Pamiat" have never succeeded in becoming serious political forces. Only two factors may jeopardize the national accord in Ukraine: deterioration of relations with Russia (with all the ensuing economic and territorial consequences) and attempts to paint a primitive picture of struggles to overcome "Russification" and the complex problem of revival and development of Ukrainian culture.

The Ukrainian ruling elite's overt hostility to democratic reforms makes Russian democrats suspect that its chief aim is to oppose radical economic reforms in the hope that procommunist forces might be returned to power in Russia. Hence the lack of political restraint on the part of quite a few democratic leaders of Russia who support chauvinists in their territorial claims to Ukraine, thus provoking the hostility of Ukrainians who cannot remain indifferent to the unfriendly and sometimes even insulting tone of many public statements. The same holds true for the Ukrainian democrats who are well aware of the reserve that has been displayed by the Russian authorities and the press in cases where the rights of Russian minorities have in fact been violated.

Such selectivity could trigger an aggravation of interethnic relations in Ukraine, which hitherto have been relatively stable, with no apparent seats of national conflicts. The absence of overt conflicts by no means excludes the existence of covert tension, which may reveal itself under extreme conditions and lead to a confrontation of political and nationally oriented forces. The studies carried out in 1991 by the Central Ukraininan division of the Center for the Study of Public Opinion and by the Institute of Sociology of the Ukrainian Academy of Sciences, with the participation of the authors of this report, make it possible to judge the extent to which such covert tension is characteristic of the Russian minority in different regions of Ukraine and to assess social awareness of the Russians.

Table 5.1

Structure of Settlement of Ukrainians and Russians in Ukraine (in %)

Types of settlement	Russians	Ukrainians
Kiev	7	5
Regional centers	42	28
Other cities	34	32
Villages	17	35

Results of the following studies were used in the report: (1) a public opinion poll among the Russian population of the Ukraine conducted by the Center for the Study of Public Opinion under the program "Russians in Ukraine" (August 1991) in which a total of 1,138 people were polled (eastern region—276; central and southern regions—200; Galicia—462; Bukovina—105; Crimea—95); and (2) representative public opinion polls among Ukraine's population conducted by the Ukrainian Institute of Sociology in September (1,660 respondents), October (1,780 respondents), and November 1991 (1,752 respondents) and April 1992 (1,752 respondents) on issues relating to people's attitude toward the prospects of socioeconomic and political development of Ukraine.

2. Social and Demographic Characteristics of Russians in Ukraine

The average level of education among the Russian population is slightly higher than that of Ukrainians. Thus, for example, the share of people with a higher or incomplete higher education among adult Russians is 19 percent and among Ukrainians 13 percent; for specialized secondary education the figures are 18 percent and 16 percent, respectively. The share of people with an incomplete secondary education among Russians is lower.

The reasons for this situation become clear when one analyzes the different places of settlement of the Russian and the indigenous Ukrainian populations (Table 5.1).

It is an open secret that the level of knowledge of inhabitants of rural areas who finish school is lower, on the whole, than that of their urban counterparts, which is why the latter have greater opportunities for higher education. Thus, other things being equal, Russian boys and girls enter higher and specialized secondary schools more often than Ukrainian youth (as a percentage of the total population of the given nationality). In our view, these differences lead to differences in the structure of the employed population of Russians and Ukrainians (Table 5.2).

It may be noted that the share of people with a high professional level (managers, specialists with higher and specialized secondary education, skilled workers, and others) is slightly larger among Russians than among Ukrainians. The Ukrainian population has a higher percentage of unskilled manual workers.

Table 5.2

Structure of Employment of Russians and Ukrainians (in %)

Occupation	Russians	Ukrainians
Managers of different levels (of enterprises, offices, departments, etc.)	4	2
Specialists with a higher education	21	19
Employees with a technical education	13	12
Peasants (collective farmers, farmers, etc.)	4	8
Skilled workers	23	22
Unskilled workers	4	7
Servicemen (including Ministry of the Interior, Committee of State Security, etc.)	2	1
Students (of colleges, higher schools)	7	6
Retired persons (housewives)	17	18
Temporarily unemployed	4	3

Table 5.3

Wages and Per Capita Incomes of Russians and Ukrainians in Different Types of Settlements (in rubles)

Type of settlement	Wage rate		Per capita income	
	Russians	Ukrainians	Russians	Ukrainians
Kiev	387	284	309	272
Other cities of Ukraine	361	347	274	255
Villages	265	263	205	189

As concerns the economic situation of the Russian population, we can state on the basis of sociological research that Russians, according to their own responses, have higher monthly earnings (grants, benefits) than Ukrainians—346 and 314 rubles respectively (data for September–October 1991) as well as higher per capita income—265 and 232 rubles respectively. An analysis of the levels of incomes and wages of Russians and Ukrainians living in different types of settlements yields interesting results (Table 5.3).

The data show that the Russian population enjoys better material conditions than the Ukrainian. However, this assertion may come under question when we consider that family income is made up not only of wages, extra earnings, pensions, student grants, and so forth, but also of revenues from other sources often hidden from researchers—subsidiary household (country house with a plot of land), foodstuffs provided by parents or relatives living in the countryside, privileges accorded certain groups of the population and members of the managerial organs, connections to the service and trade spheres, and so forth.

Table 5.4

Russians' and Ukrainians' Evaluation of Their Social Status (in %)

Social group	Russians	Ukrainians
Higher	0.5	0.3
Upper middle	14.0	8.0
Lower middle	37.0	37.0
Workers	36.0	40.0
Difficult to say	12.5	14.7

Self-appraisals of the material status of Russians and Ukrainians virtually coincide. For example, the following question was put to respondents in a November poll: "To what extent are you satisfied with the situation of your family?" The responses were rated on a ten-point scale: 1 meaning fully unsatisfied, 10 indicating complete satisfaction. The answers of Russians and Ukrainians were identical—4.38 points.

As to social characteristics of the Russian and Ukrainian populations, it is interesting to analyze the social ranking to which Russians and Ukrainians feel they belong. It is notable that Russians more often think they belong to the upper middle group, usually a sign of social prosperity and adaptation to the existing situation. (See Table 5.4.)

At the present time, therefore, one can say that the objective living conditions of the Russian minority in Ukraine and their self-awareness do not create prerequisites for a feeling of national restriction and a desire for radical change. The attitude of Russians toward Ukrainian state sovereignty is strongly influenced by this factor.

3. Attitude of Russians to Ukraine's Sovereignty and the Ukrainian Language

The results of the referendum on the "Resolution on the Independence of Ukraine" showed that the majority of both the indigenous and the Russian populations were in favor of Ukrainian sovereignty. Even in the Crimea, where Russians constitute the majority of the population, the resolution was supported by the majority of those who took part in the December 1991 referendum. This very fact testifies that the sovereignty of Ukraine is a much more complicated phenomenon than mere Ukrainian self-affirmation.

Even Russians in Ukraine for whom Russia is an irreplaceable cultural touchstone were in favor of Ukrainian sovereignty, raising the obvious question: What factors were stronger for them than the "voice of blood" and the natural wish to preserve a common space of communication with the people of their nationality residing in Russia and other republics? To answer this question, one should analyze the problem of identification with the country in which people live.

According to a study done by the Moscow Center for the Study of Public Opinion in 1991, most Russians in Ukraine do not feel themselves strangers there. Ninety percent of the Russians in the Crimea, 89 percent in the eastern region, 86 percent in the central and southern regions, 72 percent in the southwestern region (Bukovina), and 68 percent in Galicia answered in the affirmative when they were asked: "Do you agree with the statement 'I do not feel myself as a stranger in this Republic'?"

Most Russians felt closely connected to the life of Ukraine, from 69 percent in Galicia to 91 percent in Bukovina. The Russians do not see any marked differences between their way of life and that of the Ukrainians. Asked whether Russians live better or worse than Ukrainians, an overwhelming majority said that they lived "practically the same way." Russians also do not see marked differences in the level of education and culture between themselves and Ukrainians.

Such identification with the native population is quite natural, since most Russians are indeed closely related to Ukrainians: 45 percent of those polled in Galicia, 52 percent in Bukovina, 53 percent in the Crimea, 62 percent in the central and southern regions, and 73 percent in the eastern region said that they had close relatives of Ukrainian descent. The fact should be noted that in the central, eastern and southern regions and in the Crimea there are no Russians (at least among those polled) biased against close relationships with Ukrainians, whereas in the western regions 11–12 percent of men and 15 percent of women are opposed to mixed marriages.

The Russian population's support of Ukrainian independence is not explained by psychological identification alone. Also of great importance is the economic factor, specifically, the Ukrainian citizens' feeling that Ukraine gave more to the Union than it received. Most of the people polled said that Ukraine made a net contribution to the Soviet Union; only 4 percent said that it gave less. Two-thirds of the Russian respondents said that life in Ukraine was better than in Russia, and three-fourths expressed a firm decision to stay in Ukraine under any circumstances. Only 15 percent said they would leave Ukraine immediately if under threat of physical violence. None wished to leave if Ukraine seceded from the USSR (only in Galicia did 3 percent plan to do so).

At first glance, it seems rather strange that most Russians say they would not leave Ukraine even under the threat of physical violence. However, not only is the threat itself still abstract, but the fate of Russian refugees from ethnic conflict in other republics raises the doubt that Russia would welcome them in such difficult times. Russians in all regions of Ukraine feel their ties with life in Russia to be rather tenuous.

The aforementioned data suggest that support for Ukrainian independence is prevalent among the local Russian population. However, the sort of ambivalence that is characteristic of people living in a transitional period was evident in the attitude of Russians to an alternative—the existence of Ukraine within a Union or as an independent state. Thus, in August 1991, three out of five respondents supported the signing of a new Union Treaty (73 percent in the Crimea, 67 percent in the central and southern regions, 60 percent in Galicia and Bukovina, 59 percent in the eastern region). At the same time, over two-thirds of the respondents believed that Ukraine had to escape Moscow's *diktat* and achieve real independence. Though it is quite evident that "to live in the Union and be free from it" is impossible, precisely that variant of Ukraine's future would correspond to the prevailing orientations of not only the Russians, but the Ukrainians as well, most of whom had supported the idea of preserving a reformed Union in the March 1991 referendum.

Of course, the answer to the question of whether Ukraine should be independent involves more dramatic feelings on the part of the Russians than among Ukrainians, who are not threatened with the fate of becoming a national minority. These feelings are particularly apparent in the answers given to the following question: "Will the declaration of Ukraine's independence lead to violation of the rights of other nationalities?" The question was asked in a public opinion poll conducted in the republic in October 1991. The results of the poll were that 61 percent of Ukrainians and only 44 percent of Russians answered in the negative; 12 percent and 15 percent respectively had certain doubts; 7 percent and 20 percent answered in the affirmative; 20 percent and 21 percent were uncertain. Sixty-two percent of Ukrainians believed that Ukraine's independence would contribute to building a democratic society; among Russians the share of optimists was much smaller (42 percent).

Doubts concerning the democratic character and national tolerance of a future independent state were also reflected in the attitude of Russians to the September 1991 "Resolution on the Independence of Ukraine," which was supported by 46 percent of the Russians and 69 percent of the Ukrainians; 32 percent and 13 percent respectively were against independence. However, in October the attitudes of Russians changed, with 58 percent supporting the independence of Ukraine, while the share of opponents dropped to 18 percent. In November the situation remained practically unchanged: 60 percent were for Ukrainian independence and 15 percent opposed.

Such changes in the attitudes of Russians during 1991 were to a great extent the result of a campaign by the central authorities aimed at discrediting the idea of Ukraine's independent development in 1991 while also displaying the more accommodating style of relationship that would be adopted if Ukraine were to remain under the leadership of a renewed Union. At the same time, the Supreme Soviet of Ukraine passed laws guaranteeing observance of the rights of national minorities, including the right to use the Russian language in all spheres of activity. Thus, a decisive step was taken to remove the fears of the Russian population associated with the prospect of forced "Ukrainization."

The Russian language and culture in Ukraine traditionally hold very strong positions. The vocabulary and intonation of the Russian language used in Ukraine differ from the canonic Moscow standard, and in this respect it is quite correct to speak about its "Ukrainization." A special sociocultural value of the "Ukrainized" Russian language is that it serves to facilitate communication between Russians and Ukrainians who, as a rule, have no difficulties in understanding each other even if each speaks in his own language.

Of course the widespread use of this variant of the Russian language presents a certain threat to the Ukrainian literary language, since the former is a universal means of communication in many regions, particularly in big cities. This may be explained not so much by the policy of "Russification" pursued by the authorities (although this is a factor) as by the real cultural and linguistic closeness of the two nations, which has given rise to the peculiar phenomenon of a Russian-language Ukrainian culture which serves to link the two cultures.

This culture is most widespread in major cities (excluding the western Ukraine), which serve as crucibles for the development of the dynamic part of Ukrainian culture and civilization. Any attempts to restrict the development of this culture through administrative methods would lead to the provincialization of society, and hence to its stagnation and degradation. Due to what may be considered a legacy of historical injustice in the imperial relations between Russia and Ukraine, the main nutritive medium of high Ukrainian culture was conservative rural culture, while that of the Russian-language Ukrainian culture was more dynamic and urban. One can well understand the pain of those Ukrainian intellectuals for whom Russian-language Ukrainian culture symbolizes Ukraine's dependence, its provincialism, even under the guise of sovereignty. However, one can hardly accept the appeals of national radicals for resolute "de-Russification" or for administrative restriction of the influence of Russian culture upon the Ukrainian people.

Though such appeals have not been supported so far by most of the representatives of legislative and executive power, they raise apprehensions among Russians in Ukraine. For instance, in answer to the question "Will Ukraine's independence insure full freedom for development of all national languages?" only 39 percent of the Russians who took part in the poll in October 1991 said "yes." The rest were uncertain (22 percent), expressed doubts (19 percent), or answered in the negative (20 percent). Most Russians in all regions of Ukraine agreed that they ought to know the Ukrainian language.

An overwhelming majority of Russians supported the idea of Ukrainian national revival (from 88 percent in western Ukraine to 96 percent in the central region), emphasizing their positive attitude to the renewal of local national traditions, holidays, and customs. Most of the respondents positively assessed the influence of the Russian culture upon that of the local population. It is noteworthy that answers of "practically no influence" were most frequent in Galicia (31 percent) and the eastern region (28 percent)—areas with diametrically opposite degrees of interethnic integration.

On the whole, Russians in Ukraine are characterized by great tolerance to the language and culture of the native population. At the same time, apprehensions that development of their own language might be restricted as a condition of establishing Ukraine's independence are expressed rather frequently.

4. Attitudes Toward Russians and Social and Interethnic Tensions

The numerous interethnic conflicts in the former union republics, in which Russians are ever more frequently involved, draw attention to the problem of interethnic relations in Ukraine, where there exist both historical conditions for the emergence of anti-Russian sentiments and a degree of social tension brought about by the lowering of living standards and manifestations of national conflicts and contradictions.

As for the Russians, they explain the difficulties they experience not so much by the aggravation of interethnic relations as by the economic crisis, although regional differences influence their general assessment of the situation. In the central region, 12 percent of Russians believe that the main reason for hardships lies in the fact that extreme nationalists came to power; in Galicia this number increases to 32 percent. However, 90 percent of the Russians in all regions are convinced that the entire population of Ukraine, both Russians and Ukrainians, experience equal difficulties.

In assessing the relations among different nationalities residing in Ukraine, no one actually regarded them as hostile. Most of the respondents considered them to be normal, and only in Galicia did 29 percent regard these relations as "tense." The problem is perceived differently in different regions: in Galicia the problem of an aggravation of relations was mentioned by 38 percent of the respondents; in the central region and southern region by 19 percent; in Bukovina it was mentioned by 6 percent; in the east by 17 percent; and in the Crimea by 16 percent. As for attitudes toward Russians, many believe that over the past two or three years they have worsened in the western regions, especially in Galicia. In the eastern regions only 9 percent think that attitudes toward Russians have worsened; in the central region, 14 percent; in the Crimea, 18 percent; and in Galicia, 59 percent.

The direct question "Are the Russians oppressed in Ukraine?" was answered in the negative in most regions except Galicia. Only 2–4 percent of the respondents answered in the affirmative (25 percent in Galicia). This is not surprising since 82 percent of the Russian population in Galicia answered in the affirmative to the question of whether they ever witnessed manifestations of national hostility to Russians in everyday situations (in the street, transport, queues). In Bukovina, the Crimea, and the central and eastern regions the percentages were 42, 25, 24, and 15 respectively. Russians experience unfriendly attitudes on the part of state officials much less frequently, though the tendency is the same in the above-mentioned regions: 38 percent in Galicia, 11 percent in Bukovina, 8

Table 5.5

Attitudes of Russians and Ukrainians Toward People of Different Nationalities (in %)

Nationality	Would accept relationship through marriage		Would not admit to Ukraine	
	Russians	Ukrainians	Russians	Ukrainians
Ukrainian	69	84	0	0
Russian	67	34	1	2
Belarusian	38	25	0	1
Ukrainian living abroad	18	25	0	1
Pole	17	15	5	4
Jew	14	7	10	10
Hungarian	12	8	5	4
American	12	11	6	4
French	12	8	5	4
German	12	7	5	5
Romanian	10	6	9	8
Arab	6	2	20	16
Japanese	5	4	7	4
Crimean Tatar	4	3	17	17
Vietnamese	3	2	18	13
Gypsy	3	3	36	36

percent in the Crimea, 6 percent in the central region, and 3 percent in the eastern region.

The above data indicate that Russians in Ukraine find themselves in relatively favorable conditions when it comes to observance of their rights by state bodies. Even in Galicia, a negative attitude on the part of state officials is much less frequent than in other regions of the former USSR.

One of the important psychological prerequisites for national conflicts is mutual intolerance of people of different nationalities, especially in conditions of increased social tension, deterioration of the economic situation, and an aggravated confrontation of various political forces.

In research conducted in April 1992, the social attitude of Russians and Ukrainians toward members of their own and other nationalities, evaluated on the basis of the Bogardus scale, was taken as a basic index of national intolerance. When asked to what social position or post one is prepared to admit a representative of another nationality, a respondent's answer reveals the social distance he would like to preserve between himself and a given ethnic group. The list proposed for respondents comprised 16 nationalities (Ukrainians, Russians, Jews, and some other nationalities of the former USSR, East European countries, and countries of the West, Asia, and Africa), as well as Ukrainians living abroad. The data cited in Table 5.5 reflect the attitude of Russians and Ukrainians toward people of different nationalities from two points of view in the context of national tolerance: readiness for a close relationship through marriage and unwillingness to admit any member of a given nationality to Ukraine in general.

The results of this research allow us to call into question a number of contemporary stereotypes, first of all those concerning the prevalence of anti-Russian attitudes ("Russophobia"). Thus, only two out of a hundred Ukrainian respondents showed extreme intolerance toward Russians, and more than one-third were ready for a close relationship. This percentage is, of course, not very high, but we should keep in mind the fact that attitude toward a relationship in marriage, even to members of one's own nationality, is characterized by heightened sensitivity among peoples of all nationalities. Thus, only one-fourth of Ukrainians would admit a Ukrainian living abroad as a family member in marriage, whereas Russians living nearby are admitted more readily than "overseas" members of their own nationality. The widespread notion that marriages to foreigners, especially those from developed countries, become particularly attractive in times of social crisis has not been confirmed.

The low level of national tolerance shown in the attitude toward certain nationalities is only one manifestation of a low national tolerance in general. Xenophobia has become a real factor during the disintegration of the totalitarian system. From under the weight of communist ideology and the total suppression of dissent has shot up a spirit of intolerance and distrust of "aliens" and of other social groups and strata, including people of other nationalities. And here the positions of the indigenous population and Russians in Ukraine differ little. In some aspects Ukrainians are less tolerant toward mixed marriages, whereas Russians (however paradoxically) are less prepared to admit "aliens" to the Ukraine. As for the mutual relations of Russians and Ukrainians, they are most tolerant when compared with their attitudes toward other nationalities.

The high level of mutual tolerance of Ukrainians and Russians residing in Ukraine is explained by, among other things, their approximately equal socioeconomic status, which precludes any envy or hostility associated with social injustice. In Russian society, such injustice is identified with unequal chances for different categories of the population in terms of social promotion and distribution of material goods. As was noted above (Table 5.4), the researchers found no major differences in the identification of Russians and Ukrainians with different social strata.

A certain difference in the identification of Russians and Ukrainians with the upper middle class is explained by the high concentration of the Russian population in big cities, where there are more favorable conditions for social promotion. However, this advantage is negligible and has nothing to do with Russians' and Ukrainians' self-reporting of their incomes. Two percent of Russians and 5 percent of Ukrainians state that their income is higher than average; 37 percent and 38 percent, average; 55 percent and 53 percent, lower than average; and 6 percent and 4 percent, respectively, found it difficult to assess their incomes. As we see it, Russians and Ukrainians share one paradoxical feature: they feel, in general, that both nations are worse off materially than some abstract "average individual."

This "equality in poverty" experienced by Russians and Ukrainians is an integrating yet potentially conflict-generating factor in their relations. It will perform an integrating function only if Russians and Ukrainians continue to believe that life in Ukraine, despite all hardships, is better than in Russia and in other former union republics. But should it become clear that radical economic reforms in Russia are yielding positive results, while the conservative economic course of the Ukrainian administration results in a deepening economic crisis, this "equality in poverty" will inevitably result in an aggravation of national relations in Ukraine. That is why radical economic transformations in Ukraine are the main prerequisite for solving not only economic problems but also those of relations between different nationalities.

5. Conclusions

In conclusion, we would like to underscore the fact that the relatively stable and favorable position of the Russian minority in Ukraine is due to both mutual tolerance of Ukrainians and Russians and the reliable observance of rights of national minorities on the part of the Ukrainian authorities. The less favorable position of Russians in some western regions of Ukraine is the result of historical factors that are deeply rooted in the imperial past and reveal themselves much more strongly in many other former union republics than in Ukraine.

Russians in Ukraine are characterized by a high degree of identification with the country in which they live. While they support independence, local Russians at the same time have certain doubts as to whether the rights of national minorities will be properly observed in the new state, especially the right to use the Russian language. Another potential source of aggravation is the real distinction between Russia and Ukraine, which puts Russians into an ambivalent position fraught with serious inner conflict between national and civic stands. To prevent the large-scale spread of this conflict and its manifestation in relations between nations, a harmonization of relations between Ukraine and Russia is indispensable. In this context, Russia must renounce any territorial claims to Ukraine and drop its "big brother" attitude, while Ukraine should firmly support the economic and political reforms in Russia. All this will help both countries advance to a democratic society.

Note

1. N.V. Panina and E.I. Golovakha, "Interethnic Relations and Ethnic Tolerance in Ukraine," *Jews and Jewish Topics in the Soviet Union and Eastern Europe*, 1 (14), Spring 1991, pp. 27–30.

6

Russians in Moldova

Vladimir Solonar and Vladimir Bruter

1. The History of Settlement and Certain Social Features of Russians Residing in Moldova

The Republic of Moldova is the heir of the Moldavian SSR, which was formed on August 2, 1940, by decision of the Supreme Soviet of the Soviet Union. The Moldavian SSR included the greater part of Bessarabia[1] and the Dniester region of the Moldavian Autonomous SSR, which had been part of the Ukrainian SSR.[2]

In July 1940, after enlisting the support of Nazi Germany (the Molotov-Ribbentrop Pact), the Soviet Union issued ultimatums for the return of Bessarabia and northern Bukovina,[3] to which Romania was forced to agree. The postwar frontiers between the Soviet Union and Romania were determined by the Paris Agreement of February 10, 1947, signed by Britain, France, the United States, the Soviet Union, and other Allied nations.

The difference in the historic destinies of the Bessarabian and Dniester parts of the republic underlies many of the present-day territorial problems of Moldova.

Slavic people settled in Bessarabia and the left bank of the Dniester long ago, back in the sixth century. From the ninth to the thirteenth centuries their cultures acquired the features typical of ancient Russian culture. However, nomadic raids devastated these territories in the thirteenth and fourteenth centuries.

A Romanized population first appeared here in the late fourteenth century. As they settled this territory the Moldavians assimilated the remnants of the Slavic population. Still, even in later periods, the East Slavic people played an important part within the local population. The influx of Slavs from beyond the Dniester continued in the sixteenth and seventeenth centuries. Russians as such appeared here much later, in the eighteenth century. The terms "Rus" and "Rusin" applied to the local East Slavic people in earlier periods should not mislead the reader; these were the names given to the ancestors of those who later were called Ukrainians. The first Russians who settled the territory of the

Moldavian state, including Bessarabia, were Old Believers who fled from the persecution of tsarist authorities.

After Bessarabia was annexed to Russia, Turks and Tatars left. At the time, the territory was populated by approximately 250,000 people.[4] The overwhelming majority (78.2 percent, according to V.S. Zelenchuk) were Moldavians who lived mostly in the villages in the north and the center. The urban population was mixed—Armenians, Greeks, Moldavians, Jews, and others.

The annexation of Bessarabia to Russia was followed by a powerful influx of migrants: Ukrainians and Russians from beyond the Dniester; Moldavians from beyond the Prut who came in search of a peaceful life; and Bulgarians and Gagauz. According to V.M. Kabuzan, in 1858 the population of Bessarabia amounted to 1,018,000, of whom 51.4 percent were Moldavians, 21.3 percent Ukrainians, 10 percent Bulgarians, 7.25 percent Jews, and 4.28 percent Russians.[5]

Russians arrived in Bessarabia in three basic ways. First, they came illegally, as runaway serfs (there was no serfdom in Bessarabia). Some of these peasants were caught and sent back to their owners, but some, obviously, managed to escape and settled in the area, sometimes disguised as local people, even taking their names. Second, Russians came to Bessarabia in accordance with the plan of the local administration, approved by St. Petersburg in 1825, "On the Settlement in the Bessarabian Region of Twenty Thousand State-Owned Peasants from the Central Provinces." This plan was only partially realized.[6] And third, many Russian military men and officials with their families stationed in Bessarabia settled there. Moreover, Old Believers continued to immigrate to Bessarabia. Some of them even came from abroad.

As a result of constant wars, the population of the left-bank Dniester region was sparse and unstable up until its annexation to Russia. In the 1860s in the southern part of this region Moldavians constituted half of the population. Ukrainians were the second most numerous group.[7] The joining of the territory to Russia was followed by a sharp increase in the influx of Slavs, especially Ukrainians, while the percentage of Moldavians dropped. In 1782, Russians founded the town of Tiraspol and a number of villages.

In the second half of the nineteenth century, the intensity of immigration flows sharply decreased. The growth in population was accomplished mostly as a result of natural increase. The intensified construction of railways and industrial upsurge that characterized Russia in the late nineteenth and early twentieth centuries had their effect on Bessarabia as well. Still, industrial development here was slower than in central Russia. However, there was a certain flow of migrants from central provinces of Russia, primarily to the cities.

According to the all-Russian population census of 1897, there were 155,800 Russians living in Bessarabia, or 8.1 percent of the population. However, at the time all educated people who had good command of the great Russian language were considered Great Russians. As has been estimated by Zelenchuk, there were at that time actually 123,100 Russians in Bessarabia, or 6.4 percent of the population.[8] I.V. Tabak is of the opinion that there were even fewer—not more than 100,000, or 5.2 percent of the population.[9]

Russians in the countryside were more often than not surrounded by Moldavians or Ukrainians, and in such cases they assimilated rather quickly. The intensity of assimilation processes in Bessarabia is borne out by the great number of Moldavians bearing Russian surnames.

In the late nineteenth and early twentieth centuries, Russians were the most urbanized ethnos in Bessarabia: more than 60 percent of Russians lived in towns and cities.[10] This can be explained by the fact that army detachments, state offices, and industrial enterprises were concentrated in towns and cities. According to N.V. Babilunga, 40.6 percent of urban Russians were employed in industry, 16.7 percent in state offices, 14.2 percent were engaged in agricultural handicrafts, 27.5 percent in trade, and 7.4 percent lived on incomes from their capital or were state-subsidized. At the same time, 55.5 percent of urban Ukrainians and 51.2 percent of urban Moldavians were employed in farming. Only 34.7 percent of Moldavians and 29.9 percent of Ukrainians were industrial workers.[11]

The class representation of the Russians was as follows: they were 41.5 percent peasants, 41.8 percent petit bourgeois, 8.5 percent noblemen and officials, 1.7 percent clergy, and 2.2 percent merchants and honorary citizens. Russians were obviously overrepresented in the top strata: 60 percent of all the noblemen and officials of the province were Russian.[12]

It is impossible to determine the number of Russians who lived on the left bank of the Dniester in the territory of present-day Moldova in the late nineteenth and early twentieth centuries. According to I.I. Zharnutskii, at the turn of the century 28,700 Russians, or 17.9 percent of the population, lived along the Dniester in the Tiraspol region of Kherson Province. Of this number, 16,500 lived in towns and cities (32 percent of the urban population) and 12,200 in the countryside (11 percent of the rural population). There were 65,900 Moldavians, or 41.3 percent of the population, of whom 55,000 lived in the villages and 10,900 were townsfolk.[13]

In the early years of World War I, many cadre railwaymen from central Russia and military men arrived in Bessarabia. The number of new settlers increased, especially in towns and cities. On the other hand, mobilization led to a decrease in numbers of the local able-bodied population. However, no accurate data on that score are available.

The Romanian period (1918–40) witnessed a very slow population increase in Bessarabia, from 2,642,000 to 2,864,000. The causes lay in the high mortality rate (higher than in the rest of Romania and one of the highest in Europe—23.6 per thousand) and emigration (in the period from 1922 to 1930 about 300,000 people left Bessarabia).[14] Characteristic of Bessarabia of that period were economic decline, high unemployment, and stagnation of the urban population: in 1918 there were 368,000 urban dwellers; in 1930, 371,000.[15]

According to the universal Romanian population census conducted in 1930, there were 351,900 Russians in Bessarabia, or 12.3 percent of the population.[16] Such a huge increase as compared with the early twentieth century—accompanied incidentally by a sharp "reduction" in the number of Ukrainians in certain districts—could be explained by the fact that many Ukrainians who called themselves "Russians" or "Rusins" were registered as Russians.[17] Even if the arrival of a certain number of émigrés from Russia is taken into consideration, the number of Russians in 1930, as Tabak has aptly remarked, could have hardly reached 200,000.[18]

According to the 1926 census, the population of the Moldavian Autonomous SSR living along the Dniester amounted to 256,400 people, of whom 35,900, or 13.7 percent, were Russians. Some 23,500 people lived in the countryside (10.1 percent), while in the towns of Rybnitsa and Tiraspol there were 12,400 Russians (39.7 percent of their residents).[19]

According to the survey of the population of the left-bank regions of Moldavia conducted in October 1940, there were 38,000 Russians (13.4 percent of the population).[20] These data testify to the absence of significant migration processes at the time.

The events of 1940–41 resulted in radical changes in the composition of the population of the Moldavian SSR. The shifts in the structure of the population were caused by the forced emigration of Romanian officials and intellectuals in 1940, Stalin's repressions of 1941, the departure of Germans to Germany and evacuation and flight of the population following the attack on the Soviet Union by Germany and Romania, the extermination of Bessarabian and left-bank Jews and Gypsies, and finally, a new wave of immigration after the end of the war.

According to Zelenchuk, within this period the republic's population was reduced by 350,000 and amounted to 2,257,000 in 1945.[21] In the view of P.M. Shornikov, over 90,000 people died during epidemics[22] and over 100,000 died from hunger.[23] Most gravely affected were the southern regions of the republic and cities such as Kishinev and Bendery. The prewar level of the population was achieved only in the mid-1950s.

In the period from 1940 to 1950 the number of Russians in Moldavia grew from 188,300 to 232,000, or from 7.2 to 10.2 percent of the population.[24] Obviously, the most important factor here was played by migration processes.

From the 1950s to the early 1970s, Moldavia was the scene of tempestuous urbanization processes, which were accompanied by an increase in the percentage of the urban population. From 1959 to 1966 the annual average growth rate of the percentage of urban dwellers in the Moldavian SSR was 4.1 percent (2.3 percent for the Soviet Union as a whole), which was the highest among the union republics.

While in 1930 the urban population in Bessarabia was 13 percent, in 1959 in Moldavia it reached 22 percent, and by 1989 it was 47 percent.[25]

High rates of industrialization and urbanization, also attributable to political and ideological factors (Moldavia was the face that the Soviet regime showed to the neighboring Balkans), necessitated the mass import of labor from other republics of the Soviet Union, primarily from Russia and Ukraine. Within the period under consideration, the urban population in Moldavia grew mostly (by more than a half) at the expense of migrants, of whom at least 40 percent came from other republics of the USSR.[26] In the period from 1959 to 1970 Russians constituted 34 percent of all migrants to Moldavia.[27]

As a result, the number of Russian residents in Moldavia rose in the period from 1959 to 1989 from 292,900 to 562,100, that is, from 7.2 to 13 percent of the population.[28] According to Tabak, from 1959 to 1970 the share of the natural increase in the general increase was 37 percent, and from 1970 to 1979 it was 28 percent. This means that over twenty years, 142,200 Russians migrated to Moldavia and in 1979 constituted 28 percent of the total population.[29] Within the same period the percentage of Moldavians in the republic's population dropped from 65.4 percent (1959) to 63.9 percent (1979).

After the mid-1970s immigration became less intensive, although by all appearances the real change in the situation occurred only in 1990.

In the opinion of the authors, who support Tabak's estimates, not more than a third of the Russians now living in Moldova were resident there, or descend from people who were resident in this territory, prior to 1940, the rest being migrants or children of migrants of the Soviet period.[30] At least half of the people in this category were born in Moldavia.

Russians rank second in the republic (after Jews) in level of education. For instance, while in 1970 the average number of people in the republic with a secondary or higher education was 23 per 1,000 of the population, among Jews the figure was 47, among Russians 37, among Ukrainians 22, and among Moldavians 11. This pattern in the indicators for different nationalities has persisted.[31] The professional status of the Russians employed in the national economy of the republic was rather high, at least higher than that of the Moldavians, as is borne out by the data in Table 6.1.

Among the top managers of industrial enterprises and organizations in construction, farming, transportation, and communications, the situation was as follows (January 1,1990):[32] Moldavians—46.8 percent, underrepresented by 27.4 percent; Ukrainians—24 percent, overrepresented by 73.9 percent; Russians—14 percent, overrepresented by 7.6 percent.[33]

The influence of the "Russian factor" in the life of Moldova is much greater than one might expect if the percentage of Russians in the republic's population alone is taken into account. For almost two centuries the Russian language and culture played an exceptionally important part in Bessarabia and the Dniester region. In the postwar period knowledge of Russian was obligatory for the entire able-bodied population, irrespective of nationality. There were two types of general secondary schools: Russian and Moldavian. The first was attended by children of all nationalities, with a small percentage of Moldavians (in the late 1980s about 10 percent, mostly children from mixed marriages), and the second by the

Table 6.1

National Composition of Specialists with Higher and Secondary Specialized Education Employed in Various Branches of the National Economy (November 15, 1989; in %)

	Moldavians	Russians	Ukrainians	Jews
Total for republic	52.3	20.0	17.6	3.4
Including industrial enterprises	32.8	31.0	25.1	5.1
Agricultural organizations and enterprises	69.9	6.1	13.6	0.3
Public education establishments	61.6	16.6	13.2	2.4
Scientific and affiliated establishments	34.3	33.1	20.9	7.0
State and economic bodies, management bodies of cooperatives and public organizations	54.8	19.9	17.7	1.6
Ministerial bodies and departments	41.4	31.0	17.2	3.4

Source: Express-Information of the State Statistical Board of the Moldavian SSR, February 23, 1990, no. 07-13-10.

majority of the Moldavians. Although Russian-language instruction was standard in Moldavian schools, there was only a pretext of Moldavian-language instruction in Russian schools. Moldavian-language textbooks were of extremely low quality and almost no vocabulary or teaching aids were available. In the republic's higher schools there were groupings for instruction in either Russian or Moldavian, but the percentage of students in the Moldavian groups was lower than the percentage of Moldavians in the republic's population. In 1988, for instance, 46.3 percent of the students were registered in the Moldavian groups at Kishinev (now Moldova) University, 38.2 percent at the Kishinev Polytechnical Institute, 54.05 percent at the Kishinev Pedagogical Institute, 50 percent at the Beltsy Pedagogical Institute, and 48.3 percent at the Tiraspol Pedagogical Institute.[34]

If we add to this the complete dominance of Russian in the mass media and the fact that a good command of the Russian language was considered a manifestation of political loyalty, it becomes clear why, despite the outward appearance of bilingualism in the republic, the actual situation was obviously asymmetrical. This is borne out by the data in Tables 6.2 and 6.3.

The policy of Russification pursued by the communist regime thus led to a gap between the two basic communities in Moldavia—the Moldavian and the non-Moldavian[35]—in the matter of language. This gap gave rise to a category of

Table 6.2

Distribution of Population by Nationality and Language

| | Percentage of people of a certain nationality who consider its language their mother tongue | | | | Percentage of people of a certain nationality who have good command of a second language of the peoples of the USSR | | | | | |
| | | | | | Romanian | | Russian | | Other | |
	1959	1970	1979	1989	1979	1989	1979	1989	1979	1989
Entire pop.	94.2	93.0	90.4	88.9	4.0	3.9	40.6	45.3	3.2	3.7
Moldavians	98.2	97.7	96.5	95.4	1.2	1.7	46.2	53.3	0.6	0.5
Ukrainians	86.3	79.4	68.5	61.6	12.9	12.8	43.3	43.0	6.4	8.8
Russians	98.6	99.1	99.2	99.1	10.6	11.2	0.5	0.6	3.8	4.2
Gagauz	96.8	95.7	91.7	91.2	6.3	4.4	68.4	72.8	0.9	1.8
Bulgarians	91.5	88.6	80.2	78.7	7.3	6.9	66.9	68.3	0.8	1.3
Jews	50.0	44.7	33.1	26.0	14.9	15.2	30.4	23.2	9.6	11.4
Germans	69.5	64.3	57.5	31.1	2.1	5.0	53.4	30.5	1.2	2.3

Source: Economis nationala a Republicii Moldova: anuar statistic. 1990 (Chisinau, 1991), p. 25.

"Russian-speaking population," which generally embraces all non-Moldavians and those Moldavians who either do not know or have only a poor command of the Moldavian language. However, is the use of this term justified from the sociological point of view?

"Russian-speaking" people first emerged as a social group with a community of interests and a capacity for joint action in 1989 during the discussion and adoption of the language laws that gave the status of a state language to the language of the majority ethnos. Although no sociological surveys were conducted at the time, analysis of the republican press and personal observation suggest that practically the entire Russian-speaking population insisted that the status of state language be given to both Moldavian and Russian, while the Moldavians favored the status for the Moldavian language only.

The 1990 elections, which took place under conditions of acute interethnic tension, demonstrated a high degree of solidarity among the Russian-speaking population, who almost everywhere voted for representatives of national minorities rather than for Moldavians, except in the case of a Moldavian nominee who was considered to be on the side of the Russian-speaking population and was recommended by their political organizations. In the March 1991 referendum on the fate of the Union—which was prohibited by decision of the Moldova parliament but was conducted nonetheless by a number of local soviets, work collectives, and public and political organizations[36]—it became clear that the Russian-speaking population constituted an independent political factor. Since

Table 6.3

Distribution of Population by Language Use (in %)

	Total (including mother tongue)	Of own nationality	Moldavian	Ukrainian	Russian	Gagauz	Bulgarian
Entire pop.							
1970	100	93.0	0.4	0.3	6.3	0.02	0.01
1989	100	88.9	0.5	0.2	10.3	0.0	0.0
Moldavians							
1970	100	97.7	—	0.2	2.0	0.01	0.01
1989	100	95.4	—	0.2	4.3	0.0	0.0
Ukrainians							
1970	100	79.4	1.1	—	19.4	0.01	0.03
1989	100	61.6	1.6	—	36.7	0.0	0.1
Russians							
1970	100	99.1	0.6	0.2	—	0.02	0.03
1989	100	99.1	0.6	0.2	—	0.0	0.1
Gagauz							
1970	100	95.7	0.9	0.2	3.2	—	0.1
1989	100	91.2	1.1	0.1	7.4	—	0.2
Bulgarians							
1970	100	85.9	1.7	0.3	9.1	0.4	—
1989	100	78.7	2.4	0.3	18.1	0.4	—
Jews							
1970	100	44.7	0.6	0.1	54.5	—	—
1989	100	25.9	0.8	0.2	72.9	0.0	0.0

Source: Express-Information of the State Statistical Board of the Moldavian SSR, February 17, 1990, no. 07-13-11.

complete and reliable data on the results of the referendum are not available,[37] it is impossible to analyze its results thoroughly. However, there is no doubt that the significant majority of the Russian-speaking people voted for preservation of the Union. According to the authors' estimates, about 80 percent of Russian-speaking voters intended to take part in the referendum (although not all of them had the opportunity), while only 20 percent of the Moldavians planned to participate.

These data fully correspond to the results of the survey conducted by the Center for the Study of Public Opinion in early 1990. At that time 43.1 percent of the population favored the preservation of Moldavia within the Soviet Union, while 41.8 percent were for independence. Supporting the Union were 29.9 percent of Moldavians, 76.1 percent of Russians, 72.6 percent of Ukrainians, 94.7 percent of Gagauz, 88.8 percent of Bulgarians, and 66.9 percent of "others." For independence were 54.8 percent of Moldavians, 8.8 percent of Russians, 8.4 percent of Ukrainians, not a single Gagauz, 11.5 percent of Bulgarians, and 26.4 percent of people of other nationalities. Favoring the unification with Romania were 3.9 percent of Moldavians, 2.7 percent of Russians, 1.6 percent of Ukrainians and no Gagauz, Bulgarians, or people of other nationalities.[38] Thus the non-Moldavians have demonstrated a high degree of unity on the main political question of the time—the question of statehood.

The unity of non-Moldavians appeared to be much higher than that of Moldavians on the same question, but it should be added that the people who took upon themselves the organization of the referendum were practically all non-Moldavians, for the referendum was conducted almost exclusively in those settlements overwhelmingly populated by national minorities.

The differences the survey revealed in the level of pro-Union sympathies of Russians and Ukrainians and, say, Bulgarians, was so small that it could be ignored, while the exceptional pro-Union sympathies of the Gagauz could probably be explained by their special position in the conflict zone.

All of these considerations lead to the conclusion that Russian-speaking people constitute a real sociopolitical community in Moldova. In the authors' opinion (although further studies are necessary), within the framework of this community the political and cultural differences among its basic "components" are less significant than the differences between, say, old residents and new settlers or city dwellers and rural residents of the same nationality.

The disintegration of the Soviet Union and the collapse of the "Union identity" have led to a search for a "new identity" among the national minorities in Moldova. With the worsening of their position in the republic and the strengthening of the national-state centers, the attractiveness of national-state ideas and national cultures is bound to grow. It may lead to a gradual erosion of the "Russian-speaking" community and the disappearance of the community of interests and purposes among members of various national minorities in Moldova. Such processes are already under way, especially among Jews and Germans, who are leaving Moldova on a scale that makes it possible to foresee their complete exodus. To a lesser extent, the same is true for Bulgarians. However, most Ukrainians intend to stay where they are. At present the category of "Russian-speaking population" has preserved a kind of operational value, although to distinguish Russians from the Russian-speaking community is difficult or impossible.

2. The Collapse of Soviet Communism and the Fate of Russian and Russian-Speaking Minorities in Moldova, 1988–92

The post-communist liberalization in Moldova quickly gave way to nationalistic dictatorship. Within the period from 1988 to 1992, Russians and Russian-speaking people changed from citizens of the totalitarian Union into a suspected, persecuted, and oppressed minority.

The democratization and political mobilization of the masses in Moldova, which started, as in the other republics of the former Soviet Union, on the eve of the Nineteenth Party Congress in the spring of 1988, took place under national and nationalistic slogans. In demanding recognition of the identity of the Moldavian and Romanian languages (which was denied by party ideologists despite its obviousness), transfer of the Moldavian language to the Latin alphabet and the status of state language, the new Moldavian political leaders hit upon extremely attractive slogans that proved to be effective mobilizers. The heated discussion of the language problems in the republican press in 1988–89 was accompanied by a great number of openly Russophobic publications, which often contained only slightly disguised appeals to ethnic violence.[39] It became evident that the nationalistic-minded Moldavian leaders had chosen a strategy for deepening the ethnic-linguistic split in society and considered the flare-up of interethnic strife advantageous to their own advancement to the highest posts in the leadership.

As a response, political organizations with Russian-speaking members were formed under the usual "internationalist" slogans.[40] The leaders and active members of these movements understood internationalism as the preservation of national equality as well as of the state political status quo, although the latter idea was not made very explicit. This ideological and symbolic division of society further aggravated the situation.

August–September 1989 witnessed the first confrontation, when during a session of the Supreme Soviet of the Moldavian SSR language laws were adopted at the behest of the Moldavian national movement. This event coincided with a strike of Russian-speaking workers and employees who demanded official status for the Russian language alongside Moldavian. According to the data of the strikers' committees, over 200 work collectives (200,000 people) took part in the strike.

The first free (relatively) and universal elections in Moldavia, in February–March 1990, were conducted largely along ethnic-linguistic lines, as has already been mentioned. However, a high degree of competition among the nominees

Table 6.4

The Rating of Radicals Among Russian-Speaking and Moldavian Voters in Moldavian Cities of Republican Subordination
(results of the 1990 parliamentary elections; percentage of votes cast)

	Moldavians	Russian-speaking people
Kishinev	58.8	64.3
Beltsy	57.4	62.3
Bendery	—	53.3
Dubosary	—	60.8
Kagul	49.5	63.2
Orgeev	61.5	63.2
Rybnitsa	—	55.55
Soroki	52.2	—
Tiraspol	—	53.3
Average	*56.8*	*59.7*

Note: The table shows the percentage of voters (Moldavians or Russian-speaking) who preferred to cast their votes (in those districts where there was an alternative) for a radical nominee against a nominee from the nomenklatura. (The 1989 election law envisaged the nomination of candidates by work collectives and meetings of citizens and polling in accordance with individual programs. The party lists had not been institutionalized.) The absence of a figure means that in a certain town or village there was no competition between the radicals and nominees from the nomenklatura among the respective ethnic-linguistic part of the electorate.

was observed between the Moldavian and Russian electorates. By the time of the elections, the ideological monopoly of the party had been undermined, although formally the party remained the most united and powerful organization in the republic both financially and organizationally. The actual struggle thus occurred between, on the one hand, nominees who represented the party and top economic officials and who often had their own clientage and, on the other, radicals enjoying the support of various organizations—the Popular Front among the Moldavians and the Intermovement and United Councils of Work Collectives.

Analysis of election results demonstrates that the Russian-speaking and Moldavian voters in cities of republican subordination preferred radicals; in the countryside, the elections mostly boiled down to competition among the clientages. The authors' estimates are displayed in Table 6.4.

These data refute the frequent allegations, at least for Moldavia, that Russians in the union republics were more loyal to the old party and state apparatus than were voters who were members of the titular nations. It is noteworthy that in the cities with a predominantly Russian-speaking population and where their organizations enjoyed mass support, the positions of the old nomenklatura were completely undermined in the course of the 1990 elections. Nevertheless, the

Table 6.5

National Composition of the Leadership in the Government, Ministries, and Departments of the Republic of Moldova (September 1, 1991)

Post	Total	Moldavians	Percentage of total
Government leadership	77	71	92
Ministers and chiefs of departments	17	15	88
Deputy ministers and deputy chiefs of departments	66	47	71
Chiefs of departments	14	14	100
Deputy chiefs of departments	25	20	80

radicalism of the Russian-speaking population had a conservative character and a rather "reddish" ideological hue.

Following the elections, the situation in the parliament was determined by the correlation between two basic blocs—the Moldavian national organization, centered on supporters of the Popular Front, and the Russian-speaking international bloc. A total of 370 people were elected to the new parliament,[41] 90 of whom were firm supporters of the Popular Front and about 60 staunch supporters of the internationalist bloc. Further development depended on the position taken by the soft center, the "agrarian-clientage swamp."

The Popular Front won in the struggle for power. By exploiting the acuteness of the contradictions between the two basic ethnic-linguistic groups, presenting the Russian-speaking deputies and the population as enemies, building up nationalistic hysteria, and even resorting to direct physical violence against their opponents,[42] the Front succeeded in forming the "Moldavian Bloc," which consisted of both radical deputies and deputies from the nomenklatura who were Moldavians by nationality. This bloc united 65 percent of all the parliamentary deputies.

However, the unity of the bloc was not strong and after a year it disintegrated due to internal disputes. Still, in the spring and early summer of 1990 it was this coalition that formed the new government and the leading bodies of the parliament —the presidium and the standing commissions. The chance to procure a top post directly depended on the candidate's nationality, as is borne out by the data contained in Tables 6.5 and 6.6.

At that time there were fifty-four Russians in the parliament, including one member of the presidium. The conditions under which the top leadership of the republic was elected and the actual results of the elections left no doubt that in the Republic of Moldova the practice of discrimination against ethnic minorities —that is, Russian-speaking people—was being established. This provoked a very sharp reaction. On August 19, 1990, the First Congress of the Gagauz People proclaimed the formation of the Gagauz Republic. On September 2,

Table 6.6

National Composition of the Deputies' Corps, Standing Commissions, and Parliament Presidium of the Republic of Moldova (June 1991)

	Total	Moldavians	Percentage of total
Total deputies	373	261	70.0
Members of standing commissions on wages	49	46	93.9
Chairmen of these commissions	15	15	100.0
Vice-chairmen and secretaries	15	15	100.0
Members of the presidium	25	21	84.0

1990, the Second Congress of People's Deputies of all levels of the Dniester region decided to form a Dniester Moldavian Soviet Socialist Republic (since October 1991—the Dniester Moldavian Republic).[43] The interethnic conflict first turned into a territorial and then an interstate conflict, which later assumed the form of military confrontation.

The Dniester problem deserves a separate, thorough analysis. In this article the authors will deal only with the basic problems confronting Russian and Russian-speaking people living in the main territory of Moldova, where they are in the minority. These problems are as follows.

1. *Discrimination in the workplace.* Formation of the republican leadership was immediately followed by a purge of the state apparatus and state institutions during which people of non-Moldavian nationalities and those considered not loyal were fired. Russian workers and employees were either dismissed or demoted. Knowledge of the state language was considered a sine qua non for professional suitability, although the law envisaged a four-year period for the transition to the new system of languages. Since then the practice of discrimination based on nationality has become permanent and widespread.

2. *Limitation of educational opportunities in Russian.* The new administration has chosen to phase the Russian language out of the system of education, both higher and secondary. Russian schools were closed down or turned into Moldavian schools, and admission to Russian groups in republican schools of higher learning was reduced or closed altogether.[44] As a result, today many parents who communicate with their children in Russian decide to send them to Moldavian schools.[45] On the other hand, the graduates of the Russian schools are faced with a choice: either to resign themselves to reduced opportunities in life (admission to higher schools is strictly limited) or to emigrate.

3. *Limited access to and dissemination of information.* In June 1990 the republic's new leadership placed republican radio, television, and regional newspapers under its strict control and set up new publications (first of the parliament

and then of the government). The publication of Russian-language periodicals was either disrupted or stopped, and acts of terrorism against their employees were encouraged.[46] Today the Russian-language independent press in Moldova is practically nonexistent and Russian-speaking leaders have no access to radio and television.

4. *Ethnic violence.* The use of violence for political purposes is an important weapon of the present Moldovan leadership. As a rule, violence is directed against political opponents of the regime, including deputies, both Russian-speaking and Moldovan. There have been cases of uncontrolled, street-level violence against ordinary people, mostly those who do not speak Romanian. For instance, on November 15, 1990, there was a massacre of the Russian-speaking population in Kishinev which claimed dozens, perhaps hundreds, of victims. No measures have been taken against the perpetrators of this massacre.

One can ascertain the scale of ethnic violence from the survey data. For instance, the survey conducted by the Center for the Study of Public Opinion in early 1991 registered a high rate of acts of violence against members of ethnic minorities (25 percent of the respondents experienced aggression from nationalistic groupings) as well as the respondents' fear of acts of violence on ethnic grounds (more than half of the respondents considered the danger quite real). Over 70 percent of the Russian-speaking respondents thought that the cardinal problem was the aggravation of interethnic relations, while 58.3 percent of Moldovans considered the main problem to be the lowering of living standards.

After the conflict in the Dniester region turned into an open military confrontation (March 1, 1992), many facts were made public concerning the training of groups of saboteurs by the Ministry of National Security of Moldova, which also took upon itself the supervision of operations (murder, arson, kidnapping, etc.) intended to destabilize the situation. In addition, the terrible crimes perpetrated by the Moldovan Army in the town of Bendery in June 1992 justify the statement that the present Kishinev government is a regime of state terrorism.

3. The Future of Russians in Moldova: Preliminary Estimates

For the majority of Russian and Russian-speaking people now living in Moldova the alternatives are rather harsh: either leave the republic for other countries of the Commonwealth of Independent States and concentrate on preparing for departure or stay in Moldova and reconcile themselves to their position as second-class citizens. A survey conducted in June 1991 by the Institute of Economic Studies of the Academy of Sciences of the Republic of Moldova in Kishinev among Moldovans, Russians, and Ukrainians revealed attitudes toward the problem of emigration (see Table 6.7).

Table 6.7

**What Are Your Intentions Concerning Your
Further Stay in Moldova?** (in %)

	Moldavians	Russians and Ukrainians
Do not want to leave	82	39
Ready to leave for some other republic	1	29
Ready to go abroad	2	1
Have not decided yet	9	31

Thus, even before overt military actions, about a third of the Russians and Ukrainians living in Kishinev wanted to leave Moldova, and 90 percent of the respondents in this category named growing interethnic tension as the main reason for mounting migration.

According to data from the State Statistical Board, the year 1990 was a turning point in the history of migration processes: that year the net departure was 9,944 people, while the next year 22,682 people emigrated. The year 1992 witnessed the appearance of refugees from Moldova, especially from areas of military clashes. The migration processes of recent years are basically ethnic in character. Thus in 1990, 6,000 more Moldavians came to the republic than departed, and in 1991, 3,500 more. At the same time the net departure of Russians was 2,998 in 1990 and 4,077 in 1991; for Ukrainians—1,706 and 2,410 respectively. Russians left mostly for Russia (66.85 percent in 1991 and 66.2 percent in 1991) and Ukraine (27.9 and 29 percent, respectively). In 1990, 28 percent of the Ukrainians left for Russia and 68.1 percent for Ukraine; the respective figures for 1991 are 27.4 and 69.2 percent.

However, the absolute scale of emigration seems insignificant compared with the total number of Russians (and Ukrainians) living in Moldova as well as the scale of immigration in the 1950s through the 1970s. It is obvious that the main obstacles to the plans of Russian-speaking people living in Moldova to emigrate to other republics of the former Union are the difficult economic situation and political instability. It would be unrealistic to expect a sharp turn for the better in this respect in the near future. That is why a quick and painless solution of the "Russian question" in Moldova through emigration of its Russian-speaking citizens to their historic motherland is simply impossible. Equally unlikely is the integration of the Russian-speaking population into the political life of Moldova and reconciliation of the two basic ethnic-linguistic communities. Thus the "Russian question" is bound to remain the main problem in the republic—that is, of course, unless a full-scale civil and international war, a mass-scale expatriation or flight of the civilian population, or the absorption of Moldova by Romania should take place.

Notes

1. Bessarabia—a historical territory located between the rivers Dniester, Prut, and Danube.

2. The Moldavian Autonomous Soviet Socialist Republic (area 8,100 sq. km., population 1,545,400) was formed by decision of the Central Committee of the All-Russian Communist Party (Bolsheviks) in 1924 in the area between the Dniester and Southern Bug rivers, with the capital first in the town of Balta and then in Tiraspol. Although at that time Moldavians were in the minority, they were still numerous—28.5 percent of the population. The purpose of this move was to "compromise the rule of Romanian bourgeoisie in Bessarabia . . . and . . . in the rest of Romania" (K. Mialo, "Strasti po Moldavii," *Novoe vremia,* 1990, no. 40, p. 24).

3. From the eleventh to the fourteenth centuries, northern Bukovina was part of Kievan Rus and the Galitsk-Volynsk Principality, becoming a part of the Moldavian state with its appearance in 1356. In 1775 it was incorporated into Austria (after 1866, Austria-Hungary). In 1918 it was annexed by Romania. In 1940 a relative majority of the population of the territory (44.9 percent) were Ukrainians. Now it is part of the Chernovtsy Region of Ukraine (as well as a part of northern Bukovina).

4. See V.S. Zelenchuk, *Naselenie Bessarabii i Pridnestrov'ia v 19-om veke* (Kishinev, 1979), p. 98.

5. V.M. Kabuzan, *Narodonaselenie Bessarabskoi oblasti i levoberezhnykh raionov Pridnestrov'ia* (Kishinev, 1974), pp. 54–55.

6. See I.V. Tabak, *Russkoe naselenie Moldavii: chislennost', rasselenie, mezhetnicheskie sviazi* (Kishinev, 1974), p. 27.

7. Kabuzan, *Narodonaselenie Bessarabskoi oblasti,* p. 27.

8. Zelenchuk, *Naselenie Bessarabii,* p. 173.

9. Tabak, *Russkoe naselenie Moldavii,* p. 59. According to the census, the population of the province was 1,935,000 people, of whom 47.6 percent were Moldavians, 19.6 percent Ukrainians, 8.1 percent Great Russians, 5.3 percent Bulgarians, 3.1 percent Germans, 0.6 percent Poles, 0.1 percent Greeks, 11.8 percent Jews, 2.1 percent Gagauz, 0.1 percent Armenians, 0.5 percent Gypsies, and 0.35 percent people of other nationalities (L. S. Berg, *Naselenie Bessarabii: etnograficheskii sostav i chislennost'* [Petrograd, 1923], p. 44).

10. See the data of V.N.Butovic, whose research led to the compiling of an ethnographic map of Bessarabia, and I.V. Tabak. According to the 1897 census, 44.8 percent of Russians lived in cities and towns. They were the most urbanized ethnos. See N.V. Babilunga, *Naselenie Moldavii v proshlom veke: migratsiia? assimilatsiia? russifikatsiia?* (Kishinev, 1990), p. 57.

11. Ibid., p. 59.

12. Tabak, *Russkoe naselenie Moldavii,* p. 47.

13. According to I.I. Zharnutskii, *Spiski naselennykh mest kak istochnik k izucheniiu dinamiki naseleniia Tiraspolskogo uezda (1859–1905). Problemy istochnikovedeniia istorii Moldavii perioda feodalizma i kapitalizma* (Kishinev, 1983), pp. 186–87.

14. Tabak, *Russkoe naselenie Moldavii,* p. 67.

15. Ibid.

16. According to the census, the population numbered 1,610,800, of whom 56.2 percent were Romanians (Moldavians), 11 percent Ukrainians, 7.2 percent Jews, 8.7 percent Bulgarians, 3.4 percent Gagauz, 2.8 percent Germans, 0.5 percent Gypsies, and 0.9 percent people of other nationalities. See *Recensamantul General al populatiei Romaniel,* vol. II (Bucharest, p. xxviii). The growth in the number of Romanians (Moldavians) could be explained by the resettlement of Romanians from the Old

Kingdom and Transvaal organized by the Romanian government (although on a rather small scale: in 1930 there were about 80,000 new settlers; see S.K. Brysiakin, *Kul'tura Bessarabii (1918–1940)* [Kishinev, 1978], p. 20) as well as by the fact that many Ukrainians, Russians, Bulgarians, and other non-Romanians called themselves Romanians, especially if they knew the language.

17. Tabak, *Russkoe naselenie Moldavii*, pp. 68–71.

18. Ibid.

19. According to the All-Union Population Census of 1920, vol. I–XIII: Ukrainian Soviet Socialist Republic (Moscow, 1929), pp. 182–83. I.V. Tabak is mistaken in citing the figure 27,400 for Russians. Grigoriopol and Slobodzeia, which are now towns, were at that time considered villages.

20. V.S. Zelenchuk, *Naselenie Moldavii: Demograficheskie protsessy i etnicheskii sostav* (Kishinev, 1973), p. 40. The frontiers of the republic at the time did not fully coincide with the boundaries of the regions.

21. Ibid., p. 42. P.M. Sornikov, extrapolating the birthrate for 1840 to 1941–44 increases the figure to 600,000. See P.M. Sornikov, *Kogo vybirala smert? O "belykh piatnakh" v istorii Moldavii perioda Velikoi Otechestvennoi Voiny* (Kishinev, Gorizont, 1988), no. 9, p. 57.

22. P.M. Sornikov, "Zabytaia tragedia," *Kommunist Moldavii*, 1990, no. 1, p. 90.

23. B.G. Bomesko, *Zasukha i golod v Moldavii, 1946–1947* (Kishinev, 1990), p. 43.

24. Zelenchuk, *Naselenie Moldavii*, p. 42.

25. Tabak, *Russkoe naselenie Moldavii*, p. 76.

26. Ibid., p. 85.

27. Ibid., p. 34.

28. *Economia nationala a Republicii Moldova: anuar statistic, 1990* (Chisinau, 1991), p. 24.

29. Tabak, *Russkoe naselenie Moldavii*, pp. 82–83.

30. Ibid., p. 118.

31. Ibid., p. 78.

32. See *Express-Information of the State Statistical Board of the Moldavian SSR*, February 23, 1990, no. 07–13–10.

33. In 1989 the Moldavians' representation among party leaders was as follows: secretaries of city and regional party committees—69.7 percent; first secretaries of city and regional party committees—69.4 percent; chiefs of departments of city and regional party committees—64.6 percent; chairmen of city and regional executive committees—74 percent; and chairmen of rural and village soviets—66.7 percent, which means that almost everywhere they constituted the majority (*Sovetskaia Moldova*, January 18, 1990).

34. Data of the Ministry of Science and Education of the Republic of Moldova.

35. According to the 1989 census, the population of Moldavia numbered 4,335,400, of whom 64.5 percent were Moldavians, 13.9 percent Ukrainians, 13 percent Russians, 3.5 percent Gagauz, 1.5 percent Bulgarians, 1.5 percent Jews, 0.5 percent Belarusians, 0.3 percent Gypsies, 0.2 percent Germans, 0.1 percent Poles, and 0.6 percent other nationalities (*Economia nationala a Republicii Moldova*, p. 24).

36. Their actions were in accordance with a decision of the Supreme Soviet of the USSR, which gave the right to local soviets, work collectives, and public organizations to organize a referendum in the Soviet Union if the republican government refused to do so.

37. According to data of the Referendum Central Commission, a total of 943,000 people voted in the republic, including 114,000 in Kishinev.

38. See *Golos naroda* (Kishinev, 1991), no. 10, March 12.

39. For instance, on August 31, 1989, the popular newspaper *Literatura si arta*, the

organ of the Writers' Union of the Moldavian SSR, published a poem by Petr Kerare titled "Unwelcome Visitor":

> There is a thief in our home,
> With whom we sit at one table.
> Only yesterday he blocked our way
> With ideas and guns.
> Today he is snatching a piece of bread from our hands.
> And there is other news:
> You must call him "brother."
> But instead of bread
> Better give him a block of *dynamite*.

During that period many talented Moldavian authors, such as Grigore Vieru, indulged in this kind of writing. The frequency of such publications, and the strong language used by leaders of the Moldavian national movement, testified to the fact that Russophobia was considered an important mobilizing factor in political strategy, a kind of escalator leading to the summits of power.

40. Those were: Unity Internationalist Movement in Defense of Perestroika (Intermovement) in Kishinev, the United Council of Work Collectives in the cities of Rybnitsa, Bendery, Tiraspol, Dubosary, and Beltsy, and Gagauz-khalky, an organization of the Gagauz. They were formed in 1989.

41. The number of deputies differed, since the mandates of some of them were not recognized and some rejected their mandates, so additional elections had to be organized, and so forth.

42. In April–May 1990 the beating of Russian-speaking deputies at the entry to the parliament became a common occurrence.

43. The territory of the Dniester Moldavian Republic embraces the left-bank regions along the Dniester and the city of Bendery, located on the right bank of the river. The area is 4,163,000 sq. km., and the population is 712,000, of which 39 percent are Moldavians, 26 percent Ukrainians, and 24 percent Russians.

44. Table 6.8 (next page) illustrates the scale of the decline in educational opportunity in the Russian language in the republic's higher schools.

45. For instance, in the current year (according to the data of the Ministry of Science and Education) 65 percent of the parents in Kishinev decided to send their children to Moldavian schools, although in Kishinev the ratio between Moldavians and non-Moldavians is 50 : 50.

46. Most notorious is an incident involving the newspaper *Molodezh' Moldavii* (Moldavian Youth). The newspaper's office was destroyed by extremists in September 1990 and burned down in October. Newspaper employees were threatened with physical violence and some fell victim to such violence. The newspaper staff subsequently underwent radical changes, as did the overall political tone of the paper. Government bodies not only did not prosecute the offenders, they even expressed their solidarity with them. For instance, in May 1991 President Mircea Snegur declared: "In my view, the newspaper has drawn the right conclusions from such lessons. Now read it with pleasure, for it has completely changed" (*Moscow News,* May 19, 1991).

Table 6.8

**National Composition of Students in Schools of Higher Learning
of the Republic of Moldova** (in %)

Nationality	Year	MSU	KSPI	KPI	BPI	TPI	EFI
Moldavians	1988	66.0	49.0	70.0	69.1	65.0	—
	1989	77.8	64.6	70.6	81.1	70.5	—
	1990	81.7	68.4	68.9	79.6	66.8	—
	1991	89.0	77.0	78.8	83.5	60.4	83.0
Russians	1988	15.0	22.0	12.0	10.0	11.0	—
	1989	10.5	18.1	10.3	5.6	10.2	—
	1990	6.0	14.6	6.9	6.4	10.2	—
	1991	3.9	9.7	4.1	4.8	15.7	8.0
Ukrainians	1988	12.8	16.0	10.0	14.8	9.1	—
	1989	7.0	9.6	5.7	8.8	10.1	—
	1990	5.1	11.2	5.8	11.4	—	—
	1991	3.8	7.9	3.9	8.3	15.3	5.8
Bulgarians	1988	2.0	2.0	2.0	0.4	2.5	—
	1989	1.8	1.3	4.4	0.2	3.2	—
	1990	1.9	1.5	2.6	0.4	—	—
	1991	1.0	1.5	2.8	0.2	3.6	0.9
Gagauze	1988	2.0	2.0	2.0	0.7	2.7	—
	1989	0.9	1.0	7.3	0.4	2.3	—
	1990	1.2	1.4	3.3	0.8	—	—
	1991	0.4	1.2	3.2	—	2.3	1.2
Jews	1988	3.0	5.0	2.0	2.9	—	—
	1989	1.2	4.3	0.7	1.5	—	—
	1990	0.6	2.6	0.4	—	—	—
	1991	0.4	1.2	0.2	0.4	—	—

Source: Kishinevskie Novosti, April 24, 1992.

Key: MSU: Moldavian State University; KSPI: Kishinev State Pedagogical Institute;
KPI: Kishinev Polytechnical Institute; BPI: Beltsy Pedagogical Institute; TPI: Tiraspol
Pedagogical Institute; EFI: Economic Financial Institute

7

Russians in Lithuania

Vladis Gaidys

There are advantages to studying the situation of Russians in Lithuania as compared with the other regions examined in this book, since in Lithuania the process of the change in roles of the national groups involved has already been completed, passions have subsided, and the situation has stabilized. This provides an opportunity for a more dispassionate analysis of the actual state of affairs and leaves room for hope that this chapter will not become outdated in the near future. The chapter supplies an analysis of several objective and subjective characteristics of the Russian minority in Lithuania as well as some data concerning the Russian minorities in Latvia and Estonia. The situation in the latter two states is much more problematic, however, and an accurate account of the processes taking place there would require much more space.

This analysis is based on population censuses, current statistics, and data from surveys conducted by the Survey Research Center of the Institute of Philosophy, Sociology, and Law of the Lithuania Academy of Sciences, which has conducted regular surveys since the spring of 1989 (for details see Appendix 1 to this chapter). Data from the Center's surveys of the Russian population have not as yet been either analyzed or published.

We also draw on data from cooperative studies in Lithuania, Latvia, and Estonia (also known as Baltic Surveys). In Lithuania these studies were conducted by the Survey Research Center of Lithuania, in Latvia by LASOPEC Ltd., and in Estonia by EMOR Ltd. Unfortunately, the author does not have at his disposal data on the Russian population specifically, so the term "others" (meaning non-Latvians, non-Estonians) is used. Since in both Latvia and Estonia, Russians constitute the majority of the non-Latvian and non-Estonian population, the ambiguity is not significant.

1. The National Composition of the Population of Lithuania

In the early fourteenth century the Grand Duchy of Lithuania was an agglomeration of Lithuanian and Slavic territorial and tribal formations that maintained

Table 7.1

National Composition of the Lithuanian Population
(population census data; in %)

	1897	1923	1959	1970	1979	1989
Lithuanians	61.6	69.2	79.3	80.1	80.0	79.6
Russians	4.8	2.5	8.5	8.6	8.9	9.3
Poles	9.7	15.3	8.5	7.7	7.3	7.0
Ukrainians	0.1	—	0.7	0.8	0.9	1.2
Jews	13.1	8.3	0.9	0.8	0.4	0.3
Others	6.0	4.3	1.0	0.5	0.8	0.9
	95.3	99.6	98.9	98.5	98.3	98.3

rather close ties. It was quite common to find Slavs living in urban settlements of ethnographic Lithuania. The second half of the seventeenth century witnessed a movement to Lithuania of some Old Believers who left Russia because of religious persecution.

After Lithuania was incorporated into the Russian Empire, the number of Russians living there grew. Among these were many officials who in the nineteenth century engaged in active Russification of the indigenous population (for instance, in the period from 1864 to 1904 the Lithuanian alphabet was strictly prohibited and those who disobeyed this rule were persecuted). At the time of the first population census in 1897, Russians constituted less than 5 percent of the population. Many Russians returned to Russia during World War I, but some of them came back after the revolution, fleeing the Red terror. In 1939 only 3 percent of the Lithuanian population was Russian. After the annexation of Lithuania in the wake of World War II, the influx of Russians into Lithuania intensified (see Table 7.1).

Several factors precipitated the postwar growth of the Russian population: (1) a planned influx of Russians to ensure control over strategic points (repressive bodies, transport junctions, industrial enterprises, etc.) and a required percentage of Russians in the capital; (2) planned growth in order to man large industrial enterprises; (3) a spontaneous influx of people in search of higher living standards and a better way of life.

Russians settled mostly in large cities. According to the 1989 census, Vilnius was 20.2 percent Russian (116,318), Klaipeda 28.2 percent (57,204), Kaunas 8.3 percent (34,823), Šiuliai 10.5 percent (15,343), and Sniečkus, with its nuclear power station, 64.2 percent (20,812).

After the establishment of Soviet rule, the inflow of Russians to Latvia and Estonia was even greater than to Lithuania (Tables 7.2 and 7.3).

At the time of the 1989 census, only 36.5 percent of Riga residents were

Table 7.2

National Composition of the Latvian Population
(population census data; in %)

	1935	1959	1970	1979	1989
Latvians	77.0	62.0	56.8	53.7	52.0
Russians	18.8	26.6	29.8	32.8	34.0
Others	4.2	11.4	13.4	13.5	14.0
	100	100	100	100	100

Table 7.3

National Composition of the Estonian Population
(population census data; in %)

	1934	1959	1970	1979	1989
Estonians	87.8	74.6	68.2	64.7	61.5
Russians	8.2	20.1	24.7	27.9	30.3
Others	4.0	5.3	7.1	7.4	8.2
	100	100	100	100	100

Latvian, while in Tallinn only 47.4 percent were Estonians. Within a single generation both Latvians and Estonians had been taken to the brink of demographic catastrophe. While prior to the annexation they were small but culturally and economically developed nations, over the last 50 years they ceased to be masters in their home countries and were helpless before the processes of migration and Russification, although they were fully aware of the gravity of the situation.

The fact that a smaller number of Russians moved to Lithuania than to other Baltic states can be explained by three factors: (1) Lithuania's more persistent resistance to Moscow's policies (thanks primarily, to Antanas Sniečkus, who ruled over Lithuania until 1974); (2) a comparatively low level of industrialization; (3) the decentralization of large industrial centers carried out since the early 1960s and their replacement with regional centers that attracted labor from the countryside. Since 1989, when the national movement reached its highest point (recall the Baltic Line on the day of the fiftieth anniversary of the Molotov-Ribbentrop Pact), the net migration of Russians to Lithuania has been negative (−700 people in 1989, −6,221 in 1990, and −5,504 in 1991).[1] The same was true of the other Baltic states. For instance, while in 1989 the net migration to Estonia was still +914, in 1990 it was already −2,048.

Although in-migration has stopped, the imbalance it created has led to many problems, including the immigrants' difficulty in adapting, troublesome inter-

Table 7.4

Persons over 15 with a Higher or Specialized Secondary Education
(per 1,000 of the population in 1989)

	Lithuanians	Russians	Poles	Belarusians
Higher	101	168	45	109
Specialized secondary	193	230	257	237

ethnic relations in the Baltic states, and the political difficulties in relations with Russia.

2. The Educational and Professional Level
   of the Russian Minority

The real state of interethnic relations, and the fate of the nation itself, depends largely upon the social position of a national minority and the social niche it occupies. Compare the area under study with Jewish communities, the Armenian diaspora, or Gypsy life. As a rule, the tendency is to stay in the middle, neither striving for the upper strata nor sinking to the lowest.

What is the educational level of Russians in Lithuania? It should be noted that the popular stereotypes of the uneducated Russian is far from accurate.

As is clear from Table 7.4, the percentage of Russians with a higher or specialized secondary education is higher than that of Lithuanians. The situation is approximately the same among the urban and rural populations.

Russians also have a higher level of education in Latvia, the corresponding indicator for Latvians being 96 and for Russians 143.[2]

Now let us consider the professional composition of the Russian minority, citing only those trades in which Russians do best.

The majority of Russians live in large cities. This to a certain degree explains their social and professional composition: more Russians are engaged in mental labor; there are more office employees among them and consequently fewer of them work in agriculture. The high percentage of Russians among engineers, technicians, and skilled workers at engineering plants should be particularly stressed.

Noteworthy is the gap between Russians and Poles engaged in nonphysical labor (40.9 and 21 percent respectively) and those engaged in physical labor (59.1 and 79.0 percent). The respective figures for motor transport workers are 4.8 and 10 percent, and for those working in the trade and service sectors, 2.9 and 4.5 percent. In Vilnius, 6.2 percent of municipal workers are Poles and only 3.3 percent are Russians (see Table 7.5).

It is characteristic of the aforementioned sectors (motor transport, trade, ser-

Table 7.5

Nationality-Occupation Distribution in Lithuania (1989 census; in %)

	Lithuanians	Russians	Poles
Nonphysical labor	33.4	40.9	21.0
Engineers and technicians	8.3	13.7	5.5
Medical workers	3.6	2.7	1.5
Scientists, teachers	6.2	5.1	3.2
Other	1.7	7.3	1.5
Physical labor	66.6	59.1	79.0
Engineering, metal-working	12.0	17.5	17.1
Farming	11.0	2.8	10.3
Transport	7.2	4.8	10.0
Trade and public catering	3.8	2.9	4.5

vice) that those employed in them are always in contact with the public, facing customers and clients on a day-to-day basis. Russians, Poles, Belarusians, and Ukrainians in these professions, who have no distinct anthropological differences and all of whom speak Russian, tend to be lumped together. So the members of these professions are responsible to a certain extent for the image of "Russian-speaking" people, including Russians, although there actually are not so many of the latter either behind the wheel or behind the counter.

Strange as it may seem, even today when all the statistics are available, it is difficult to determine the share of those serving in the army or working at military bases who are Russian (it is stated that as of the beginning of 1992 there were at least 35,000 officers and men of the Russian army in Lithuania[3] and 130,000 in Estonia, Lativa, and Lithuania taken together).[4] There is, however, a mysterious column in the 1989 population census titled "Other nonphysical occupations," which includes 7.3 percent Russians, as opposed to only 1.7 percent Lithuanians and 1.5 percent Poles.[5] Obviously, this column includes army personnel.

The professional composition of Russians in Latvia is similar to that of Lithuania.[6] The main problem there lies not in the Russians' social structure, but in their greater number. The same goes for Estonia, especially for its northeastern region, where the "tempestuous growth" of power engineering and the shale and chemical industries in Narva and Kohtla-Järve resulted in a labor shortage. Local workers were in short supply, so, as usual, workers were hired in other areas, in this case in the neighboring regions of the Russian Federation.[7]

Lithuania was fortunate in not having similarly high concentrations of Russians, with the controversial exception of Sniečkus, which is the site of a nuclear power plant and to which Lithuania can be seen as a hostage. For instance, in February 1992 an employee of the nuclear power station, a highly skilled computer specialist who was suspected of intentionally introducing viruses into the computers monitoring the operation of the reactors, was arrested.[8] But on the whole, this town does not cause any truly serious problems, mainly because Lithuania needs it and its residents are eager to integrate into Lithuanian society.

Russians, who are employed mostly at large plants, shipyards, and power-engineering enterprises, may be subject to varying fates. For example, the nuclear power station and oil refineries that were on the verge of closing down under pressure from the Green Movement are today considered to be of vital importance for Lithuania. On the other hand, some large industrial enterprises are not very competitive and may be unprofitable to operate. Thus, problems of restructuring the economy have turned into problems of nationalities.

It is also worth mentioning that the majority of Russians are well educated, professionally skilled, and maintain close ties with people living in the territory of the former Soviet Union. Still, for a variety of reasons their desire to be employed by state structures has diminished and the majority of them have no intention of returning to the land of their forebears.

All of the above helps Russians to be successful in the field of private business, a characteristic that is especially evident in Latvia and may well prove yet another cause of tense interethnic relations.

Overall, it is to be expected that, despite the departure of some Russians, especially the military, others will remain and smoothly integrate into a new socio-occupational structure.*

However, there may be a new spiral of migration in the future. It may be assumed that the process of reforms will be quicker in Lithuania and consequently bear fruit sooner. The whole of Europe is now witnessing the resettlement of less skilled people prepared to do more demanding jobs for less pay, from the east to the west, from the south to the north. In this respect Lithuania is a more advantageous place for Russians since the technologies are less complicated than in the West. Moreover, Lithuanians can speak Russian and some Russians still maintain certain ties here to relatives and friends who can help them to find at least an "illegal" job. Under conditions of free enterprise it would be difficult to put up barriers to this flow (Lithuanians themselves will be interested in an inflow of cheap labor). This will be followed by still another "alienation reaction" of the "Lithuania for Lithuanians" type, and the anti-immigrant tendencies so widespread in the European countries are bound to strengthen.

3. Attitudes of Russians to the Lithuanian Language and the Independence of Lithuania

Unfortunately, census data supply only an approximate picture of the linguistic map. Moreover, these data are often wrongly interpreted. For example, the "percentage of people having good command of a language" was an average indica-

---

*The Russian troop withdrawal was completed on August 31, 1993.—Eds.

Table 7.6

**Share of Russians in the Soviet Republics Fluent in the Language
of the Indigenous Population and Considering It Their Mother Tongue**
(according to data from 1979 and 1989 censuses)

	1979	1989
1. Lithuania	37.4	37.5
2. Ukraine	31.6	34.3
3. Armenia	27.4	33.6
4. Belarus	30.9	26.7
5. Georgia	16.2	23.7
6. Latvia	20.1	22.3
7. Estonia	12.9	15.0
8. Azerbaijan	9.3	14.4
9. Moldova	11.2	11.8
10. Uzbekistan	5.9	4.6
11. Tajikistan	2.7	3.5
12. Turkmenistan	2.1	2.5
13. Kyrgyzstan	1.1	1.2
14. Kazakhstan	0.7	0.9

tor covering all age groups, including babies who obviously know no other language. As a result, figures that greatly distort the real state of affairs are common. For instance, according to the 1979 census, 52.1 percent of Lithuanians could speak and write Russian (according to the same census, the figures for the group "up to seven years of age" was 2.5 percent, and for those from 20 to 29 years old, 81.6 percent). According to the 1989 census, only 34.7 percent of Lithuanians have a good command of the Russian language.[9] Apart from being an average figure, this statistic was distorted by the political boycott of the Russian language during the census.

There is another factor that renders the results of the census inaccurate. Since a respondent had to name only one such language, the result obtained was significantly reduced (the figure of 15.5 percent for the Poles knowing Lithuanian is patently ridiculous).

The above-mentioned drawbacks of the censuses increase the importance of taking sample surveys of the adult population. According to the Survey Research Center of Lithuania, in September 1991, 50 percent of Russians stated that they knew Lithuanian well. Only 5 percent could not speak it; the rest knew "a little" or "were studying it." The indicator is consistent for a transitional period. Still, to compare the situation in the republics of the former Soviet Union, the author has nothing to rely upon but the far-from-perfect data of the censuses.

As can be seen from Table 7.6, Russians in Lithuania rank first in the Soviet Union in level of knowledge of the language of the indigenous population, despite great linguistic differences between the two languages. This is due basically to: (1) the relatively low proportion of Russians among the population; (2)

the absence of large compact Russian territorial communities; (3) the smaller influx of Russian immigrants; (4) the preeminent role played by the Lithuanian language in the life of the nation.

The situation is quite different in both Latvia and Estonia, where more Russians migrated and their proportion of the population is consequently greater. There the level of knowledge of the local language is much lower (although it cannot be compared with the situation in the Asian republics). The poor knowledge of the Estonian language as well as the linguistic Russification of the Estonians served as a pretext for the "singing revolution" there. [10]

Although the status of state language has undergone significant changes, the language problem nevertheless remains in Latvia and particularly in Estonia, where many Russians failed to learn the Estonian language. Lack of knowledge of the native language has now become an obstacle to citizenship or employment in state organizations. In Lithuania, passionate debates are still being waged on whether Russians should be obliged to know the state language.

It is tempting to conclude that all the problems of Russian minorities boil down to knowledge of the language of the indigenous population. This is not so. Suffice it to recall that perfect knowledge of the Russian language and culture did not help the Jews in the Soviet Union to escape the consequences of answering the notorious "Item No. 5," the question on all application forms that asked one's nationality.

Until Lithuania was recognized by the world community in September 1991, its entire political life centered on one basic issue—the question of independence. The attitude of Russians toward Lithuanian independence was reserved, not only in 1989 but also after its declaration in 1990. The situation in Estonia with non-Estonians is very similar (EMOR data): April 1989—5 percent "for," September 1989—9 percent "for," January 1990—17 percent "for," March 1990—21 percent "for," and May 1990—26 percent "for."[11]

Why were Russians against independence? There were many factors both conscious and subconscious at work here so one could hardly expect a coherent (and not stereotypical) answer to this question from a respondent. The author attempts to describe at least some of the reasons:

1. *"My Motherland is the Soviet Union."* Since the beginning of the twentieth century (with the exception of the short period from 1918 to 1940), Russians have identified proudly with the territory stretching from the Pacific to the Baltic Sea. Now the notion "Russia" (including the distinction between Russia and the Russian Federation) has yet to be defined. In a survey of young people in Vilnius in 1987, 51 percent of the Russians answered the question about their Motherland with "the Soviet Union" and 16 percent with "Russia." The frontiers between the republics seemed conventional (and this was actually so). The possibility of changing identity (from a citizen of the USSR to something else) was bound to encounter resistance.

2. *"I am not an émigré."* The stereotype of the hardships of Russian, Jewish,

and Lithuanian émigrés, widespread over the years, has left its imprint.

3. *Anxiety over "national minority" status.* It has been difficult psychologically for Russians to consider themselves a national minority; in their view this notion is more suited to Yakuts, Jews, and the like. They have had to give up their Big Brother role. Moreover, they fear they would become a persecuted minority, especially having had direct experience with the notorious Item No. 5 in the Soviet Union.

4. *"The end of socialism."* Russians believed in socialism more strongly than Lithuanians. When asked "What economic system would you prefer for future Lithuania?" 20 percent of Lithuanians and 39 percent of Russians answered "socialism" (Lithuanian Survey Research Center, October 1989). Obviously, the independence of Lithuania was viewed by many as an end to socialism.

5. *Economic fear.* The argument that Lithuania would be unable to exist on its own, without the USSR, was employed by many propagandists. However, it was only a ruse on their part, for very few really believed that Lithuania lived at the expense of the USSR. This idea was more widespread among Russians. During an April 1988 survey conducted under the author's guidance among Vilnius workers (the respondents included 320 Lithuanians and 183 Russians) a question was posed about economic ties between Lithuania and the USSR. Nineteen percent of the Russians and 6 percent of the Lithuanians answered that Lithuania received more from the USSR than it contributed to the all-Union budget, while 28 percent of the Russians and 65 percent of the Lithuanians said that it was the other way around.

6. *Political fear.* A certain segment of the Russian population living in Lithuania was associated with the repressive and ideological infrastructure. This segement is quite large, especially if family members, relatives, and pensioners are included in the count (although no estimates have been made as yet). These people could expect not only trouble from independence, but even punishment for their former activities.

7. *Political-economic fear.* The above-mentioned strata of the population realized that they would lose all their privileges along with their means of existence.

8. *"The Lithuanian language is difficult to learn."* Some Russians could neither speak nor write Lithuanian and experience has shown that the process of teaching adults to speak the language is rather ineffective. The fact that it was becoming increasingly difficult to manage without knowing Lithuanian intensified the Russians' fear, especially in the older age group.

While considering Russians' attitude toward independence, mention should be made of the events of January 13, 1991. The coup attempt organized by the army and the Communist Party was abetted by Russian-speaking workers who took part in the provocations before, during, and after that tragic night. Nevertheless, a telephone survey conducted by the Lithuanian Survey Research Center on January 17 showed that the majority of Russians supported the Supreme Soviet of Lithuania. Naturally, we did not overestimate the reliability of data collected over the telephone at such a tense moment, but a qualitative shift in the consciousness of Russians had definitely taken place. Had they wished to do so, Russians could have significantly affected the results of the referendum of February 9, 1991, but the outcome was striking—94 percent of the votes were "for independence" (76 percent of registered voters took part in the referendum). Still, one must recall that it was a period of very intense political passions; before and after this night, Russians' attitudes toward the question of Lithuanian independence were rather reserved. Now that all Baltic states have become independent, Russians are more worried about other things, such as their status, their rights, and their future.

4. The Party Affiliation and Ethnic Identification of Russians and Their Loyalty to the New Government

As in the entire postcommunist world, the formation of political parties in Lithuania has proceeded with difficulty. Economic interests have not been determined as yet and the level of political culture is low. It is very difficult for an ordinary respondent to find his bearings in the swirl of political metamorphoses.

I shall cite one curious example. In October 1989, when asked what party they would vote for during the elections, 13 percent of Russians and 5 percent of Lithuanians named the Party of Democrats. The figure seemed unreasonably high, since this party had never stood for the Russians. A little bit later we tried to clarify the point. It turned out that the Russians knew nothing of such a party, which was exactly what was to be expected. But for them the notion "democrat" was associated with something good, democratic and just. The name of the party sounded neither communist nor nationalist. Not only the Russians but Lithuanians as well often swallow such linguistic tricks.

Naturally, the main political forces were distinguished rather clearly. Up until the collapse of the USSR they could be divided according to their attitude toward the independence of Lithuania: against independence—the CPSU and the "Unity" Movement; for gradual withdrawal—the Communist Party of Lithuania (later renamed the Democratic Labor Party); for immediate secession—Sajudis.

If the initial attitude of Russians toward Sajudis was positive, it later became sharply negative. It should be pointed out that the Sajudis program also has undergone radical changes—from general democratic slogans and the demand for a "cost-accounting for Lithuania" to purely nationalistic demands, including secession from the USSR. At first Russians might have considered Sajudis as part of Mikhail Gorbachev's perestroika, but they later realized that it threatened the stability of their way of life. The sympathies of Russians were with the Communist Party of Lithuania, not Sajudis.

In December 1989 the Communist Party in Lithuania divided into two branches—the Communist Party affiliated with the CPSU and the Democratic

Table 7.7

Voting Preferences Among Lithuanians and Russians (January 1992; in %)

	Russians	Lithuanians
Democratic Labor Party	20	14
Lithuanian Future Forum	9	2
Sajudis	10	18
Difficult to say	35	33

Labor Party (led by Algirdas Brazauskas). The Russians' assessment of these two parties was roughly similar, though not high. In their view, the first had some advantages, for it openly defended Russians and supported the preservation of the USSR. Still, it was too obviously communist-oriented. The latter, although attractive for its mild economic and political reformism, did not promise to maintain the former position of Russians in society. The attitude of Lithuanians toward these two branches of the Communist Party was diametrically opposed to that of the Russians.

After the collapse of the CPSU and the recognition of Lithuania by the world community, not a single legal political grouping advocating imperial unification or socialism remained. Table 7.7 presents the data of the Lithuanian Survey Research Center for January 1992.

Almost 30 percent of Russians identified themselves with the opposition (the Democratic Labor Party) and the radical opposition (the Lithuanian Future Forum), while more than half had failed to determine their stand or were indifferent. The empirically stated support of Russians for the opposition (including opposition to the Lithuanian parliament and the government) cannot be explained by the negative attitude toward political changes alone, especially since the Russian minority is rather passive politically. Here the real issue lies in dissatisfaction with economic hardships. In all the Baltic states the opinion of Russians on the state of the economy is rather low, a fact we have come across many times in our surveys. We, together with our colleagues from Latvia and Estonia, think that the explanation is simple: Russians are alienated from the general cultural and political process, which means that the fruits of independence already enjoyed by Lithuanians (the return of cultural values, the feeling of pride for being a member of the world community, etc.) are irrelevant to Russians, who are more sensitive to economic difficulties—even though the situation in Moscow and in Russia as a whole is much worse. Many Russians must have hoped to live "as in the West" very soon.

Russians also consider their family income to be very low, although we failed to find any indication that Lithuanians were better off than Russians. For instance, in December 1991, 24 percent of Lithuanians and 31 percent of Russians said that their monthly income exceeded 1,000 rubles. Another example: in

Table 7.8

Answers to the Question: "What Is Your Opinion of the Current State of Interethnic Relations?" in Lithuania, Latvia, and Estonia (March 1992; in %)

	Lithuania		Latvia		Estonia	
	Lithuanians	Russians	Latvians	Others	Estonians	Others
Good and very good	49	44	42	27	16	21
Bad and very bad	9	16	35	43	39	40
Difficult to say	42	40	23	29	45	39

November 1991, the price of coffee in Lithuania went up 10 times and became a luxury. In the course of the December survey an equal number of Russians and Lithuanians (44 percent) said that they drank at least one cup of coffee a day. Our list of data testifying to a decent financial situation among Russians can be continued.

In Estonia, the incomes of Russians are not less than those of Estonians.[12] Yet it is notable in Estonia, too, Russians more often express dissatisfaction with their material situation (and consequently with the government), although objectively it is at least not worse than that of the indigenous population.

Naturally, there are widely varying reasons for this dissatisfaction. Some Russians suddenly began to see themselves as aliens, a perception with both subjective and objective components. It is not so easy suddenly to find oneself in another state. Lithuania has adopted a mild law on citizenship ("zero" option), while Latvia has adopted a rather tough one. On October 18, 1991, the newspaper *Diena* published the text of the law "On the Restoration of the Rights of the Citizens of the Latvian Republic and the Basic Principles of Naturalization," which stressed that people who arrived in Latvia after 1940 could become its citizens if they "can at least speak Latvian . . . and at the moment the present law comes into force had lived and been registered there for no less than 16 years." There are also other limitations. Obviously, this could not help but worry the Russian-speaking population and become a subject for debate for many years to come. Here the positions of both Latvian and the Russian-speaking sides are understandable. An individual can perceive his or her ethnic identity on different levels of social intercourse: in the street, in municipal transport (where Russians are betrayed by their accent), at one's place of work. Each of these cases should be discussed separately, but let us discuss the answers to a general question, although these responses are not as revealing (see Table 7.8).

The empirical data demonstrate that interethnic relations are strained. However, in Lithuania Russians are much more comfortable psychologically than in Latvia or Estonia. In June 1991 we asked respondents about actual interethnic conflicts. Ten percent of Russians in Lithuania, 12 percent in Estonia, and 21 percent in Latvia said that they had taken part in such conflicts in the course of

Table 7.9

Positive Answers to the Question: "Would You Like to Move Permanently or Find a Job in Another State?" in Lithuania, Latvia, and Estonia
(September 1991; in %)

Lithuania		Latvia		Estonia	
Lithuanians	Russians	Latvians	Others	Estonians	Others
3	7	1	7	1	7

several weeks. However, as a rule these conflicts had a psychological, "oral" character.

It is more serious when people begin to worry about their security. According to our data, the difference in the responses of Russians to the question "Do you fear for your personal security?" in Lithuania, Latvia, and Estonia is very slight. Lithuania lived through most of its troubled period during and after Bloody Sunday—January 13, 1991. Vytautas Landsbergis, Chairman of the Supreme Soviet, made a special appeal to the Russians in Lithuania which had a certain calming effect.[13] It should be stressed that from the very beginning the Russians as an ethnic group were not involved with the Russians who took part in the coup. At the end of January the Lithuanian Minister of the Interior said: "From the bloody night of January 13 on we got no information about any conflicts on interethnic grounds."[14]

To date there have been no interethnic clashes in the Baltic states. It seems that there will not be any.

5. Prospects for Russian Minorities in the Baltic Region

One of the basic aspects of the problem of the Russian minority is the possibility of mass emigration from the 14 former union republics to Russia, which may cause a number of political, economic, and even moral problems. It is difficult to assess the scale of the potential emigration, for there are a series of transitional nuances, from the actual readiness to move to an abstract wish involving a number of preconditions (geographical considerations, the quality of housing, the availability of jobs). So the answers differ depending on how the question is put. We have at our disposal the data presented Table 7.9.

The number of Russians who wish to move is not very high (7 percent) and roughly corresponds to the number of Lithuanians (3 percent). For Lithuanians the favored destination is either the United States or Germany. Russian respondents mentioned both Russia and the countries of the West (however, there are too few statistical data available for a proper analysis).

There are more people who want to find a temporary job in the West: 31

percent of Lithuanians and 25 percent of Russians. The countries of preference are the same—first the United States and then Germany (the situation is the same in Latvia; in Estonia most people prefer Finland and Sweden).

Russians in Lithuania constitute a small part of the population; they are definitely a minority. Besides, as already noted, they are rather well integrated into Lithuanian society, a fact demonstrated by their knowledge of the Lithuanian language (the best in the former USSR in terms of knowledge of the language of the indigenous population).

The negative feature of the composition of this minority is occupational: many of them are closely connected with the military system, while others work at large enterprises whose future is unclear (however, in Lithuania the tendency toward creating very large enterprises was not so pronounced and there is a chance that the workforce could be redistributed).

In the political arena of Lithuania today, the most serious interethnic question concerns Poles; the "Russian question" remains somewhat in the background and has to do mostly with the presence of the Russian army. It can be safely said that Russians in Lithuania are more comfortable psychologically than those Russians in Latvia or Estonia.

Of course, the Russian minority, as part of Lithuanian political life, would not support nationalist movements. Liberal or even cosmopolitan ideas are more attractive to them. It is difficult even to imagine that the idea of restoring the Russian Empire would gain much support in Lithuania.

Some Russians, especially those who are connected with ideological or repressive structures, will certainly leave Lithuania. The majority, however, is bound to integrate fully into a new society and become "Russians of Lithuania."

By contrast, the notion of "Russian minority" is hardly applicable to Latvia and Estonia, for almost half the population cannot be considered a minority. Since Russians have not lived in these countries for long but still constitute a significant part of their populations, a somewhat different description of their status needs to be devised.

When the problems of Russians living in Latvia and Estonia are discussed, often mentioned are the facts that they cannot speak the state language, that the Latvian and Estonian cultures are alien to them, and that they are employed mostly in areas that hold little or no prospect for further development. But these problems could be resolved through the creation of a new system of education, reconstruction of the economic system, and so on. The basic problem is quite different—the demographic fact of the presence of such a great number of Russian people. It is hardly likely that in the near future either Latvians or Estonians would agree to the existence of a Latvian-Russian or Estonian-Russian state. The instinct for national self-preservation would spontaneously or even irrationally make itself felt. It affects both everyday life and legislation (hence such strict laws on citizenship and naturalization in these countries). Russians there will

Table 7.10

**Number of Respondents to Surveys Conducted by the
Survey Research Center of Lithuania in 1989–92**

Date	Number of respondents	Lithuanians	Russians
May 1989	1,725	1,363	155
October 1989	1,459	1,172	131
November 1989	1,459	1,172	131
December 1989	1,616	1,277	155
April 1990	1,583	1,251	142
June 1990	1,351	1,102	128
August 1990	1,376	1,086	132
October 1990	1,383	1,111	163
December 1990	1,336	1,055	142
April 1991	1,394	1,132	123
June 1991	932	755	85
September 1991	1,383	1,093	124
December 1991	1,198	934	120
January 1992	1,347	1,064	121

always be in opposition to national parties. In contrast to Lithuania, their influence on the political and economic lives of these countries will be significant. So I see the future of these states as a continuous chain of nervous and unstable compromises with the "Russian factor." No reasonable solution, no "optimal model" can be suggested. It is well nigh impossible to change the demographic reality. The problem of Russians will continue to exist while there is national self-consciousness.

Appendix 1

The Survey Research Center of the Institute of Philosophy, Sociology, and Law of the Lithuanian Academy of Sciences regularly conducts surveys of the voting adult population (18 years of age and older) of Lithuania. The sample surveys are conducted on a territorial, multistage basis, the last stage being a systematic random sample survey, administered with the help of voters' lists. For this purpose the territory of Lithuania is divided into six geographic zones, which include regions united by historical, social, and demographic parameters. The following large cities constitute separate zones: Vilnius, Kaunas, Klaipeda, Šiauliai, Panevežis, Alytus, Marijampole, and Sniečkus. The number of polling stations and respondents are determined proportionally to the number of residents (the surveys have been conducted in all the above-mentioned cities).

Interviewers are highly skilled professionals who regularly receive instruction. After the surveys, the quality of their work is checked by conducting sample investigations (see Table 7.10 above).

Notes

1. *Statisikos Departamentas prie Lietuvos Respublikos Vyriausybes.* Lietuvos gyventojai, Vilnius, 1991, p. 88.
2. Ibid., 1989m. Visuotinio Gyventoju Surasymo Duomenys. Vol. 2. Vilnius, 1991, p. 114.
3. "Pirmieji isvyko, tukstanciai liko," *Tiesa*, 1992, no. 44 (March 4).
4. "Panorama" (Lithuanian TV), March 4, 1993.
5. *Statistikos Departamentas prie Lietuvos Respublikos Vyriausybes,* 1989m, p. 351.
6. Ibid., p. 118.
7. P. Kirkh, P. Iarve, and K. Khaiav, "Etno-sotsial'naia differentsiatsiia gorodskogo naseleniia Estonii," *Sotsiologicheskie issledovaniia*, 1988, no. 3.
8. R. Skatikaite, "Diversiia," *Respublika*, February 14, 1992, p. 1.
9. *Statistikos Departamentas prie Lietuvos Respublikos Vyriausybes. Lietuvos Respublikos Pagrindiniu Tautbiu gyventojai.* Vilnius, 1991, p. 26.
10. See the debates in *Raduga* magazine starting with 1987, no. 10.
11. J. Kivirahk, "From the singing revolution to the referendum of independence," *Quarterly of EMORC*, vol. 1, no. 1 (July–September 1991).
12. A. Kirch, "Russians as a minority in contemporary Baltic States," *Bulletin of POTCT Proposals*, vol. 23, no. 2 (1992) (in print).
13. V. Landsbergis, "U nas net strakha nenavisti. Liudi russkie i liudi drugikh natsional'nostei kotorye oshchushiaiut sebia grazhdanami svobodnoi Litvy, ia khochu pogovorit' s vami," *Soglasie*, January 17, 1992.
14. Interview with Interior Minister M. Masiukonis, *Soglasie*, 1992, no. 5 (January 29).

8

Russians in Uzbekistan

Sergei Nikolaev

Uzbekistan, according to the 1989 population census, is inhabited by members of 128 nationalities with ethnic motherlands not only within the former Soviet Union but also beyond its borders. Although such data lead one to consider Uzbekistan a polyethnic state, it would be misleading to define the polyethnic character of Uzbekistan on the basis of a simple enumeration of the nationalities inhabiting its territory. For instance, living there are members of 28 nationalities of the North (Eskimos, Chukchi, Evenk, Mansi, etc.) who altogether number 953 people, or 0.005 percent of the entire population of Uzbekistan. Peoples of the North Caucasus and Siberia similarly comprise tiny portions of Uzbekistan's population.

If we examine the population of Uzbekistan from the standpoint of nationality, language, and religion, it becomes clear that its polyethnic character is based on the interaction of three cultural areas: Turkic-Muslim, Iranian-Muslim, and Slavic-Christian. Each of these cultural areas is the sum of unique ethnocultural communities. For instance, the Turkic-Muslim area incorporates the ethnic cultures of Uzbeks, Karakalpaks, Kazakhs, Kyrgyz, Turkmen, Tatars, and other Turkic nationalities united by common language roots, tribal traditions and a single religion—Islam. According to some estimates this area incorporates fourteen Turkic peoples which jointly comprise 82.6 percent of the republic's population. Naturally, the ethnic culture of each of these nations has unique features which manifest themselves in professional, spiritual, and everyday life. Nevertheless, these ethnic cultures have developed within a single Muslim culture and have assimilated the ethics, world outlook, and morality of Islam, and hence have many features in common, a circumstance that makes it meaningful to include them into one cultural group. In Uzbekistan the dominant role in the Turkic-Muslim configuration is obviously played by the Uzbeks, whose numbers (71.4 percent of the entire population) and wide distribution throughout the republic result in the dominance of their ethnic culture in the region as a whole.

The Iranian-Muslim configuration includes the ethnic cultures of Tajiks and Persians, who jointly constitute 4.8 percent of the population.

Two of the three cultural areas mentioned above—the Turkic-Muslim and the Iranian-Muslim—are part of a "Muslim East" supersystem which forms the foundation for the polyethnic space of Uzbekistan. There is a certain rivalry between these cultural areas which finds expression primarily in ethnic competition between Uzbeks and Tajiks in regions where they live together (the Samarkand and Bukhara regions and some districts of the Kashkadaria, Surkhandaria and Namangan regions). This competition is especially keen in the workplace and in the availability of ethnic and cultural institutions (schools and other educational establishments). This competition affects interstate relations between Uzbekistan and Tajikistan—which, by the way, have no treaty on state borders because the Tajik side considers certain parts of the Bukhara and Samarkand regions as historically part of the Tajik Republic. Still, these two areas are united by Muslim roots, which has a significant effect on the establishment of the ethnic hierarchy in Uzbekistan.

The Slavic-Christian configuration is represented by the ethnic cultures of Russians, Ukrainians, and Belarusians, who together constitute 9.2 percent of the population. The formation of this cultural area began with Russia's colonization of Central Asia, followed by the Sovietization of Uzbekistan. The major share is the ethnic culture of Russians, who constitute 8.3 percent of the republic's population. Russians arrived in Uzbekistan in five large migration flows. The first is tied in with the colonization of Turkestan in the 1870s.[1] By 1912 there were 210,306 Russians living in Uzbekistan.[2] This migration had both political and economic causes: at the beginning of the century the importance of Turkestan as the principal cotton-growing region supplying raw material for the textile industry of Russia began to grow (in 1915 the percentage of Central Asia in the total import of cotton to Russia reached 77.7 percent).[3] This necessitated the creation of local production facilities for the primary processing of raw materials. Since the indigenous population lacked the necessary skills, industrial workers from Russia were brought in.

Four other migration flows of Russians occurred in the Soviet period, all connected with the creation in Uzbekistan of industries, transportation facilities, and the expansion of building and assembly operations.

Russians differed greatly from the native population of the republic in language, culture, and religion. Their need to maintain their own ethnic-cultural identity made it possible to form in Uzbekistan a specific cultural area (Slavic-Christian) which existed in Central Asia for only a hundred years.

Naturally, the polyethnic character of Uzbekistan is not exhausted by the interrelationships among the three areas mentioned above. The national (and consequently, religious) composition of the population is constantly expanding: people from other regions of the Soviet Union arrived in Uzbekistan during the period of industrialization and expansion of the irrigated farming zone. The national structure of the republic was also greatly influenced by the deportation to its territory of the repressed nations of the North Caucasus, the Crimea, and the Soviet Far East during Stalin's dictatorship. Yet, these resettlements of people to Uzbekistan did not significantly affect either the total number of the population or the established balance in the interrelationships of peoples who were earlier settlers.

Therefore, the essence of the polyethnic character of Uzbekistan boils down to the interaction of the three cultural areas mentioned earlier. It should also be pointed out that the peoples comprising these areas are estimated to constitute 96.7 percent of the entire population of the republic.

The interaction of cultural configurations in a polyethnic environment can be judged first of all by the degree of their stability in relation to each other and second by their spread. In the second case what is meant is not so much the number of ethnic groups they embrace, but the territory they occupy.

Intercultural relations in Uzbekistan are characterized by competition, which is especially evident in the case of the Turkic-Muslim and Slavic-Christian configurations. In these groups, there is a marked growth in the Uzbek population and a decline in the Russian population. This phenomenon has its consequences for both, essentially as follows:

1. The reduction in the number of Russians (both absolute and relative) in the republic's population is bound to change the ethnic composition of the electorate, that is, the voters whose support political forces seek in elections. As a result, Russians will have fewer opportunities to participate in political life. An example of this situation is the present composition of the Supreme Soviet of the republic, its highest legislative body, in which Russians constitute only 4 percent. This is the result of an electoral system in which elections to this body is based on such large electoral districts that the chances for the Russian minority to promote their deputies are limited. The Supreme Soviet of Uzbekistan consists of one chamber and thus no possibilities for nominating candidates from different nationalities are envisioned. In this way Russians are ousted from public management, while their opportunities in politics are also strictly limited.

2. A change in the ethnic composition of the republic's territory has made it more difficult for Russians to ensure their national and cultural development: the spheres of application of the Russian language are being narrowed, the opportunities for performing communal and religious rites curtailed, and the number of Russian cultural establishments reduced.

3. The eclipse of the Slavic-Christian configuration by the Turkic-Muslim configuration has led to the ouster of Russians from many fields of employment. The drop in the number of rural residents among Russians has led to the gradual devaluation of peasant life and labor by the professional culture of the Russian diaspora in Uzbekistan. These values are of great importance to the Russian ethnos as a whole, for practically the entire ethical system unifying Russians as a

Table 8.1

**Changes in the Percentage of Uzbeks and Russians
in the Population of Uzbekistan**

	Percentage of urban population		Percentage of rural population	
	Uzbeks	Russians	Uzbeks	Russians
1970	41.1	30.4	79.5	2.2
1979	48.1	24.8	82.8	1.2
1989	53.7	19.5	83.5	0.7

nation (notions of good and evil, corporal and spiritual, lofty and vile, past, present, and future) is and has been built on folk myths and images from peasant life (folk tales, heroic poems, fairy tales, proverbs, etc.). This means that the high degree of urbanization of the Russian diaspora in Uzbekistan is pregnant with the threat of loss by local Russians of the feeling of indentification with their ethnos.

4. The ouster of Russians from employment spheres affects their status in the social stratification of society and may result in their losing much of their professional culture.

To my mind, all these consequences taken together are the principal reason for the departure of Russians from Uzbekistan. Now let us analyze the above-mentioned phenomena from the statistical and sociological points of view. Due to the specific features of the demographic development of the Uzbeks and the reduction (both absolute and relative) in the number of Russians, a steady trend has been observed within the last two decades toward a change in the composition of the republic's population (see Table 8.1).

Here we are faced simultaneously with the narrowing of the habitat of the Russians and expansion of the habitat of the Uzbeks. This led to the ouster of Russians from many spheres of employment such as trade, public catering, health care, the military, credit and finance, law enforcement, and the judiciary. The rapid urbanization of Uzbeks forces them to search for new jobs that suit their background, only this time in urban conditions. This results in interethnic competition in the industrial sphere. Recent years have witnessed growth in the percentage of Uzbeks employed in food service, light industry, and transport and construction, areas that owed their earlier development chiefly to influxes of people from beyond the republic's borders. This circumstance radically affected the formation of the ethnic composition of Uzbekistan: the growth of the non-Uzbek part of the population due to the arrival of people from other republics has practically halted.

Statistical bodies in the republic have started registering the egress of non-indigenous people from Uzbekistan. The emigration of the non-indigenous population in recent years is due to the following circumstances: the repatriation of peoples that had been deported to Uzbekistan, the reduction of work opportuni-

Table 8.2

Migration from Uzbekistan (in thousands)

	1980	1985	1986	1987	1988	1989	1990
Arrived	88.6	113.9	132.2	142.9	164.8	83.9	75.7
Departed	94.6	114.4	143.1	166.9	213.6	117.7	215.6
Balance	−6.0	−0.5	−10.9	−24.0	−48.8	−33.8	−139.9

Table 8.3

Migration from Uzbekistan in 1990 (national composition; in thousands)

	Arrived	Departed	Balance
Total for the republic	75.7	215.6	−139.9
Russians	20.9	59.7	−38.8
Ukrainians	2.7	6.1	−3.4
Uzbeks	25.0	19.0	+6.0
Kazakhs	6.3	12.6	−6.3
Azerbaijanis	0.8	10.7	−9.9
Kyrgyz	1.1	2.8	−1.7
Tajiks	2.4	2.2	+0.2
Armenians	0.8	3.5	−2.7
Turkmen	0.9	1.3	−0.4
Crimean Tatars	0.6	19.7	−19.1
Jews	0.5	20.5	−20.0
Germans	0.7	5.6	−4.9
Greeks	0.2	2.2	−2.0
Kurds	0.1	0.4	−0.3
Uigurs	0.4	0.3	+0.1
Koreans	2.3	3.1	−0.8
Others	4.5	20.4	−15.9

ties for the nonindigenous population, and mounting interethnic competition in politics, the economy, and culture. Thus, the migration processes in Uzbekistan are characterized not so much by the influx of population as by its efflux, which is vividly demonstrated by the data in Table 8.2.

Emigration began to intensify in the late 1980s and reached its highest point in 1990. For the national composition of the émigrés from Uzbekistan, see Table 8.3.

As can be seen from the table, members of the majority of non-Uzbek nationalities are departing from the republic. Russians rank first in net outflow (−38,800), followed by Jews (−20,000), Tatars (−20,000) and Crimean Tatars (−19,100). The departure of the latter can be explained by their resettlement in regions adjacent to the Crimea. For the most part, Jews leave the country permanently, going abroad. As for the Russians and Tatars, their departure is caused by the

Table 8.4

**Percentages of Urban and Rural Dwellers Comprising the
Total Russian Population of Uzbekistan**

Year	Urban population	Rural population
1970	89.1	10.9
1979	93.4	6.6
1989	94.8	5.2

growing interethnic competition within the Turkic-Muslim community as well as among the ethnic areas. This circumstance has resulted in the fact that the ratio between arriving and departing Russians has tended to grow: 1989—1.78; 1990—2.87; 1991—2.12; January 1992—2.28.

All the processes mentioned above have affected not only the ethnic composition of the population but also ethnic and cultural factors influencing Uzbekistan's domestic and even foreign policy. Interrelationships among cultures in the republic have gradually led to the turning of the non-Uzbek nations into national minorities with all the ensuing consequences.

Because of the backgrounds of those Russians who migrated to Turkestan and Uzbekistan, they became highly urbanized: the percentage of this population living in cities and towns was dozens of times greater than that of people living in the countryside (see Table 8.4).

The Russians' predominantly urban environment gave them the advantages of better education and social services (health services, culture, housing, etc.) and also higher wages than average, since in Uzbekistan wages in cities and towns (especially in industry) were always higher than in the countryside. With occupational characteristics typical of the urban environment, Russians concentrated mostly around the middle stratum of the social structure: engineers, technicians, and managerial personnel in industrial enterprises; workers in industrial, power engineering, transportation, and construction establishments; skilled workers in the same establishments; workers of average skill levels without a specialized education; employees in educational, cultural, and other such facilities, and so forth. This means that the professional culture of Russians in Uzbekistan, by incorporating industrial labor skills absent among the Uzbeks, has promoted Russians to second place in the ethnic hierarchy after Uzbeks. Features of the totalitarian-unitary state (USSR) of which Uzbekistan was a part were also conducive to their promotion. The party and state administration, preaching the principle of "equality of nations," carefully monitored quota representation of members of nationalities in management bodies and structures. As a result, in both party and state agencies the second most important job was usually held by a Russian. This naturally affected the status of Russians in the ethnic hierarchy of the republic and was standing practice up until the moment

Uzbekistan gained the status of a sovereign independent state.

As has been mentioned above, the rapid urbanization of the members of the Turkic-Muslim configuration has resulted in the narrowing of the Russians' habitat. This is true both of the political-economic and cultural spheres. Conflicts and confrontation result as the mutual alienation of the members of different nationalities within one work collective grows. These tendencies have been uncovered by the Sociological Survey Center of Tashkent University. For instance, the survey conducted in 1990 (and continued in 1992) of workers at several industrial enterprises in Tashkent, Bukhara, and Fergana was aimed at determining, among other things, the level of satisfaction of workers with their jobs. Among the respondents, 29.7 percent of Russians and 30.9 percent of Uzbeks said they wanted to change jobs. But while the Uzbek workers, when asked why, mentioned "the lack of prospects" and "the discrepancy between the job and education level," 17.6 percent of the Russian respondents pointed to the "tension in interethnic relations at their place of work."

The organizers of the survey "Russians in the USSR: Realities and Stereotypes" (1991) made an attempt to find out, among other things, how 1,008 respondents felt about the threat of interethnic conflicts in Uzbekistan. Of this number 88.9 percent of the Russian respondents experienced interethnic tension at their place of residence, 55.6 percent at their place of work or study, and 27.8 percent with close friends. Among the causes of interethnic tension cited were infringement upon the rights of the non-Uzbek nationalities, the Uzbeks' dislike of the culture of other peoples, the aggressiveness of members of certain nationalities (50 percent), and the outcome of the struggle for power.

Interethnic competition in the sphere of professional activity affects Russians' choices of occupation. A study of the occupational orientations of Russian schoolchildren and their preferences conducted in 1989 and 1991 revealed that they tended to choose occupations that had not as yet become a part of Uzbek professional culture. For instance, schoolchildren in Tashkent preferred, in order, the following occupations: creative worker (writers, actors, musicians, etc.) military man, research worker in natural sciences, and industrial worker. Meanwhile the occupations from which Russians had been or were being ousted were named by only a few respondents: doctor (tenth place), engineer (eleventh place), trade worker (twelfth place), nurse (twelfth place), and police officer (fourteenth place).

During the period from 1990 to 1991 we studied the opinions of young people from various ethnic groups in Uzbekistan concerning the character of interethnic relations in the republic. A total of 1,480 people were surveyed, including 820 Uzbeks, 460 Russians, and 200 members of other nationalities. It turned out that 42.2 percent of the Uzbek respondents and 31.1 percent of the Russian respondents had a negative attitude toward other nationalities. For specific data see Table 8.5.

It is worth mentioning the obvious antipathy between Russians and Uzbeks;

Table 8.5

Nationality as the Object of Negative Attitudes Among Uzbeks and Russians
(percentage of those answering in the affirmative)

Target nationality	Uzbeks	Russians
Uzbeks	0.5	9.6
Russians	14.2	1.9
Jews	8.2	9.6
Tajiks	8.7	3.8
Armenians	16.9	13.5
Azerbaijanis	5.0	11.5
Tatars	9.6	13.5
Koreans	1.8	5.8
Karakalpaks	0.0	1.9
Turks	9.6	0.0

however, while for Russians, Uzbeks are in fourth or fifth place as objects of hostility, Russians are in second place for Uzbeks (after Armenians).

It should be pointed out that especially hostile toward Russians are residents of those regions where interethnic competition for jobs is greatest. This is borne out by the following data (percent of the Uzbeks who have negative attitudes toward Russians): Tashkent—14.3 percent; Samarkand—13.7 percent; Nukus—2.6 percent; Andijan—12.8 percent; Fergana—7.6 percent; Karshi—33.3 percent; and Urgench—10.2 percent. This circumstance has led to the departure of Russians not only from the countryside but from towns and cities as well.

Russians have the status of a national minority in the ethnic hierarchy of Uzbekistan. Where formerly the party and state apparatus, among other agents, artificially maintained the Russians' second-place status, the present sovereignty of Uzbekistan and its concomitant ties with the world economy have changed the position of Russians in the ethnic hierarchy to the point where it is possible to say that Russians have now fallen behind the Uzbeks and other Muslim peoples. This statement is also borne out by the fact that Russians today play a lesser part in the political life of the republic and their range of employment has narrowed. Consequently, Russians' influence in all spheres of life in the republic has diminished. In view of the present tendencies it is possible to predict that Russians will concentrate their efforts in those few sectors of the economy to which the influx of locals is as yet hardly noticeable, such as power engineering, railway and air transportation, the iron, steel, and metal working industries, and mechanical engineering. This is bound to lead to changes in the choice of occupations and trades by the Russians and their geographic concentration in those regions where they can find jobs that suit their skills and support conditions under which their ethnic culture can be preserved.

Table 8.6

Responses to the Question "Do You Agree That a Policy of Russification Was Carried Out in the Republics?" (percentage of affirmative answers)

	Yes	No	Difficult to say
All respondents	62.5	17.8	19.7
Uzbeks	60.0	5.0	35.0
Russians	55.6	38.9	5.5

On the other hand, the decrease in percentage and absolute number of Russians will inevitably lead to a lessening of the role of the Russian language in the life of the republic. The establishment of conditions for the ethnic and cultural development of Russians is bound to become more the Russians' than the state's concern.

The sooner the Russians are able to recognize themselves as a minority, the sooner they will be able to adapt to their new position in the ethnic hierarchy of Uzbekistan and to the new geopolitical reality of an independent Republic of Uzbekistan, whose political and economic interests will be oriented not only to the north, to Russia, but to the world as a whole. Uzbekistan has always been and continues to be a state whose residents are mostly Muslims; this will naturally determine the character of its domestic and foreign policies.

Formerly, the social, economic, political, cultural and even national interests of Russians in Uzbekistan were bound not only to the republic where they lived and their ethnic motherland, Russia, but to the Union state as a whole. The single Union ensured the use of the Russian language throughout its territory, guaranteed similar approaches to education and the upbringing of young people, promoted the uniformity of political, economic, and cultural life in all the republics, and much else. Among the basic ideogems of the single Union state was the idea of the Russian people as the "Big Brother" of all the nations and nationalities inhabiting the Soviet Union. This circumstance led Russians living in Uzbekistan to assume an arrogant attitude toward the traditions, language, customs, and habits of Uzbeks and to ignore them altogether in their everyday life. According to the results of our survey, 83.33 percent of the Russian respondents believe that the Russians play a progressive role in relationships among the country's nations, while only 5.55 percent are of the opinion that Russians have not had a decisive influence on the life of other nations.[4]

As a result of this kind of understanding of their "mission" in the life of the Soviet Union, Russians consciously kept a distance between themselves and Uzbeks as well as members of other nationalities. During our survey we asked the following question: "Do you agree that in the year of stagnation a policy of Russification was carried out in the republics?" The results are presented in Table 8.6.

Table 8.7

Manifestations of Perceived Policy of Russification
(percentage of those who answered affirmatively to the
question asked in Table 8.6)

	Uzbeks	Russians
Monopoly of Russians in key posts in party and government bodies in the republic	30.0	22.2
Infringement upon the rights of non-Russians in hiring	30.0	5.6
Contempt of Russians toward other cultures and customs	5.0	27.8
Forcing members of other nationalities to learn Russian	5.0	11.1
Not sure	30.0	33.3

Table 8.8

Perceived Role of Russians in Uzbekistan

	Uzbeks	Russians
Hold most top jobs in politics and economy	35.0	5.6
Employed in various sectors alongside other nationalities	40.0	16.7
Top jobs held by non-Russians while Russians do arduous jobs of secondary importance	15.0	61.1
Difficult to say	10.0	16.6

We then asked those who answered in the affirmative to elaborate on the manifestations of this policy of Russification. The answers are presented in Table 8.7.

These data illustrate the fact that not only Uzbeks but also the Russians were clearly aware of the detrimental character of the nationalities policy in the Soviet period.

At the same time, Russians began to feel threatened. We asked our respondents about the role Russians played in Uzbekistan and obtained the data displayed in Table 8.8.

These data show the political polarities between the views of the Uzbeks and the Russians living in the republic.

In 1989 the Law on State Language was adopted in the Uzbek SSR (the official name of the republic until 1991), according to which the Uzbek language acquired the status of an official means of communication in state and public

Table 8.9

Knowledge of the Uzbek Language by Russians

	Know the Uzbek language	
	Number of people	Percentage of Russian population
Uzbekistan as a whole	75,927	4.6
Karakalpakstan	1,037	5.2
Andijan region	5,103	11.4
Bukhara region	3,962	2.9
Jizak region	2,397	7.4
Kashkadaria region	3,432	9.1
Namangan region	3,256	11.9
Samarkand region	6,242	5.5
Surkhandaria region	2,921	7.7
Syrdaria region	3,390	6.0
Tashkent region	9,960	3.2
Fergana region	6,544	5.3
Khorezm region	2,942	24.2
City of Tashkent	24,741	3.5

Source: Results of the All-Union Population Census of 1989. The National Composition of the Population of the Uzbek SSR (Tashkent, 1990).

life. This same law gave the Russian language the status of a means of international intercourse. A term was established by the end of which all bookkeeping would be transferred to the Uzbek language. A term was also set within which officials were to have learned Uzbek. Russians reacted negatively to this law. The main problem was that at the time of the adoption of the law, very few Russians had an adequate knowledge of Uzbek (see Table 8.9).

Note that the smaller the percentage of Russian population in a particular region of the republic, the better they know the Uzbek language, which testifies to their better adaptation to existing conditions (see Table 8.10).

The Russian population of the republic responded to the adoption of the above-mentioned law with a decline of confidence in local government and an increase of confidence in Union government agencies that they considered to be guarantors of their rights (especially later, when some deputies in their speeches in the Supreme Soviet of the USSR condemned the "practice" of the adoption of language laws in union and autonomous republics). This is proven by our longitudinal survey of the political consciousness of young people (1989, 1990, 1991), the results of which are presented in Table 8.11.

The data in the table were estimated on the basis of a system proposed by the respondents: "trust completely" (+2), "trust" (+ 1), "difficult to say" (0), "do not trust" (−1), "do not trust at all" (−2).

Table 8.10

The Relationship Between the Number of Russians in Regions of Uzbekistan and Their Level of Knowledge of the Uzbek Language

	Percentage of Russians in total population	Percentage of Russians with good command of the Uzbek language
Khorezm region	1.2	24.2
Namangan region	1.9	11.9
Kashkadaria region	2.4	9.1
Andijan region	2.6	11.4
Surkhandaria region	3.0	7.7
Dzhizak region	4.4	7.7
Samarkand region	5.5	5.5
Fergana region	5.8	5.3
Bukhara region	8.2	2.9
Syrdaria region	10.0	6.0
Tashkent region	14.6	3.2
City of Tashkent	34.0	3.5

Table 8.11

Changes in the Level of Confidence Toward State and Public Bodies Among (Russian) Young People

	1989	1990
State structures of the USSR (president, Supreme Soviet)	0.37	0.60
State structures of Uzbekistan (president, Supreme Soviet)	−0.45	0.05
CPSU (Communist Party of Uzbekistan)	−0.32	−0.27
Clergy	−0.25	−0.31
Public organizations (trade unions, Komsomol)	−0.52	−0.50
Unofficial organizations	−0.09	−0.71

The data in Table 8.11 show lack of trust in those organizations that promoted radical changes in society not to the liking of the Russian population (unofficial organizations, the clergy) as well as those organizations that displayed passivity (public organizations, the Communist Party). Given these conditions, the top leadership of the republic (the president and the Supreme Soviet), aware that radical changes might weaken the existing government, condemned the actions of political forces aimed at destabilization of the situation in the republic. This in turn has raised the trust of the Russian population.

The fact that Uzbek has been given the status of state language has promoted

Table 8.12

Attitudes of Russians in Uzbekistan Toward Islam

Attitude toward Islam	Percentage of respondents
Hostility	6.3
Fear	2.9
Interest	48.6
Indifference	37.7

Table 8.13

Russians' Preferences of Situation-Normalization Measures

Measures	1989	1990
State-repressive	7.9	26.4
Liberal	63.2	19.8
Democratic	29.9	53.8

the national self-consciousness of Uzbeks and awakened interest in the nation's history and the spiritual heritage of Islam.

Russians in turn made an attempt to mobilize for the protection of their interests, forming an Intermovement Association with the aim of uniting the entire Russian-speaking population of the republic. However, the association has had no success. The authority of the former party functionaries who headed the group was very low, dooming the movement from the start. Attempts to set up branches of Moscow and St. Petersburg organizations in Uzbekistan with the purpose of uniting the Russian-speaking population also failed, due perhaps to the orientation of the Russians in Uzbekistan toward a single Union, which was not among the aims proclaimed by the majority of the radical movements in Russia.

The threat of Islamization of the internal life of Uzbekistan forced Russians to seek the "support" of the secular government.

When conducting our study "West–East: Ethnic and Cultural Attitudes in Political Behavior,"[5] we noticed the negative attitude of the Russians in Uzbekistan toward Islam (see Table 8.12).

During the same survey we studied the preferences of Russians for solutions to the republic's problems. The data obtained, as compared with the results for 1989, are contained in Table 8.13. We have conventionally divided all the measures cited by the respondents into three categories: (1) state-repressive (consolidation of power "from a position of strength," restriction of meetings and demonstrations, maintenance of order and discipline, extension of the powers of interior troops); (2) liberal (transition to a market economy, to a multiparty system, etc.); (3) democratic (complete independence of the republic, the power of law rather than individuals, the division of power, etc.).

The data shows that as Russians began to comprehend that reforms in Uzbekistan were irreversible, they came to realize the need to support those forces and leaders who would obey the law. In this they see the predictability of state policy under the new conditions of the development of a sovereign Uzbekistan.

The fate of the Russians lies primarily in their own hands. Even their departure from the republic in significant numbers would not result in their complete disappearance from the ethnic map. As already stated in this chapter, Russians in Uzbekistan are mostly urban dwellers. Russia is not prepared to receive urban populations from other republics of the former USSR; all plans concerning "migrants" envision their settlement in the countryside. This would make it necessary for Russian migrants from Uzbekistan to adapt to new, unknown conditions that are bound to change their status as well as their way of life. Are Russians now living in Uzbekistan ready for such changes? I think not. This means they must ultimately adapt to life in newly independent Uzbekistan.

Only by thoroughly comprehending their new status as a national minority will Russians gradually be able to change the character of their public activity and ensure conditions for their ethnic and cultural continuity.

There are several potential or already-existing sources of support for the Russian community that are in need of further development or exploration, such as the Russian Orthodox Church, whose role has already made itself felt: the number of parishioners has grown, more people have been baptized or married in church, more children attend Sunday school at the cathedral in Tashkent (there are already two groups of 100 children each). The Church's influence will no doubt increase, along with Russians' need for pillars of community consciousness.

A major part might be played by Russia itself, which should now consider Russians living beyond its borders as a Russian diaspora in need of patronage.

It would also be desirable to open a Russian cultural center at the future Russian embassy in Uzbekistan as compensation for the losses caused by the reduction of the Slavic-Christian cultural community in the republic.

And lastly, as the Russian diaspora in Uzbekistan is separated from Russia by state borders, it will also need international patronage, especially from those states that are based on democratic principles and observe human rights.

Notes

1. Turkestan corresponds to the present borders of southern Kazakhstan, Uzbekistan, Turkmenistan, and Tajikistan.

2. For more details, see A.I. Ginzburg, *Russkoe naselenie v Turkestane* (Moscow: Institut etnografii, 1991).

3. N.V. Chernyshev, *Sel'skoe khoziaistvo dovoennoi Rossii i SSSR* (Moscow-Leningrad, 1926), p. 100.

4. *Russkie v SSSR: realii i stereotipy,* 1991.

5. Research was conducted by the All-Union "Opinion" Program of State Education and included all regions of the former USSR. There were 3,809 respondents, including 1,067 in Uzbekistan.

9

Russians in the North Caucasian Republics

Galina Soldatova and Irina Dement'eva

Over one million Russians inhabiting the territories of the North Caucasian republics (Dagestan, Kabarda, Balkaria, Chechnia, Ingushetia, North Ossetia, and Karachai-Cherkessia) constitute numerically the largest ethnic group in the area. This makes up approximately one-fifth of the total population of this multinational region inhabited by people of nearly forty indigenous nationalities. According to the last population census, in Dagestan alone Russians are the fifth largest ethnic group after Avars, Dargins, Kumyks, and Lezgins. In three republics of the region (Checheno-Ingushetia, North Ossetia, and Kabardino-Balkaria) Russians invariably take the second place. In Karachai-Cherkessia they constitute a majority, with the most numerous indigenous nationality of the republic (Karachai) constituting only 31 percent and the share of Russians exceeding 42 percent. One may naturally suppose that Russians living in this region are a considerable force, capable of exerting a major influence on the development of interethnic relations and on the entire sociopolitical situation in the region. We shall attempt here to outline certain sociopsychological and sociodemographic features of the Russians and the role they may play in a situation in which ethnopolitical conflicts either exist or are likely to arise, as is the case in all the North Caucasian republics.

1. Demographic Peculiarities of the Russian Population in the North Caucasian Republics

During the last two decades not only have the socioethnic positions of the Russians and the native population been balanced, but the leading position formerly held by Russians has changed in many ways to favor the indigenous nationalities. In short, the demographic situation is becoming unfavorable for Russians.

The dynamics of the ethnic composition of the population in the North Caucasian republics is compared graphically in Table 9.1.[1] The growth rate of the Russian population, despite considerable increases during the postwar period,

Table 9.1

Dynamics of the Share of Indigenous Nationalities and Russians in the Total and Urban Populations in the North Caucasian Republics (in %)

	Total population			Urban population		
	1959	1979	1989	1959	1979	1989
Dagestan						
Indigenous ethnic groups	63.9	77.8	83.6	35.6	59.8	67.2
Russians	20.1	11.6	9.2	43.4	24.4	18.1
Kabardino-Balkaria						
Kabard and Balkars	53.4	54.5	57.6	16.6	36.2	43.0
Russians	38.7	35.1	31.9	69.4	49.8	43.5
North Ossetia						
Ossetians	47.8	50.5	52.9	28.8	44.1	49.3
Russians	39.6	33.9	29.9	55.4	40.5	35.0
Checheno-Ingushetia						
Chechens and Ingush	41.1	64.5	70.8	9.0	37.8	46.0

Table 9.2

Russians in North Ossetia

	Total population (thousands)	Russians (thousands)	Share of Russians in total population (%)
1939	407.8	156.1	38.3
1959	450.6	178.6	39.6
1979	552.6	202.4	36.6
1989	632.4	189.2	29.9
January 1, 1992	728.0*	186.2	25.5

 * Refugees from Georgia included.

slowed down in the sixties and by 1970 reached zero growth. Since that time the Russian population has been decreasing continuously in the entire region. These processes are taking place in various ways in the different republics. For example, the number of Russians in North Ossetia decreased by 13,200 over the last thirty years, whereas in Dagestan it decreased by 23,000 (2.4 percent), and in Checheno-Ingushetia it decreased by 42,000 (5.9 percent) over a period of only a decade (1979–89).

Although these processes are developing more smoothly in North Ossetia, the population dynamics in this territory reflect tendencies common to all North Caucasian republics (see Table 9.2).[2]

The decrease in the share of Russians in the total population of this region was caused mainly by factors related to ethnodemographic processes, interrepublican and interregional processes, and the contemporary socioeconomic development of the indigenous nationalities of the region.

Demographic changes were caused largely by higher rates of natural increase in the native population in the North Caucasus. Compared with the preceding periods, from 1979 to 1989 the population of Checheno-Ingushetia, Dagestan, and Kabardino-Balkaria grew by more than one-fourth. The decrease in the share of Russians in each of the multinational North Caucasian republics also resulted from a high rate of natural increase in other indigenous peoples in the region. At the same time there occurred a reduction in natural increase among Russians living in the North Caucasus. In North Ossetia, for example, for each thousand of the Russian population in 1979, 16.4 people were born and 9.9 died, while in 1990, 13.6 were born and 13.2 died. This means that the natural growth of the Russian population decreased more than 16 times over the last decade alone.

Another important reason for the decrease in the proportion of Russians is the large-scale interrepublican migration connected with the return of Balkars, Ingush, and Chechens to their national territories that began in 1957. The proportion of Russians in these territories had been very high. Most Ingush settled in North Ossetia, while most Chechens settled in Dagestan. The return of deported peoples has directly affected not only the ethnic composition of Kabardino-Balkaria and Checheno-Ingushetia but also the balance of ethnic groups in the neighboring republics.

The numerical decrease in Russians in the North Caucasian region is also connected with their large-scale departure from the republics in recent years. The migration of Russians is mostly forced, with the largest flow coming from Chechnia and Ingushetia: already in February 1991 a figure of 60,000 people was cited.[3] The Russians are not attracted by the prospect of life beyond the Russian frontiers in the Chechen and Ingush states. Even in North Ossetia, where relations between the indigenous population and the Russians have developed quite favorably, the 1989–91 period saw a negative migratory process, with 1,076 Russians leaving.

Census data show that the Russians constitute a major part of the North Caucasian urban population. However, the Russian urban majority has been rapidly turning into a minority. This process has been especially intensive in Dagestan, Checheno-Ingushetia and Kabardino-Balkaria. During the period from 1959 to 1989, for example, the share of the Russian urban population decreased in Dagestan by 25 percent, in Kabardino-Balkaria by 26 percent, and in Checheno-Ingushetia by nearly 33 percent (Table 9.1). The main reason for the decrease in the proportion of Russians in the North Caucasian urban population is the growth of the native urban population, caused mostly by their high internal migratory mobility from villages to cities. For example, in the period from 1959 to 1989, the proportion of Ossetians in the total urban population of North Ossetia grew 1.7 times, that of Kabard and Balkars more than 2.5 times, and that of Chechens and Ingush more than 5 times. These processes are particularly manifest in the capital cities. In Vladikavkaz, for example, the proportion of Ossetians had grown from 23.6 percent in 1959 to 40 percent in 1979, almost equaling the proportion of Russians at that time (43 percent) and exceeding the proportion of Russians in the capital of North Ossetia in 1989 (35.6 percent).

Having lost the status of ethnic majority in the cities, Russians were hard-pressed in the socioeconomic infrastructure. Migration of people from villages to cities was caused to a great extent by a wide spread orientation of the indigenous population toward nonproductive labor. This resulted in the considerable growth of the proportion of the native people in the urban population and particularly in the total number of office workers in the region. At the same time the share of Russians in this social group has decreased. For example, the proportion of Russians in the total number of office workers in the region decreased from 36 to 15 percent in the period from 1959 to 1985.

The share of Russians among engineers, technical and scientific workers, professors and teachers, and those working in the fields of literature, art and journalism is somewhat larger. The educational level of the Russian population in the North Caucasian region is substantially higher than that of other nationalities. Thus, there are 178 people with a higher education per 1,000 of the entire employed population in North Ossetia, whereas the corresponding figure among Russians is 189. Similar ratios are still more impressive in neighboring republics.

The considerable growth of the Russian population in the North Caucasus in the Soviet period took place predominantly during the wave of migration in the early thirties and the influx of skilled manpower during industrialization in the late 1950s and 1960s. It is no wonder that the Russian-speaking population (mainly non-Cossack Russians) constitutes a major part of the working class in the North Caucasian republics, which is also typical of many other regions of the former USSR. This situation has not changed despite the fact that the share of Russians in the workforce decreased by more than two-thirds in the period from 1959 to 1985. This fact points to a lack of opportunities for self-sufficiency and to the great dependence of a major part of the Russian population upon industry.

2. Social Position and Self-Consciousness of the Terek Cossacks

Recent developments have graphically demonstrated the lack of homogeneity of Russians living in the territory of the North Caucasian republics: Cossacks stay aloof from the rest of the Russian population and are exerting an appreciable influence on the social and political situation in the region. Differentiation of the Russian population has been evident especially in the "hot spots" of the region—Checheno-Ingushetia and North Ossetia. It is believed that about half a million Cossacks now live in the North Caucasian republics. In North Ossetia, Chechnia, Ingushetia, Kabardino-Balkaria, and Karachai-Cherkessia they form stable territorial and economic communities mainly in rural areas. In North Ossetia, for example, Cossacks are believed to constitute one-fourth of the total Russian population of the republic (about 47,000 people). These figures are quite credible, since according to some data, Cossacks constituted 20 percent of the total population of the Terek region before 1917, when they were registered separately from Russians and the local population.[4]

Although since the 1920s Cossacks have been officially numbered among Russians, these two groups remain divided both socially and psychologically. Therefore, in analyzing the Russian population it seems important to take into account its internal division into Cossacks and Russians proper (non-Cossacks).

An analysis of the situation shows that growing ethnic self-consciousness is typical only of a part of the Russian population, namely the Cossacks. This consciousness, which was greatly weakened in the course of the seven decades of Soviet power, is now flourishing. These processes are reflected in the social activity of the Cossacks. For example, since March 1990, when restoration of the Terek Cossacks was proclaimed, intensive work has been in progress to restore the Cossacks' organizational structure. The Cossack Circles (Councils) hold regular meetings in rural areas at which they discuss various issues, the most important and controversial being the creation of Cossack troops and the restoration of traditional Cossack community land ownership and land tenure.

An All-Terek Cossack cultural center was created to study problems of the history and ethnogenesis of the Terek Cossacks. The Cossacks insist on their right to be called a nation, an ethnic community, not a military estate abolished in 1917. The Terek Cossacks assert that they are, as part of the all-Russia Cossacks, "a unique historical phenomenon and, as such, are a subject of scientific study as an ethnic formation."[5]

The Cossacks have, apart from characteristic traits with respect to social, economic, and everyday life, specific psychological features as well. An analysis of the historical literature makes it possible to specify some typical features of Terek Cossacks which have distinguished them from the other Russian-speaking people of the North Caucasus.[6]

First, the core of the free Cossacks was represented historically by social outcasts—runaway serfs, participants in the peasant uprisings, dissenters, and so forth. All these people possessed common qualities, among them the striving for freedom and independence and a heightened social activity.

Second, their life near the dangerous frontiers of the Russian state gave rise to feelings of internal cohesion and unconditional mutual support. They themselves punished wrongdoers and observed laws and orders based on a hierarchy of military subordination.

Ethnic heterogeneity is highly characteristic of the Terek Cossacks. People of North Caucasian extraction also played a large role in forming the free Cossack population in the Terek River area. Cossacks, according to documents of that period, had friendly and even kindred relations with the Mountain people.[7] Free Cossacks were joined by those fleeing from punishment for various crimes or blood feuds in their native lands. Thus, for example, in the eighteenth century totally Ossetian Cossack settlements appeared in the Mozdok steppes whose members later joined the Mozdok Mountaineer Regiment. Today the Cossacks, although they identify themselves first and foremost with the Russian and Ukrainian peoples, still include Ossetians, Cherkessians, Nogai, and Kabard.[8] So the mixed ethnic composition of the Cossacks is part and parcel of their self-consciousness. That is why at the present time there can be no full identification of Cossacks with Russians: the Cossacks continue to find themselves in between Russians and the local indigenous population.

The non-Cossack Russians' national identification is different from that of other peoples inhabiting the Caucasus. The Russians identify themselves as a people by relating themselves not to a certain ethnic group, but to a state—until recently to the USSR, and now to Russia. In our study of ethnic and cultural orientations of several ethnic groups inhabiting the North Caucasus, Russians, in comparison with the indigenous peoples (Ossetians, Ingush, and Chechens), have displayed much less adherence to the traditional culture of their own ethnic group.[9] It was found, for example, that 56 percent of the Russian respondents do not at all know and do not observe national customs and traditions, or know them poorly. At the same time only 7 percent of the respondents in the group of North Caucasian peoples answered that they knew their national customs and traditions poorly.

3. Russian Minorities and Interethnic Conflicts in the North Caucasus

The extremely unstable situation in the North Caucasus contributes to the deteriorating position of Russians as an ethnic minority, with all the ensuing consequences. In addition to the general economic recession, structural changes in the economy, liberalization of prices, and inflation typical of all the republics of the former USSR, social stability in this region is undermined by a dangerous criminal situation, a huge number of civilians possessing arms, overpopulation caused by an influx of refugees,[10] lack of jobs as well as limited possibilities for self-support, and a consequent dependence on industry. While all the above factors cannot help but exacerbate the problems of Russians, social stability in the North Caucasian region is most adversely affected by the aggravation of interethnic tensions in the region, including tensions between the native and Russian-speaking populations. The main causes of this tension are the accelerating drives for political sovereignty and the existence of still-unsolved problems of the peoples who had been subjected to repressions and forcibly deported.

The process of political sovereignization is, as a rule, accompanied by the adoption of new laws and regulations. Their implementation sharpens not only ethnic affiliation as such, but also language and religious issues of ever-growing importance. This directly affects the interests of national minorities, primarily the Russian population, which until recently has held a privileged position in the North Caucasus.

The return of the deported peoples in the late 1950s failed to solve the entire problem. In fact, it generated a number of new and no less serious problems that have become particularly acute since the adoption of the Russian law "On the Rehabilitation of the Peoples Subjected to Repressions." For example, the issue of the forcibly displaced peoples (Cossacks in 1918–20, Ingush in 1944, Ossetians in 1920, 1944, and 1957) overlooked by the law has become particularly acute. Thus, one of the main demands of the Cossacks is their political rehabilitation in connection with their forced displacement from 1918 to 1920.

Also of great importance are problems of statehood and territorial claims resulting from the arbitrary demarcation of the borders of national territories in the North Caucasus as Soviet statehood was established. These territorial disputes emerged primarily between the indigenous peoples (Ingush versus Ossetians, Dagestani versus Chechens, Kabard versus Balkars, etc.), and they are becoming the basis both for interrepublican and internal conflicts in the region.

The Terek Cossacks have advanced with growing insistence the idea of returning to traditional land tenure. Implementation of this idea centers around the problem of restoring to the Cossacks ownership of lands that once belonged to their forefathers, since before 1917 the Cossacks acquired these lands as a reward for special military service. This, however, could engender further territorial disputes (for example, between the Cossacks and the Mountain peoples, particularly, the Ingush). One must also take into consideration the possibility that Cossacks might issue a demand for their own statehood if their efforts to promote a Cossack revival in the south of Russia are a success.[11]

Other Russians in the area mostly keep clear of territorial conflicts. However, as ethnic tensions in the region increase, Russians seek either to leave the republics or to separate from the indigenous population's territory. Such trends can be observed, for example, in certain territories that were formerly a part of Russia's southern fringe but which were forcibly separated from the Stavropol Territory and joined to the North Caucasian republics in the late 1950s (Mozdok region in North Ossetia and Kargalin, Naur, and Shelkov regions in Checheno-Ingushetia).

The direct interest of the Cossacks in the main interethnic problems in the North Caucasus makes their involvement in interethnic conflicts inevitable, but at the same time other Russians find themselves outside the main knot of interethnic problems. This situation explains the noninvolvement of non-Cossack Russians in these conflicts and their efforts to remain neutral. Nonetheless, the tension between this group of the population and the indigenous peoples is growing. This tension is largely of a secondary character and is predetermined not by the development of conflicts as such with the native peoples of the region but by the impact of the general sociopolitical situation.

Growing interethnic tension in the region lowers the overall level of ethnic tolerance. However, our studies show a high level of tolerance on the part of the indigenous population toward Russians. Conflicts among the indigenous peoples do not influence directly their attitude toward Russians. For example, the attitude of members of different ethnic groups toward Russians after the tragic events that took place in 1982 in connection with the conflict between the Ingush and the Ossetians could be characterized in general as positive.[12] This may also be illustrated by the attitude toward Russians among refugees from South Ossetia and inner Georgia who are now living in North Ossetia. Despite the general decrease in ethnic tolerance among the refugees, even toward members of their own ethnic group,[13] their attitude toward Russians remains fairly positive. The situation is different when a direct conflict between Mountain people and the Russian-speaking population of the North Caucasus flares up, as, for example, in Ingushetia and Chechnia, where Cossacks are often called "the occupiers along the Terek River." The same thing occurs when a conflict arises on the state level, as, for example, between Chechnia and Russia.

The heterostereotypes of Chechens, Ingush, and Ossetians formed by Russians account for approximately one-third of negative descriptions. However, the picture is not that simple. In conditions of coexistence of an ethnic majority and minority, the balance of mutual influence in the cultural, religious, and behavioral spheres tends to shift in favor of the ethnic majority. And the fact of a person's (or a group's) belonging to the ethnic majority (the indigenous population) or minority is important for determining one's status and influences the system of interethnic estimations and opinions. Compared with the native peoples, the Russians are more often inclined to appraise the indigenous nationalities higher than their own group. On the whole, in the structure of interethnic preferences of Russians one may observe a shift in favor of the indigenous population.

Historically the North Caucasian Cossacks have been in closest contact with the Ossetians and Ingush. Relations between the Cossacks and the Ingush developed badly from the very beginning. There were Ingush villages in the Tarskaia Valley until the early 1860s, when, at the end of the Caucasian War, the Ingush were displaced and the Cossacks settled on their lands. The result was an acute shortage of land among the Ingush and a running feud between the Ingush and Cossacks that lasted through the nineteenth and early twentieth centuries and the Civil War. In the 1920s the lowlands along the right bank of the Terek River were returned to the Ingush, and the Cossacks moved to different areas in the North Caucasus. Today a conflict is growing between the Cossacks living in the left-bank settlements along the Terek River and the Ingush living on the territory of the former Checheno-Ingushetia. The conflict was triggered by the tragic events in the Troitskaia settlement in April 1991, after which Cossacks started to leave the republic on a mass scale. In early September about 3,000 people left six Cossack settlements in the Sunzhen region and another 12,500 submitted applications for moving to the central regions of Russia.[14]

In contrast, relations between the Cossacks and the Ossetians historically developed quite favorably. This is because (besides the fact that some Ossetians formed part of the Cossacks) in 1920, under Soviet power, when the right-bank Cossacks were nearly totally subjected to Soviet repression, the left-bank Cossacks were less affected thanks to joint intervention by the Cossacks and Ossetians. It is not incidental that in the most serious interethnic conflict of the region—between the Ossetians and Ingush in North Ossetia—local Cossacks support the Ossetians. If this conflict is aggravated, the local Cossacks and the Cossacks of southern Russia may become allies of the Ossetians.

One should not forget that the overwhelming majority of the indigenous population of the North Caucasus is Muslim. The aggravation of social, ethnic, and economic problems is ever more often accompanied by actions under Islamic slogans. This is typical, first and foremost, of the situation in Chechnia and Ingushetia, where oppression on religious grounds has a long history and where only in the late 1970s were the first mosques officially opened (previously they operated underground). It is not by chance that Chechnia is seeking to lead "the national liberation movement" of the Caucasian Mountain peoples, giving it the color of Islamic revolution. Representatives of the republics where Islamic proponents are becoming especially strong are beginning to dominate also in the Confederation of the Mountain Peoples of the Caucasus. All these processes testify to the fact that confrontation on the basis of religion is likely to develop in the North Caucasus. This may greatly escalate interethnic tensions, first of all between the indigenous Moslem population and Russians (both Cossacks and non-Cossacks).

As for relations between the Cossacks and other Russian-speaking people of the region, they are characterized by the lack of any unifying impulse despite a community of language, religion, and origin. The situation in the Mozdok region of North Ossetia, home to 25 percent of the total Russian population of the republic, is revealing in this respect. Part of this population has been very active in advocating the return of the region to Stavropol. The Slavic peoples in coalition with the Cossacks form the required majority and thus could have a significant influence on the internal political situation. So far, however, the Russian-speaking population is not united enough on the issue of separation of the Mozdok region to ensure success in a referendum on this problem.

The separatist tendencies typical of the non-Cossack Russians, which grow in direct proportion to interethnic tension, are at odds with the desire of the Cossacks to live in close proximity with the Mountain peoples. If the political situation in North Ossetia should become aggravated, however, or should it separate from Russia, the Cossacks might change their position. Separatist tendencies among the non-Cossack Russians can be explained on the one hand by their interest in avoiding involvement in local interethnic conflicts, and on the other by a lack of feeling of community with the local peoples, their history, and problems.

The Cossacks are not as frightened of interethnic conflicts. Nearly five hundred years of peaceful and nonpeaceful coexistence with the Mountain peoples have given the Cossacks a strong identity in the eyes of the indigenous peoples of the North Caucasian republics. Besides, the Cossacks are psychologically bound to the lands of their forefathers. That is why the Cossacks, unlike other Russian-speakers, consider the Caucasus their historical homeland and are determined to remain there.

The lack of striving for unity between the Cossacks and other Russians manifests itself in political activities. The Cossacks are much more active in this sphere because of their origin and their history as a community. During perestroika, their unofficial traditional structures were easily restored on a large scale. That is one of the reasons why the most active social organizations of the Russian-speaking population in the North Caucasus are those set up by Cossacks. For example, a social organization called The Terek Cossack Circle is even stronger and more active than the political movements representing the indigenous peoples of some republics. These Cossack organizations do not, however, represent other Russian-speaking people of the republics, and their Cossack members do not participate in other political and social movements.

The non-Cossack Russians are represented mainly in pro-Russian social and political movements and organizations relying on support from corresponding central political parties. Purely Russian social organizations have been established in the region. In North Ossetia for example, there is a society of Slavs called Rus, which, judging by press reports, was created by former Russian nomenklatura workers primarily for purposes of self-protection.

The increase in the activity of democratic pro-Russian organizations in the North Caucasus lags behind the national movements, most of which were formed by early 1989. Non-Cossack Russians sometimes participate in these organizations, but in very small numbers and not very actively. This can be explained by the fact that the new political organizations of the North Caucasus are mainly monoethnic. In North Ossetia, for example, there are such organizations as the Ossetian society Ishtir Tanakhash, the Ingush Democratic Party, the Georgian Association, etc. In other North Caucasian republics the ethnic component is accompanied by a religious—that is, Islamic—one, which often plays a dominant role. Russians cannot participate in these social and political movements because of language and religious barriers.

As a result, the Caucasian Russians do not consolidate their ranks. Sociopolitical movements like the Interfronts do not exist there, but they might someday, especially if Cossack communities serve as a nucleus.

4. Russians in Chechnia

Today Russians in Chechnia and Ingushetia (Table 9.3) live mostly in cities and towns. Seventy-two percent of the Slavic population lives in the Chechen capital, Grozny, where they constitute 56 percent of city dwellers. Another 7.42 percent reside in three other cities—Gudermes, Malgobek, and Nazran—and urban-type settlements. The rest are rural dwellers.

Table 9.3

Ratio Between Veinakh (i.e., Chechen and Ingush) and Slavic Populations in Cities and Urban-Type Settlements (according to 1989 Census)

	Total population (thousands)	Chechens (percentage)	Ingush (percentage)	Russians (Slavs, percentage)
Cities:				
Grozny	397,258	30.5	5.4	56.0
Gudermes	37,402	59.4	0.1	35.0
Malgobek	20,179	8.4	69.6	19.6
Nazran	18,076	0.2	97.1	1.3
Argun	25,491	*	*	*
Urban-type settlements:				
Novogroznensk	8,225	95.1	0.1	3.8
Goragorsk	4,364	68.5	0.4	29.5
Karabulak	9,161	2.1	52.5	44.1
Chiri-yurt	5,075	*	*	*
Total in cities and urban-type settlements	525,231	29.7	11.0	46.6

* No data available.

Grozny has never been a Chechen city. This is borne out not only by the present composition of its population, but also by its history and origin (it was established in 1818 as a Russian fortress on the approaches to the Caucasus) and its Russian name (see Table 9.3).

Even though the major part of the non-Veinakh-speaking population is concentrated in the capital, Russians have always felt themselves masters of the city. At the same time, Grozny is home to all the republic's institutions, the majority of industrial enterprises, and practically the entire scientific elite. This circumstance sets the stage for competition for prestigious or lucrative jobs, competition that has always had a national coloring. As elsewhere throughout the Soviet Union, Russians enjoyed certain advantages in job placement and sometimes even had an exclusive right to certain jobs. A key post in every republic—usually the second Secretary of the Communist Party Central Committee—was always held by a Russian. The chief of the Republican Committee for State Security was also a Russian, as were the majority of heads of enterprises.

Restrictions in job placement due to nationality were a standard practice under the Soviet regime. The discrimination against the republic's eponymous nationalities was evident from the letter of protest of twenty-seven prominent representatives of the Chechen and Ingush peoples[15] to the CPSU Central Committee in 1973, citing restrictions on job placement of Chechens and Ingush in

Table 9.4

Distribution of Specialists Among National Groups in Checheno-Ingushetia

National group	Number of specialists	Percentage of national group	Percentage of all specialists
Chechens	37,098	5.1	38.9
Ingush	9,439	5.8	9.7
Russians	45,886	15.6	47.4
Ukrainians	1,505	16.0	2.4
Armenians	2,364	16.0	2.4

leading industries and in science. They were not given jobs or promoted to high positions in the petroleum, machine-tool, and electronic industries, to say nothing of the defense enterprises.

In the capital and other cities and towns of the republic members of the indigenous population were relegated to those sectors of the national economy where a relatively honest competition among national groups was possible— mainly trade, motor transport, and to some degree in services. This fed a contemptuous attitude among Russians, enhanced by their socialist mind-set, toward the commercial opportunism of the indigenous peoples. Although members of the indigenous population could apply their skills in construction, many sought better pay far beyond the republic's borders, to the north and east of Russia, and this did not significantly change the opinion of Russians living in the republic concerning the business and moral qualities of the native population of Checheno-Ingushetia.

Due to two circumstances—resistance to attempts to penetrate key industries and science and higher wages in trade and services, where jobs were given only to relatives and acquaintances—a great number of certified specialists, Veinakhs by nationality, did not work at the level of their qualifications. That is why, despite a high percentage of Veinakhs among certified specialists (65 percent), they had no noticeable effect on the republic's macroeconomy. At the same time, the low percentage of certified specialists among the Chechens (5.1 percent) and Ingush (5.8 percent) shows that they do not entertain hopes for a higher education.

From the data contained in Table 9.4 on the distribution of certified specialists among national groups it is clear that more than half of them are Russians, Ukrainians, and Armenians (51.35 percent).[16]

Since these groups dominate in the key industrial branches, the loss of this part of the population of the republic is bound to have a catastrophic effect on its economy. Moreover, the most skilled workers in the key industries also belong to the Russian-speaking part of the population.

Russians and Russian-speaking people constitute a minority among the rural population of the republic, and they live mostly in compact settlements. As can

Table 9.5

National Composition of Population by Region (1989 census)

Region	Total	Chechens (%)	Ingush (%)	Russians (%)
Achkhoi-Martan	59,328	96.6	0.2	1.1
Vedeno	33,142	97.2	1.2	0.7
Grozny	99,880	86.1	1.3	9.3
Gudermes	82,238	76.7	0.95	16.7
Malgobek	45,943	12.6	74.6	11.2
Nadterechn	35,449	94.3	0.08	4.3
Nazran	79,119	0.45	98.3	0.5
Naursk	46,442	59.4	0.52	37.1
Nozhai-yurt	48,842	99.5	0.01	0.2
Sunzhen	60,934	21.4	43.6	32.7
Urus-Martan	84,826	99.0	0.2	0.5
Shalinsk	136,822	96.1	0.25	2.7
Shatoisk	15,165	87.2	0.07	0.3
Shelkovsk	45,011	37.5	0.26	32.2
City of Grozny	397,258	30.5	5.4	55.9
Republic total	1,270,429	57.8	12.9	24.3

be seen from Table 9.5, the largest rural Slavic communities are in the Sunzhen, Naursk, Shelkovsk, Gudermes, and Grozny regions. In the Malgobek region, populated mostly by Ingush, and in the Shalinsk region, populated mostly by Chechens, there are also rather large compact groups of Slavs. The majority of the Russian farmers consider themselves Cossacks. Cossack villages were built long ago in the fertile land won from the Ingush and Chechens. Like the pioneers who opened up North America, Cossacks not only tilled the land but also guarded the occupied territories from raids of native peoples who did not want to submit to the conquerors. There also were ancient Cossack settlements built by freedom-loving Russian people who had escaped from serfdom, which had been introduced in the sixteenth century by Tsar Boris. The so-called Greben Cossacks—Old Believers—have lived in Chechnia for four hundred years now, are on good terms with the local population, and have assimilated many of the latter's traditions, but have preserved their faith.

The revival of the Cossack movement, although not on a mass scale, is having a real impact. On the eve of the elections for the president of the Russian Federation, such nominees as Yeltsin, Ryzhkov, and Makashev visited Cossack settlements in order to enlist their support. This movement, which seemed to come from nowhere, first proclaimed itself a national entity with the Cossacks an independent ethnos, then declared that it would defend the interests of all working people and the socialist way of development. This is not as contradictory as it may seem. All depended on the side from which support to the new and power-hungry nomenklatura was rendered. Only people of other nationalities could be the traditional enemy of the Cossacks, and they used hatred toward this enemy as a basis for rallying the Russian-speaking population of the Cossack regions.

For a long time, however, noisy Cossack chieftains, who demanded arms and sent ultimatums to the government, failed to win over to their side with chauvinistic slogans and Cossack nationalism the peasants from the Terek and Sunzha river areas who for centuries had tilled the land. Increasingly, everyday conflicts turned into interethnic ones, which aggravated the political instability in the republic. In turn, political instability led to growing interethnic tension. In such a situation, of cardinal importance is extremist propaganda—public addresses by chieftains, nervous articles in the national-patriotic as well as the Cossack press, and spontaneous rumors. Widespread, irrational fear drives people from their homes.

The character of migration in Russia (as in the USSR) is different from that in the West. A change of residence involves the need for mandatory registration at the new address. In a large city it is next to impossible to get a permit for such registration. The only means, although not available to all, is to give a large bribe to some high-ranking official in law enforcement. Although the practice of residence registration was denounced by the Constitutional Court, its decision was not implemented in a single town or village of the former Soviet Union. Another difficulty, perhaps the major one, lies in obtaining housing, which is granted rather than purchased. Although in some parts of the country the privatization of apartments is under way, there is still no housing market. Thus, a person who vacates his residence can become homeless, with no right even to add his name to the waiting list for a state apartment, for to do so one must live for a certain number of years in the new town. A specialist in whom a local enterprise is particularly interested has a chance to obtain an apartment, but such cases are exceptional.

Still another difficulty facing a potential migrant is the need to transport all furniture and household goods. Due to exorbitant prices and, most important, chronic shortages, a person can afford to buy good furniture only once in a lifetime, so only a few dare to leave it behind. The very process of transporting involves the real risk of losing one's earthly belongings. It is not by chance that the following saying of the Soviet epoch enjoys great popularity: "Moving out is like a fire during a flood." In view of the above-mentioned difficulties, one needs profound reasons for deciding to move.

All the more surprising then is the sureness with which movement of population and political movements—that is, changes in the political situation—follow one another. An incremental change in the population of Checheno-Ingushetia is a very fine political indicator.

Up until 1989 the population of the Checheno-Ingush Republic declined rather than increased, and the migration balance of both Veinakh- and Russian-speakers was negative. True, according to the 1970, 1979, and 1989 censuses the number of people of the indigenous nationality steadily grew at approximately the same rate as the Russian-speaking population decreased. However, the increase in the Veinakh and the decrease in the Slavic population over the twenty-nine years could not have been connected with interethnic relations, which were truly stable. The year 1989 saw a sharp change in the migration pattern in Checheno-Ingushetia. For the first time in many years the growth of the Veinakh population reached zero (the number of people arriving in the republic equaled the number of people departing) and then began a sharp increase.

The same year witnessed a rise in the outflow of the Slavic population. While prior to 1988 the Veinakh community in Checheno-Ingushetia lost 3,230 people every year and the Slavic community 2,470 people, the next year, as has already been mentioned, the Veinakh community did not lose a single person, while the Slavic community decreased by 3,400 people. The positive balance of the Veinakh migration reached 6,298 people, while 7,747 more Slavs left the republic than arrived. The higher rate of outflow of Slavic population and the return of Veinakhs to their motherland are closely connected with the major political event in the republic: in 1990 a session of the Supreme Soviet of Checheno-Ingushetia adopted the Declaration of Sovereignty. Within the first months of 1991 the rate of the decrease of the Slavic population remained the same as in 1990, while the growth rate of the Veinakh population dropped to almost zero. This was the period of confrontation between the United Congress of the Chechen People, headed by Air Force General Djokhar Dudaev, and the Supreme Soviet of the Republic, headed by its chairman, Doku Zavgaev. After the August coup in Moscow, the confrontation came to a head and ended in the victory of the United Congress and the election of Dudaev as president in October 1991. An attempt was made to introduce a state of emergency on November 8, but was soon canceled by the Russian parliament.

Political events had an immediate effect on the speed of migration. Within the last three months of 1991 the growth rate of the Veinakh population reached the previous year's level, while the departure of the Slavic population sharply accelerated. Despite the obvious connection between political events and the rate of migration, it is rather difficult to establish a clear-cut causal relationship. One can find many articles in Checheno-Ingush newspapers asking why the Russians are leaving. The republic's Russian-speaking residents, when asked this question directly, usually answer that it is impossible to understand their predicament without sharing their experience, or else they resort to vague anecdotes. Almost nobody mentions concrete examples of infringement of someone's national rights. The most typical answer can be found in an article in a small newspaper, *Neftepererabochik* (Oil Refinery Worker), [17] which bears the title "Why Are Russians Leaving?"

> Since the beginning of perestroika, with each passing year Russians feel increasingly less protected. . . . Today a top official who is Russian by national-

ity is a rarity in the republic. Practically no Russians are employed in trade and services or in the departments of the Ministry of Internal Affairs. . . . The new rulers promise to guarantee the protection of citizens' rights irrespective of nationality. . . . But if you walk in the street even in broad daylight you will notice that drunks harass Russian girls, not Veinakh ones, and insolent youths test their fighting skills on a Russian boy, not a Veinakh one—all of this under the indifferent glances of passers-by.

The last words are probably the key to understanding the psychological reasons for leaving.

Most important among the restraining factors are housing and jobs. The majority of the Russian able-bodied population is employed in oil drilling and refining, and the management and science connected with these industries. Many of them were born in the North Caucasus and are practically locals. Still, they suffer either consciously or unconsciously from the loss of their position as "representatives of the empire" and for the first time feel alien and uncomfortable. So what makes them move is not only their fear of the potential aggravation of the situation, but also their accustomed secure position in life.

The president and parliament of Chechnia have assumed a declarative attitude toward the Russian population. It may even be said that their attitude is contradictory. It seems that their hands are full with other matters, although the mass exodus of Russians could have drastic consequences for the republican economy, since it would take time to train specialists to replace the Russians. Moreover, the excessively emotional and impulsive statements of Dudaev concerning Moscow, which refuses to recognize Chechnia's independence, make Russians feel even less secure. Granted, the problem of crime threatens not only Russians, but it is bound to lead to an increase in migration. Although in general the Veinakh population does not encourage the persecution of Russians, it has already begun to reconcile itself to such a possibility. Still, there has been no mass exodus of Russians and Russian-speaking people from Checheno-Ingushetia. In 1991, which was the worst year in this respect, the negative balance of the migration of the Slavic population was 7.16 percent of the 308,985 people living there (1989 census). It is also worth mentioning that despite everything, 4,747 people of Slavic origin moved to the region.

Notes

1. The following statistical data were used in the article: the 1959, 1970, 1979, and 1989 all-union population censuses; data of the statistical departments of the North Caucasian republics; data of the State Central Archives of North Ossetia; and data on the economic and social development of the union and autonomous republics, autonomous regions, and areas (1989), etc.

2. *Natsional'nyi sostav naseleniia Severo-Osetinskoi ASSR* (Vladikavkaz: Goskomstat RSFSR, 1990).

3. *Terskii kazak,* 1991, no. 2 (February).

4. I.P. Omel'chenko, *Terskoe kazachestvo* (Vladikavkaz, 1991).

5. *Terskii kazak*, 1991, no. 4 (April).

6. See A.A. Gordeev, *Istoriia kazakov* (parts 1–3) (Moscow, 1992); L.B. Zasedateleva, *Terskie kazaki (seredina XVI–nachalo XX v.): Istoriko-etnograficheskie ocherki* (Moscow, 1974); S.A. Kozlov, "Popolnenie volnykh kazach'ikh soobshchestv na Severnom Kavkaze v XVI–XVII vv.," *Sovetskaia etnografiia*, 1990, no. 5, pp. 47–56; Omel'chenko, *Terskoe kazachestvo*; S.M. Solov'ev, *Istoriia Rossii s drevneishikh vremen* (Moscow, 1960).

7. N.G. Volkova, *Etnicheskii sostav naseleniia Severnogo Kavkaza v XVIII–nachale XIX veka* (Moscow, 1974).

8. *Terskii kazak*, 1991, no. 3 (March).

9. G.U. Ktsoeva, "Issledovanie mekhanizmov etnicheskogo samosoznaniia," *Sovremennye sotsial'nye i etnicheskie protsessy v Severnoi Osetii* (Ordzhonikidze, 1987), pp. 109–22.

10. North Ossetia held second place in Russia in 1989 in density of population after Moscow and the Moscow region.

11. At the end of May 1992, the Union of Cossacks of the Russian South was created with the goal of uniting the Cossacks of the Don, Kuban, and Terek regions.

12. See G.U. Ktsoeva, "Ethnic Stereotyping: An Empirical Study," *Psikhologicheskii zhurnal*, vol. 7, no. 2 (1987), pp. 224–35; G.U. Soldatova, "Interethnic Communication: The Cognitive Structure of Ethnic Self-Awareness," *Soviet Psychology: A Journal of Translations*, vol. 29, no. 3 (May–June 1991), pp. 48–65.

13. G. Soldatova and Kh. Dzutsev, "Refugees from Georgia in North Ossetia," *Soviet Refugee Monitor*, vol. 1, no. 2 (1992), pp. 14–17.

14. *Moskovskie novosti*, 1992, no. 42.

15. *Spravedlivost'* (Grozny), 1989, no. 3.

16. 1989 population census data.

17. T. Ankundinova in *Neftepererabochik* (Grozny), no. 14 (750), November 25, 1991.

III

Flight from Diaspora

Causes and Consequences of the Failure
of Social Adaptation of Russians
to Alien Ethnic Milieus

10

The New Social and Cultural Situation and the Ouster of the Russian-Speaking Population from the Former Union Republics

Tatiana Marchenko

After the disintegration of the USSR, the former union republics started building new independent states under democratic slogans. But the dominant ideas of national revival soon led to the replacement of democratic slogans with national and nationalistic ones. In their rush to do away with the past, some new states, equating the categories "Soviet," "imperial," and "Russian," pursue a policy of rejecting everything Russian.

The cultural sphere is extremely politicized with a strong nationalist cast and creative work has more than ever become an arena for sharp ideological struggle. The subject of this study is the new social and cultural situation in which Russian minorities in the former republics have found themselves.

This chapter will examine the new cultural policy proclaimed in the republics' legislative acts, trends and processes in the cultural life of the new states as well as the attitudes of the Russian population and their patterns of behavior in various regions.

The basic sources of information for this chapter were 1989 census data, statistical yearbooks, findings of sociological research carried out by the Center for the Study of Public Opinion, and publications in the central and republican press.

1. Language Laws and the Actual Linguistic Situation in the Republics

Official policy in the sphere of interethnic relations and culture was originally proclaimed in the language laws, which therefore merit detailed analysis.

Language is undoubtedly the main cultural value, the basis of the culture of any nation, and at the same time an instrument for preserving, reproducing, and developing this culture. It is noteworthy that national revival in all the republics began with language issues, while demands for national and political sovereignty remained in the background.

Since none of the republics, except Belarus, have adopted laws concerning culture, language laws remain the main legislative acts in this sphere. The majority of the republics adopted their language laws in 1989–90, while the Transcaucasian republics had included articles concerning the status of national languages in their constitutions as far back as in 1978.[1] In the preceding period there had been no legislative acts concerning language, and this reflected a specific policy. This led to the narrowing of the sphere of usage of national languages in the republics; moreover, their popularization was regarded as manifestation of nationalism.

The adoption of language laws, undoubtedly a reaction to these negative trends, was in fact the first step on the road to building new independent nations. The importance of this step for national consciousness is demonstrated by the fact that in some republics—Georgia, Lithuania, Moldova, Tajikistan, and Turkmenistan—the days when the language laws were adopted were proclaimed Language Day by the republican supreme soviets and considered holidays.

According to language laws of all the republics, the status of official language is granted to the language of the eponymous nation of a republic. Only in Kazakhstan did the local soviets of people's deputies get the right to introduce a "local official language" in places where there is a compact settlement of people speaking another language (Article 19). In many other republics the language problems of such compact settlements are being solved in a different manner.

On the whole, the attitude toward the Russian language as stated in the laws of the new independent states varies by republic. Kazakhstan and the republics of Central Asia recognize Russian as the language of interethnic communication and support the development of bilingualism. In the laws of Estonia, Latvia, and Ukraine, the Russian language is regarded as a means of interethnic communication parallel to official language. In the Transcaucasian republics and Lithuania, the status of Russian is not specified at all.

It is noteworthy that the laws of all the republics stipulate that knowledge of the official language is necessary for occupying certain posts. These posts include heads of organizations (in Lithuania, Article 6 and in Ukraine, Article 6), all civil servants (in Belarus Article 4), and people employed in public services (in Estonia, Latvia, Moldova, Uzbekistan, Tajikistan, Krygyzstan, Turkmenistan). The list also includes workers in the fields of education, culture, mass media, and so forth.

The terms for bringing the language laws into force vary from three to five years in the majority of republics to as many as eight years in the Central Asian republics. However, none of the republics has all the necessary facilities (teachers, textbooks, language courses, etc.) to ensure mass and speedy instruction in the official language.

Thus language has become an instrument for implementing a specific policy aimed at excluding people who speak another language from employment in government agencies, management, and culture.

Perhaps the most important prognosticator for the future of a language is its status in the area of education. According to law the official language is the principal means of education and training in the majority of republics. The strictest laws in this respect were adopted in the Baltic states, where the official language alone is to be used in education, culture and science.

In some republics (Belarus, Moldova, Tajikistan, Turkmenistan) some subjects in secondary and higher schools are taught in Russian as well. The list of these subjects is fixed by the councils of ministers of these republics. A democratic principle of free choice in the language of instruction is proclaimed only in the laws of Kazakhstan, Uzbekistan, Krygystan, and Ukraine. It should be kept in mind that in the mid-1980s students of nontitular nations constituted a significant part of secondary-school students in many republics: 49 percent in Latvia, 39 percent in Tajikistan, and about 33 percent in Belarus and Moldova.[2]

As regards the learning of the language, in the republics of the Central Asia, Kazakhstan, and Moldova, provision is made for studying both the official and the Russian languages in all educational institutions. According to the language laws of Ukraine and Belarus, learning the Russian language is obligatory only in general education schools, while in the Baltic republics and Georgia, Russian is in fact equated with all other foreign languages, and studying Russian is not obligatory. Thus a policy of curtailing the learning of Russian and its further expulsion from all spheres of social life is legislatively fixed in some republics.

In the field of culture and in the mass media in Lithuania and Estonia, only the official language is to be used. The laws of these republics, as well as of Belarus, also favor the development of the national cultures. In some other republics the official language is declared the principal language in the mass media and book publishing (Uzbekistan, Kyrgyzstan).

Let us consider the real ethnic and linguistic situations in which these laws were adopted.

According to 1989 census data, Russians in all the republics except Armenia, Georgia, Moldova, and Tajikistan ranked second in population to the indigenous population group. The actual language situation was as follows: in four republics (Ukraine, Belarus, Moldova, and Kyrgyzstan) Russian was practically as widespread as the native language, and in Latvia and Kazakhstan it was much more so (see Table 10.1).

All the republics were to a certain extent bilingual. This was the case primarily because of the members of the indigenous population, who as a rule knew a second (the Russian) language. The Russians, on the other hand, were mostly monolingual. But the level of their knowledge of the native language varied by republic, ranging from practically nil in Kazakhstan and in the Central Asian republics to 11–14 percent in Moldova, Estonia, and Azerbaijan, 21–25 percent

Table 10.1

Knowledge of National and Russian Languages in the Republics

	People who know national language (thousands)	Percentage of total population	People who know Russian	Percentage of total population
Ukraine	40,140	78.0	40,340	78.4
Belarus	7,885	77.7	8,400	82.7
Moldova	2,904	67.0	2,968	68.5
Latvia	1,662	62.3	2,176	81.6
Lithuania	3,136	85.3	1,737	47.3
Estonia	1,055	67.4	921	58.8
Georgia	4,169	77.2	2,223	41.2
Armenia	3,214	97.2	1,466	44.4
Azerbaijan	6,072	86.4	2,694	38.4
Kazakhstan	6,612	40.2	13,686	83.1
Uzbekistan	14,939	75.4	6,617	33.4
Kyrgyzstan	2,283	53.6	2,416	56.7
Tajikistan	3,392	66.6	1,851	36.3
Turkmenistan	2,631	74.7	1,025	29.1

Source: Calculated on the basis of: *1989 All-Union Population Census Data. National Structure of the Population*, vol. 7, part 2 (Moscow, 1992).

in Latvia, Belarus, and Georgia, and 33 percent in Ukraine, Lithuania, and Armenia (see Table 10. 2).

Russians are often accused of covert chauvinism, scornful attitudes toward people of other nationalities, and unwillingness to learn the culture and languages of others. When we compare Russians to members of other nationalities whose members are likewise spread throughout the republics, such as Jews and Ukrainians, we see that Jews in all regions and republics indeed know the language of the title nation much better than the Russians do. Obviously, the long history of persecution of this far-flung nation has forced its members to acquire the experience of survival and adaptation in a different national milieu.

But in contrast to Jews, Ukrainians everywhere know the language of the indigenous population to a much smaller extent than Russians. Even in Belarus, which is very close to Ukraine in language and culture and where 25 percent of the Russian population knows the Belarusian language, only 16 percent of Ukrainians know Belarusian. The difference is also substantial in the Baltic republics. In Lithuania, 37.5 percent of the Russians, 42 percent of the Jews, and only 20 percent of the Ukrainians know the native language. Yet the Ukrainians have not been accused of nationalism.[*]

*It should be noted that until recently Ukrainians and Belarusians living beyond the borders of Ukraine and Belarus were not regarded as specific ethnic groups and in fact were identified with the Russians—Eds.

Table 10.2

Knowledge of the Official Language Among Various National Groups (in %)

	Russians	Ukrainians	Jews	Others
Ukraine	34.4	—	48.6	29.4
Belarus	26.7	16.1	29.5	48.2
Moldova	16.5	14.3	15.2	12.7
Latvia	22.2	8.7	26.3	24.6
Lithuania	37.5	20.0	42.5	37.0
Estonia	15.0	6.3	28.0	19.5
Georgia	23.8	15.4	60.0	24.0
Armenia	34.0	27.5	—	33.7
Azerbaijan	14.4	6.3	23.6	38.4
Kazakhstan	0.9	—	—	2.8
Uzbekistan	4.5	3.3	6.2	21.5
Kyrgyzstan	1.2	1.9	—	4.7
Tadjikistan	3.6	2.4	30.0	14.6
Turkmenistan	2.4	1.7	—	15.8

Source: Calculated on the basis of: *1989 All-Union Population Census Data. National Structure of the Population*, vol. 7, part 2 (Moscow, 1992).

It should also be noted that members of other national minorities have universally chosen Russian as their second language. Among national minorities, Russian is sometimes much more widespread than the official language of the republic. Thus, for example, 45–48 percent of the members of the national minorities in Kazakhstan and Kyrgyzstan (Germans, Ukrainians, Uzbeks, Tatars, Uigurs and others) know Russian and about 3–4 percent know the Kazakh and the Kyrgyz languages.

This shows that until recently the real situation in the republics was such that there was no need to learn another language in any sphere of life—employment, education, or culture. On the contrary, knowledge of Russian considerably widened one's opportunities in all spheres of life. Besides, the Russian language was and remains the only language of interethnic communication.

2. New Tendencies in the Cultural Life of the Republics

The movement for national revival in the former Soviet republics gave rise to dangerous social trends. Development of the national culture, freed from all implanted and traditionally alien features, has become the main aim of that movement. Everything foreign, primarily Russian, in culture and art is to be rejected out of hand.

Thus, for example, in the republics of Central Asia classical music (opera, ballet, symphonic music) is deemed a departure from the purity of national traditions, so local composers are called upon to reflect and develop national traditions in their works.[3]

In Ukraine, similar trends are seen in demands to give priority to Ukrainian operas in the repertoire of all theaters and to perform Russian and West European operas only in the Ukrainian language.[4]

It is noteworthy that the methods of implementing a new national policy hardly differ from the former administrative methods used to impose ideological directives. An example of this was the proposed resignation of the Estonian minister of culture, Lepo Sumera, because "under the guise of the so-called liberal ideology he has failed to contribute to the development of Estonian national culture and has been responsible for the disruption of cultural life."[5]

Parallel with the rejection of Russian culture in the former Soviet republics, general trends in the republics' cultural contacts are being reconsidered and changed, with Russian culture increasingly being replaced by the cultures of nations that are related from the point of view of ethnic origin, language, and religion. Active contacts are being developed between Moldova and Romania, Azerbaijan and Turkey, the Baltic republics and the Scandinavian countries, and so forth.

Changes in cultural orientations can be seen in the sphere of book publishing. From 1986 to 1990, as a result of growing financial and material difficulties (paper shortages, price increases, etc.), the number of publications and editions declined everywhere. However, this reduction came at the expense of Russian-language publications. Editions in the official languages were growing and, except in Ukraine and Belarus, the publication of books in foreign languages was increasing—3–3.5 times in Moldova, Azerbaijan, and Kazakhstan, 1.5 times in the Central Asian republics, and in Latvia, Estonia, and Georgia by 20–30 percent.

The same trend is confirmed by data on translations into native languages. Editions of books translated from Russian—mostly children's books, educational literature, and fiction—were cut 1.5–2.5 times from 1986 to 1990 in the Baltic and Transcaucasian republics and Moldova; in Lithuania, for example, editions of translated Russian children's books were cut by 95 percent, from 1.5 billion to only 70,000 copies by 1989. At the same time editions of translated foreign literature were rising in all the republics.

The mass media, especially television, also reflect this shift to new centers of attraction. Estonia broadcasts three programs from Finnish television, in Lithuania they show Polish programs, and in Moldova Romanian programs are shown. In the Muslim republics information contacts with the eastern countries— Turkey, Iran, Iraq, India, Pakistan, and others—are being broadened.[6]

Estrangement from Russian culture is accompanied by the reappraisal of historical and cultural values, often from nationalistic and anti-Russian positions. A most striking example of this is the attitude toward Russian classical literature. In works by Tolstoy and Pushkin, the authors' attitudes toward the national liberation movement in tsarist Russia's outlying provinces, as well as these writers' efforts on behalf of particular nations, are being emphasized.[7] On the other hand, of statues Pushkin's have been desecrated in several cities in Moldova under the pretext that some of the poet's lines were regarded as insulting by the new defenders of the Moldovan people.[8] Similarly, Ukrainian nationalists defiled Mikhail Bulgakov's memorial plaque in his native town of Kiev, accusing the writer of being part and parcel of Russian imperial culture.[9]

National feeling often turns into intolerance and boils down to a striving to degrade or humiliate everything Russian. "We were too long humiliated—now our time has come."[10] These words of a Georgian writer seem to express the feelings of many involved in the field of national culture.

Blaming Russians for all their problems, radical nationalists in some republics (especially the Baltic states) are pursuing a policy of ejecting Russians. One of the instruments of this policy is cultural discrimination against the Russian minority. While the rejection of Russian culture is widespread, its intensity varies in different regions and different aspects of culture. The sphere of education causes the greatest concern, because the Russian language is disappearing from the lives of younger generations. The number of Russian schools and institutions of higher education where instruction is conducted in Russian is diminishing. In some republics Russian is regarded as a foreign language, which leads to substantial cuts and lower quality of Russian-language instruction. In the Lvov region (Ukraine), the number of hours of Russian-language instruction had been already halved by 1991.

The transition to instruction in the official languages means a sharp restriction of opportunities to receive an education and choose a profession for Russian and Russian-speaking youth. This tendency is typical of the Baltic republics and western Ukraine, and is now beginning to be felt in the Transcaucasian republics.[11]

It should be emphasized that the spread of the Russian language and culture is being curtailed without heed, often in opposition to real social and cultural demands. An analysis made in Ukraine and Belarus showed that people who borrowed books from libraries preferred books in Russian (Table 10.3), particularly because this gave them greater opportunities to read technical literature and fiction by authors from other countries.[12]

The statistical data on what kinds of books and magazines people borrowed in public libraries in 1988 also showed that the majority of the population in Moldova, Kazakhstan, and Kyrgyzstan definitely preferred books and magazines in Russian, on an average 68–88 percent, with an even a higher percentage in cities (Table 10.3).

Not only is the output of Russian books being cut everywhere, but library stocks themselves are being revised in some republics. For example, the Moldovan Minister of Culture and Religion issued an order to withdraw a large quantity of Russian books from the libraries, including "the books of Russian

Table 10.3

Book Stocks and Borrowed Books in the Republican Libraries in 1988 (in %)

	Number of books and magazines		Borrowed books and magazines	
	in Russian	in language of titular nation	in Russian	in language of titular nation
Ukraine	61	38	62	37
Belarus	82	16	88	12
Moldova	69	30	68	31
Latvia	47	46	55	41
Lithuania	31	64	27	68
Estonia	35	58	39	55
Georgia	42	55	24	71
Armenia	43	52	28	66
Azerbaijan	31	68	20	80
Kazakhstan	79	20	78	21
Uzbekistan	52	44	40	57
Kyrgyzstan	77	20	69	29
Tajikistan	63	29	45	41
Turkmenistan	65	33	45	54

Source: Narodnoe obrazovanie i Kul'tura v SSSR (Moscow, 1989), p. 274.

authors that are not considered to be part and parcel of world literature and are thus not in the curricula of educational institutions."[13]

Discrimination in matters of information, aggravated by the break-up of an integral information space, causes great concern to the Russians in the republics. Until recently Russians' access to information differed little in the various republics. They watched the same TV programs, read the same newspapers, and went to see the same films in all regions of the country. Russians everywhere felt themselves at home largely due to the existence of an integral information and cultural space. Now this space is breaking up.

According to data from the Center for the Study of Public Opinion, Russians in all republics read the central press regularly, preferring *Argumenty i fakty, Izvestiia, Komsomol'skaia pravda*, and *Trud*, just as in Russia.

New state borders, the disintegration of former organizational structures, increasing financial and transportation difficulties, the lack of paper—all of these things considerably exacerbated the predicament of the daily press and periodicals in the republics, and thus constricted the public's access to information.

The central press is not available in the republics on a regular basis.[14] Material difficulties led to reductions in circulation and even to the closing of several Russian-language newspapers and magazines (*Belorusskaia Niva, Minskaia pravda*, youth newspapers in Moldova, Georgia, etc.).[15] In search of financial support, newspapers appeal to their readership and set up "survival funds" with their assistance.[16]

The well-known and very popular Russian-language Baltic magazines *Daugava*, *Rodnik*, and *Tallinn*, which have found themselves isolated from the majority of their subscribers (80 percent of them were always in Russia), are on the verge of closing. The state barriers that have been raised due to the policy of isolationism have blocked subscriptions to these periodicals from beyond the borders of the republics and have thus led to the loss of their principal readership.[17]

Russians in the republics, like other citizens in the country, watch mainly programs on the Central Television (CT). According to data from the Center for the Study of Public Opinion, nearly 80 percent of the respondents watched Central TV programs every day and the remaining 20 percent at one time or another. The programs on Russian TV (RTV) have been less popular, but on the whole 85 to 90 percent of the Russians in the republics watch RTV daily or occasionally.

Until recently, television audiences in all regions of the former Soviet Union could watch a full schedule of CT and RTV programs. Now the republics seem to regard both channels as the voice of Moscow, which does not often coincide with the political and cultural orientations in the new independent states. As a result, virtually everywhere republican TV uses Central TV and RTV time for its own programming.[18]

As for local television, in many republics it is designed exclusively for the indigenous population, with programs wholly in indigenous republican languages. In the Baltic republics, Moldova, and Ukraine, only ten to fifteen minutes of airtime are devoted to the news and sometimes to showing Soviet films in Russian. Much important information is thus not made available to the Russian-speaking population.[19] Discrimination in matters of information causes concern among Russians in other republics as well.[20]

Thus, as a result of official policies of the newly independent states, Russian minorities find themselves isolated from Russia as well as from the indigenous population, putting their future prospects into serious question.

3. Russians in a New Social and Cultural Situation

The official proclamation of a new national and cultural policy in republics that were formerly parts of an integral state, particularly the adoption of language laws, gave rise to heated discussions everywhere, while in the Baltic region and Moldova it provoked demonstrations and strikes among the nonindigenous (chiefly Russian) population. The main motive behind those actions was the demand for bilingualism, or the recognition of Russian as an official language equal in status to the native languages.[21]

Proponents of this position referred to world practice as well as experience at home. Indeed, the languages of minorities—which constitute less of the population than the Russians in the republics—have a certain official status in the world's democratic states. The proclamation of a national language as official in regions where the Russian-speaking population constitutes an absolute majority—for example, in the eastern part of Ukraine and in the Crimea, in the city of Daugavpils in Latvia, and other places—therefore runs counter to the standards of democratic countries. Besides, both Soviet and post-Soviet history provide examples of solutions to the official-language problem. For example, the Constitution of the Turkmen Soviet Socialist Republic of 1925 recognized both Turkmen and Russian as official languages. The Abkhazian Constitution recognizes three languages—Abkhazian, Georgian, and Russian—as official, reflecting the real language situation in the republic.[22]

However, despite the resistance of the nonindigenous population, language laws, with some amendments, were adopted.

What was the attitude of the Russians to the new language and cultural situation in the republics? According to data from the Center for the Study of Public Opinion (August 1991), although the absolute majority of the Russian city-dwellers in all republics did not know the language of the indigenous nation, they wanted their children to learn the language. Therefore, in the Baltic republics a significant number of children and grandchildren of Russian respondents knew two languages. In Lithuania, for example, Russian children speaking both Russian and Lithuanian totaled 29 percent, exceeding the corresponding percentage even in Ukraine (25.7 percent).

Thus, despite discriminatory laws concerning language, citizenship, and so forth, Russians in the Baltic republics are inclined to adjust to new conditions. Thus, the overwhelming majority of the resident Russians consider it obligatory to learn the official language. At the same time only one-third of the Russians in Lithuania believe that Lithuanians should know the Russian language (37 percent in Estonia and 46 percent in Latvia).

In the Central Asian republics and Kazakhstan the situation is quite the opposite. Russians who consider the study of the official language obligatory are in the minority—from 36 percent in Turkmenistan to 18 percent in Kyrgyzstan—whereas from 52 to 62 percent of Russians in this region are inclined to demand knowledge of Russian from the indigenous population. Obviously, a milder language policy in these republics gives the local Russians the opportunity to preserve their monolingual position.

Only in Azerbaijan and Ukraine did the majority of Russians (about 55 percent) deem it necessary for both the Russians and the indigenous population to know each other's languages.

It should be noted that a new national policy does not provoke the Russians' anger against the culture of the indigenous population (see Table 10.4). According to data from the Center for the Study of Public Opinion, only from 0.5 to 5 percent of the respondents in different republics experienced a negative attitude toward the renascence of local national traditions, customs, and holidays. Only in Uzbekistan, Kazakhstan, and Kyrgyzstan is their share slightly larger.

Russians by no means agree in their evaluation of the role and significance

Table 10.4

Attitudes of Russians Toward Their Own and Native Cultures (in %)

	Est	Lat	Lith	Ukr	Mol	Az	Kaz	Uzb	Kyr	Taj	Turk
Are the Russians in your republic on the whole more or less educated than others, or do you think they do not differ?											
Do not differ	46.4	56.6	69.3	78.5	40.7	50.0	51.5	38.2	35.6	31.1	38.7
More educated	7.2	10.1	2.3	7.6	46.2	30.0	28.3	45.5	36.9	44.7	47.9
Less educated	21.1	7.3	13.1	0.5	0.7	1.7	3.8	1.2	6.8	2.7	0.3
Hard to say	24.5	18.7	15.3	13.2	12.4	18.3	15.6	14.8	20.7	21.1	12.8
No answer	0.8	0.3	0.0	0.2	0.0	0.0	0.8	0.4	0.0	0.4	0.3
What is your attitude toward the restoration of local or national traditions, holidays, and customs in the republic?											
Positive	84.0	91.1	84.7	94.9	85.4	88.1	72.6	77.8	60.7	73.3	81.0
Negative	5.1	1.5	2.8	0.5	4.1	1.5	7.5	6.0	12.1	4.2	2.1
Hard to say	9.7	7.0	12.5	4.6	9.8	10.2	19.9	16.0	27.3	16.5	16.9
No answer	1.3	0.3	0.0	0.0	0.7	0.2	0.0	0.2	0.0	6.0	0.0
What is the influence of the Russian culture on the culture of the indigenous population of the republic?											
Positive	29.1	36.4	21.6	52.3	64.3	60.4	60.6	63.2	68.6	64.2	81.0
Negative	1.7	3.4	1.7	2.7	1.4	1.7	1.5	1.9	2.3	1.5	0.0
Almost none	37.6	28.7	40.3	20.0	15.1	23.3	20.1	23.7	17.4	17.8	10.3
No answer	2.1	0.0	0.0	0.2	0.9	0.0	0.2	0.2	0.2	0.2	0.0

of their own culture. The majority of the respondents in the Baltic republics see no essential difference in educational and cultural levels between the Russians and the indigenous population, yet a significant number of them (21 percent in Estonia and 13 percent in Lithuania) are prepared to recognize the priority of the indigenous population in this sphere. Moreover, nearly 40 percent of the Russians in these republics think that their own culture does not influence the native culture in any way.

On the other hand, a majority of Russians in all the other republics are convinced of the positive influence of their culture and consider their educational and cultural level to be much higher than that of the indigenous people, except in Ukraine, where Russians regard Ukrainians as absolutely equal to them in education and culture.

Having recognized after the August 1991 events the irreversibility of the political processes at work, Russian minorities turned for models of adjustment to the experience of Russian communities in Europe and the United States "that lived first and foremost by their own culture."[23]

The process of setting up national and cultural societies has begun first of all in the Baltic republics and less actively in Moldova and Ukraine. This is natural, since it was in the Baltic region that the building of independent national states began; besides, in these republics the majority of the Russians are not inclined to emigrate and are trying their best to adapt themselves to the new situation.

These new cultural centers call on Russians to give up politics and to re-arrange their lives and revive their national culture. Emil Smekhov, chairman of the Russian Society of Latvia (RSL), the largest and strongest organization of its type, stressed: "The RSL is created not against, but only for. . . . The Russians are uniting not against the Latvians but for the consolidation of the Russians, not against the Latvian state system and sovereignty but for the equal rights of the Russians in this process, not against the self-determination of the Latvian nation, but for the preservation of the Russians in Latvia as a nation."[24]

Russian cultural societies consider the following spheres of activity most important: education, publishing, culture, and business—this last as a material basis for Russian communities and a source for financing culture.[25]

These societies help Russian-speaking young people to get an education. For example, the Technological University with its technological, economic, and pedagogical departments was established under the aegis of the Russian community in Latvia in 1991.

Publishing is directed mainly toward overcoming discrimination in the sphere of information. The RSL founded the newspaper *Russkii put´*, and the Slavonic Fund in Moldova is issuing *Slavianskii vestnik.*

Emphasizing the idea of the continuity of Russian culture in a given region, the societies are engaged in studying and popularizing the legacy of Russian cultural figures whose lives are associated with a particular region. It should be noted that these societies exist without any state subsidies. Until recently they have been receiving financial aid from large regional industrial enterprises which mainly employ mostly Russian workers, but with the worsening economic situation this aid has all but stopped. That is why the cultural centers are not only seeking sponsors but also trying to do business themselves.

* * *

Analysis of the national and cultural policies of the newly independent states allows one to group the republics, as follows, according to level of radicalism, orientation toward the adoption of one official language and development of the national culture, and discriminatory attitude toward Russian minorities: (1) the Baltic republics and Georgia; (2) Ukraine, Belarus, and Moldova; and (3) the republics of Central Asia and Kazakhstan.

Resistance to Russian culture exists in all the republics, but its intensity is determined not by a region's cultural cohesion or level of westernization, but by the dominance of the national idea and the propensity toward ethnic interaction, the latter being a function of the ostensible threat to the national interests posed by Russian minorities and the appealing idea of "managing without Russians."

But the position and sentiments of Russians in the republics are determined not mainly by linguistic or cultural factors, but by the severity of interethnic conflict and the degree of any real threat. Russians, like any other group, are worried most by the aggravation of national conflicts in regions where armed clashes have taken place (Azerbaijan and Moldova) as well as in the Central Asian republics, where ethnic bloodshed has also occurred.

Deep cultural differences are most probably the basis for these conflicts and apprehensions, and it is only by taking into account this basic factor that one can assess the attitude of the Russians to their new sociocultural position in the republics. Only then can one understand the desire of the Russians to leave the Central Asian republics or, in the case of the Baltic republics, to adapt themselves to the new context, learn the native language, and continue to live there.

Notes

1. The language laws of the republics cited in this chapter and their respective sources are as follows [in Russian]: Zakon Estonskoi SSR "O iazyke," *Sovetskaia Estoniia,* January 24, 1989; Ukaz prezidiuma Verkhovnogo Soveta Litovskoi SSR "Ob upotreblenii gosudarstvennogo iazyka Litovskoi SSR," *Vedomosti Verkhovnogo Soveta i Pravitel'stva Litovskoi SSR* (Vilnius), 1989, no. 4; Zakon Latviiskoi SSR "O iazykakh," *Sovetskaia Latviia,* September 5, 1989; Zakon Moldavskoi SSR "O funktsionirovanii iazykov na territorii Moldavskoi SSR," *Kommunist Moldavii,* 1989, no. 10; Zakon Kazakhskoi SSR "O iazykakh Kazakhskoi SSR," *Vedomosti Verkhovnogo Soveta Kazakhskoi SSR* (Alma-Ata), 1989; Zakon Kirgizskoi SSR "O gosudarstvennom iazyke Kirgizskoi SSR," *Vedomosti Verkhovnogo Soveta Kirgizskoi SSR* (Frunze), 1989, no. 17; Zakon Tadzhikskoi SSR "O iazyke," *Kommunist Tadzhikistana,* May 5, 1989; Zakon Uzbekskoi SSR "O gosudarstvennom iazyke Uzbekskoi SSR," *Pravda Vostoka,* October 24, 1989; Zakon Ukrainskoi SSR "O iazyke v UkSSR," *Pravda Ukrainy,* November 3, 1989; Ukaz

prezidiuma Verkhovnogo Soveta Gruzinskoi SSR ob uchrezhdenii ezhegodnogo prazdnika Dnia gruzinskogo iazyka 14 aprelia, *Vedomosti Verkhovnogo Soveta Gruzinskoi SSR* (Tbilisi), 1990, no. 4; Postanovlenie prezidiuma Verkhovnogo Soveta Litovskoi SSR ob ob"iavlenii 1990 goda Godom Litovskogo iazyka, *Sovetskaia Litva,* October 27, 1989; Postanovlenie Verkhovnogo Soveta Moldavskoi SSR ob uchrezhdenii 31 avgusta ezhegodnogo natsional'nogo prazdnika "Limba noastre" (Nash iazyk), *Sovetskaia Moldavia,* June 24, 1990; Postanovlenie Verkhovnogo Soveta Tadzhikskoi SSR ob ustanovlenii ezhegodnogo prazdnika Dnia iazyka 22 iiulia, *Kommunist Tadzhikistana,* July 30, 1989.

2. See, for example, *Narodnoe obrazovanie i kul'tura v SSSR* (Moscow, 1989). These figures, though obsolete to some extent, can be used because according to the statistics the number of students in the country as a whole and in the republics changed little in the course of the 1980s (*Narodnoe obrazovanie,* p. 193).

3. "Oboidemsia bez baleta i simfonii," *Kommunist Tadzhikistana,* June 14, 1990.

4. Ia. Gordeichuk, "Ne dollarom edinym," *Muzyka,* 1991, no. 4; A. Mokrenko, "Kommertsializatsiia iskusstva—absurdna!" *Kul'tura i zhitiia,* June 29, 1991.

5. "Ministru kul'tury predlozheno podat v otstavku," *Estonia,* January 18, 1992.

6. "Zachem liudei trevozhit'," *Teleradioefir,* 1991, no. 10.

7. "Pogovorim bez torzhestvennykh krasok," *Russkii iazyk i literatura v azerbaidzhanskoi shkole,* 1991, no. 3.

8. G. Piatov, "I moldovanno, i toshno. . . ." *Literaturnaia Rossiia,* June 7, 1991.

9. A. Bobrov, "Shtraf—Pushkinu," *Literaturnaia Rossiia,* June 7, 1991.

10. S. Zaitsev, "Glubina i pena," *Literaturnaia Rossiia,* May 6, 1991.

11. "Trebuietsia li ekzamen po natsional'noi prinadlezhnosti?" *Soiuz,* 1991, no. 8.

12. S. Kratsiuk, "Chitatel' belorusskoi knigi—kakoi on?" *Literatura i mastatstvo,* April 11, 1990; "Pro razvitok natsional'nykh kul'tur na Doneccini," Respublikanska biblioteka URSR, inform. centr z pitani ta mistetstva, 1991, vyp. 12/4.

13. N. Ianovskaia, "Seans gipnoza ili samozvantsev," *Literaturnaia Rossiia,* August 9, 1991.

14. V. Sarkisian, "Soiuz pechati i nerazberikhi," *Soiuz,* 1991, no. 9.

15. "Belorusskiie gazety snizaiut tirazhi do . . . 1 ekzempliara," *Izvestiia,* February 8, 1992.

16. "K nashim chitateliam," *Pravda Ukrainy,* February 15, 1992.

17. "Russkii zhurnal bez Rossii?" *Literaturnaia gazeta,* December 11, 1991; "Slukhi o nashei smerti neskol'ko preuvelicheny," *Estoniia,* January 21, 1992.

18. "Chto vyrezaiut na TV?" *SM,* January 24, 1992; E. Iakovlev, "Kto govorit i chto pokazyvaet?" *Izvestiia,* March 4, 1992; N. Jonušaite, "Telezritel' plachet slezami rabyni Izaury," *Letuvos Ritas,* January 24–31, 1992.

19. Ia. Tolstikov, "V sinkhronnom perevode na russkii . . . ," *Estoniia,* January 15, 1992; N. Medvedev, "Zhit' v soglasii," *Ekho Litvy,* June 21, 1989.

20. K. Smailov, "Radi spravedlivosti," *Kazakhstanskaia pravda,* February 8, 1992.

21. "My za dvuiazychie," *Pravda Ukrainy,* October 6, 1989; N. Kyvyrzhik, "Daesh' armiiu perevodchikov?" *Sovetskaia Moldaviia,* May 19, 1989; A. Korshunov, "Preniia po dokladu 'O proekte zakona Uzbekskoi SSR o gosudarstvennom iazyke Uzbekskoi SSR,' " *Pravda Vostoka,* October 25, 1989; V. Plekhanov, "Vystuplenie v preniiakh po dokladu."

22. E. Dadevosian, "Chto takoe gosudarstvennyi iazyk," *Politicheskoe samoobrazovanie,* 1989, no. 5.

23. Z. Niva, "Talisman emigranta," *Literaturnaia gazeta,* February 20, 1991.

24. "Sud'ba russkikh v Latvii zavisit ot russkikh," *SM,* November 27, 1990.

25. B. Tykh, "Chto delat'?—Ne po Chernyshevskomu i Ul'ianovu," *Estoniia,* January 12, 1992.

11

Demographic Problems of Russian Adaptation in the Republics of the Former Soviet Union

Vladimir Mukomel

The disintegration of the USSR has placed Russians living in the republics in a difficult position: some of them have found themselves outside the borders of the Commonwealth of Independent States (CIS), others within the independent states of the Commonwealth, and still others in state formations with a disputed status (Chechnia, Tataria, the Dniester region, etc.). Now they must make a choice: to adapt themselves to the rapidly changing situation, to resist change, or to leave for other regions, primarily in Russia.

Some members of the Russian community for whom life is becoming difficult are leaving for Russia but plan to return. For now, Russians (in fact, the entire Russian-speaking population) are being driven from the republics.[1] There are grounds for argument that to a certain extent this was provoked by the expansionist and demographic behavior of Russian communities and is a response to such behavior, although not always commensurate.

The present report deals with the demographic behavior of Russians in ethnic and territorial formations, with emphasis on: (1) the role played by ethnic distinctions in the behavior of Russians and members of the indigenous population of republics in the aggravation of interethnic relations and growth of social tensions; and (2) evaluation of the prospects for change in the demographic behavior of Russians in the republics, and the ethnic and social consequences of such changes.

Factors of Maladaptation of Russian Minorities

Interethnic gaps in demographic behavior. Differences in the demographic behavior of the members of the indigenous nationalities and Russian newcomers constitute an important factor in the exacerbation of ethnic relations and the growth of social tensions in the republics. The demographic behavior of Russians differs from that of indigenous ethnic groups (mostly due to ethnic and cultural differences) and is perceived as a destruction of the cultural environment and as anomie. An argument about the right to such behavior inevitably centers on ethnic relations.

Let us examine, for instance, migratory behavior. The massive influx of Russians has considerably changed the ethnic composition in the republics. Quite often the indigenous population had no time to adjust. Changes in life style introduced by the migrants were not always acceptable to the local people, while the migrants themselves often disregarded local standards and traditions.

The mentality of people who are accustomed to being constantly on the move does not meet with understanding in the republic of their destination. A sociologist from Estonia, K. Kutas, writes: "The life style of that [superadaptive] population group is characterized by its striving to consume to a maximum degree and to give back to a minimum degree. This mode of behavior in certain circumstances may have deplorable effects."[2]

The situation was aggrvated by the fact that Russian migrants arrived and stayed mostly in the cities of these republics, thus changing their established ethnic and cultural environment. For instance, in Lvov, where before the war Poles, Jews, and Ukrainians accounted for 97 percent of the population, already by 1959 Russians accounted for about 40 percent; their share in the population of Riga grew from 7.4 percent in 1935 to 47.3 percent in 1989.

On the other hand, there also arose a trend toward the isolation of the Russian community from the indigenous population. Thus the first line of demarcation was drawn between the "occupied" cities and the countryside where the indigenous people are in the majority. The contrast between cities as small islands inhabited by an alien culture, on the one hand, and the countryside as a stronghold of the native culture, on the other, creates a precondition for interethnic confrontation. This potential is particularly dangerous in Central Asia, where the indigenous population is increasingly concentrated in the countryside.

It is important to note that Russians are a "new urban nation," distinct, for instance, from Armenians or Jews. The colonial mentality of Russian migrants is due to their lack of experience in traditional patterns of communication in a multiethnic urban environment. Today the lack of such traditions affects developments in the northeastern part of Estonia, the Dniester region and other areas. At the same time sociologists believe that "without a developed model of intracommunity solidarity and ethnic interaction constituting the essence of such traditions, without an established structure for surrogate interethnic conflict," the threat of real conflicts is growing, and this, incidentally, was one of the causes of the Sumgait tragedy.[3]

It is hardly accidental that in a survey of people of Caucasian extraction that when asked which migrant nationalities they preferred, Russian migrants came last, with preference given to Jews and Armenians, peoples with centuries-old traditions of interethnic communication in an urban environment.[4]

Sociological surveys show that the view that migration greatly strains tensions between people belonging to different nationalities is deeply rooted in social consciousness.[5] A negative reaction to migration is typical first of all of members of a republic's indigenous nationality.[6]

Ethnic differences in reproductive patterns are also conducive to the aggravation of interethnic and social tensions. High birth rates among members of non-indigenous nationalities directly provoke accusations of demographic intervention. For example, in the Baltic states differences in the reproductive patterns of the indigenous nationalities and migrants of Slavonic stock, particularly appreciable in the 1950–70 period, have contributed to shifts in the ethnic composition of the population. In some years a negative natural population growth among Latvians resulted in the share of Russians in the natural population growth of Latvia exceeding 100 percent.[7] However, in most regions the situation is radically different: the birth rates of Russians are generally among the lowest and do not ensure even a simple succession of generations, as is also the case with the Ukrainians, Georgians, Latvians, and Jews. In practical terms this means that Russians living outside Russia are doomed to a steady reduction in their share of the population of the republics (except Ukraine) due to ethnic differences in reproduction. A particularly significant decrease is expected in Central Asia, Kazakhstan, and Azerbaijan. It is estimated that by the year 2019 the total number of Russians and Ukrainians will, in fact, remain the same, while that of Belarusians, Latvians, Estonians, and Lithuanians will increase by 4 to 9 percent, Tajiks will increase 2.7 times, Turkmen, Uzbeks, and Kyrgyz, 2.4 times, Kazakhs will double and Azerbaijanians will increase by 70 percent.[8]

Such differences in reproductive behavior are assuming the form of an ethnocultural confrontation. The orientation toward a family with few children typical of Russian inhabitants of the republics is negatively viewed by those among the indigenous population who advocate large families, and vice versa. According to one demographer, the only thing as preposterous as a Muscovite father with many children is a Central Asian father with one child.

The widely accepted norms of reproductive behavior of the Russian-speaking population, such as its attitudes toward childbirth out of wedlock and family planning (including contraception and artificial interruption of pregnancy) are totally at variance with the traditions of the nations that are in the initial stages of demographic transition. And it is virtually impossible even to imagine that in a Tajik village two out of three pregnancies might end in abortion, as is the case in Russia today.[9]

Family planning is particularly balefully regarded by supporters of large families. They see such planning not only as an encroachment upon the private life of the family and on Muslim traditions, but also as a kind of barbaric instrument of Western policy directed against the growth of the indigenous population. In certain circumstances this idea can be successfully used by nationalist radicals. The dangers of this situation are dramatized by the experience of India, where the clumsy steps of Indira Gandhi's first government in implementing family-planning programs became one of the key reasons for its resignation in the late 1970s. In the Central Asian republics, where there is a tremendous interethnic gap in the norms of reproductive behavior, the situation is much worse. The 1991 civil disturbances in Uzbekistan were triggered by absurd rumors concerning restriction of the number of children in a family to no more than four; this suggests the potential explosiveness of this issue.

Birth out of wedlock is not unusual among Russian inhabitants of Central Asia, Kazakhstan, and Azerbaijan, but for the indigenous population extramarital childbirth is an incomprehensible and unacceptable abomination which Russians take far too lightly and indulge in far too often.

The situation in the republics of the Russian Federation is even more complicated: the large-scale influx of Russian migrants, which included many "social deviants," radically deformed the traditional norms of reproductive behavior. Births out of wedlock in the Russian republics are a real scourge: in Tuva more than a third of children are born out of wedlock, while in Chechnia and Ingusheti and the Buriat Republic the figure is one-fourth.[10] There are serious apprehensions that sooner or later revulsion toward the worst examples of the demographic behavior of newcomers will turn to interethnic confrontation, especially in the countryside with its predominantly indigenous population.

No less significant is the interethnic gap in norms of matrimonial behavior, particularly in the Muslim countries of Central Asia. Despite official bans, all efforts to eradicate early marriages and polygamy have failed. Recently there have been signs of the resurgence of polygamy in the wake of a return to the traditions of Islam. Thus, in Kazakhstan in June 1991, the League of Muslim Women was registered as a party demanding the recognition of polygamy.[11] Today the parliament of the republic is preparing a bill legalizing polygamy.[12] The institution of marriage itself is also subject to great differences of opinion between Russians and the indigenous population, with its strongly implanted Muslim traditions. Rare instances of divorce among the indigenous population demonstrate its adherence to the Muslim tradition, which does not approve of divorce.[13]

Observance of religious guidelines is also demonstrated by the strong orientation among indigenous Muslims to extended rather than nuclear families. The nuclear family of the Russian population is regarded as an imposed model alien to Oriental traditions and culture, while the natural process of nuclearization of the family, which is also under way in the Orient, is regarded as the destruction of the family. In Muslim society the traditional family performs vital social functions (economic, social, educational, religious, etc.), and family-clan relations predominate over individual ones.

The perceived destruction of the family brought about by the spread of stereotypical matrimonial and reproductive behaviors among Russians (which not only are essentially different from the traditional norms and principles of the indigenous population, but in many cases are banned by law) fits into a larger dooms-day scenario in which fundamental pillars of Muslim life—culture, religion, the small socioterritorial community (*mahalya*), and other social institutions—are seen as being chipped away.

Of special importance are interethnic differences in death rates, which are particularly noticeable in Central Asia. Death rates among Russians in all age groups living in Central Asia are lower than those among members of the indige-nous populations. Particularly striking is the difference in infant mortality rates: less than 18 out of every thousand Russian children under one year of age die, whereas among Turkmen the figure is 58, Tajiks—41, Uzbeks—38, and Kyrgyz—25. Specialists link these differences with the prevalent influence of specific ethnic-cultural norms and the traditions of everyday life.[14] However, public opinion associates high mortality rates of members of indigeneous popu-lation exclusively with the ecological situation. This assertion is easy to explain: in Karakalpakia, an ecological disaster area, more than 60 per thousand new-borns die.[15] The very fact of interethnic differences in death rates makes accusa-tions of discrimination in living conditions, even ethnocide, more forceful and acrimonious.

A no less difficult situation faces Russian communities in those republics of Russia where the traditional mode of life of the indigenous population has been transformed under Russians' direct impact. Three republics—Mari, Udmurtia, and Bashkiria—have the highest suicide rates in the Russian Federation. Mortality is also very high due to homicides (for instance, in 1989 in Tuva the murder rate was 5.2 times higher than the average in Russia), accidents, poisoning, and injuries.[16]

Interethnic marriage and mixed families. Interethnic marriage and the ethni-cally mixed family is becoming a major factor destabilizing ethnic relations and exacerbating social tensions in the republics. The explosive growth of the num-ber of mixed families was facilitated by urbanization and large-scale migration, growing contacts among different ethnic groups, breaches in the sexual patterns of those groups, the policy of assimilation pursued by the Soviet regime, and so forth. In 1959–89, the number of ethnically mixed families grew from 5.2 mil-lion to 12.8 million and their share in the total number of families rose from 10.2 to 17.5 percent.

The overwhelming majority of mixed families (81.4 percent) are families in which one of the spouses is Russian. Almost half of them (42.1 percent) are Russian-Ukrainian couples and 29.6 percent are couples in which one of the spouses is Russian and the other is the titular nationality of the republic in question.[17] In the republics of Central Asia and Kazakhstan marriages of mem-bers of the titular nation with Russians are exceptionally rare (2–12 percent of the mixed families). Most frequently they are to be found in Ukraine, Belarus, and Armenia (about half). In other republics the figure varies from 20 to 33 percent.

In Ukraine, Belarus and Lithuania, indigenous women are more often married to Russian men due to the numerical superiority of women of marital age. A comparable situation is observed in those republics of Russia that had been places of exile or influx of Russian immigrants: lack of Russian brides was the cause of mixed marriages involving women from indigenous nationalities.

By contrast, in Transcaucasia, Central Asia, and Kazakhstan, women of indigenous nationalities marry Russians 3–5 times less often than men belonging to indigenous nationalities marry Russian women.[18] The greater endogamy of Russian men in the Central Asia, compared with Russian women,[19] is largely unnatural: ethnic and cultural traditions, and the Koran in particular, forbid a Muslim woman to marry an "infidel," whereas men have the right to marry women of other monotheistic religions.

In recent years the attitude toward mixed marriages has undergone certain changes, even in republics with frequent interethnic contacts. For example, in Kazakhstan "over the last 5–10 years one could see not just the traditional ethnic isolation . . . . Mixed marriages have become a rare phenomenon."[20] According to data provided by A.A. Susokolov, that process began in Central Asia and Kazakhstan in the early 1970s.[21] Recent sociological surveys attest to the importance of nationality in selection of spouses by young people of the indigenous nationality and an obvious trend toward endogamy, both among members of the indigenous nationality and among Russians.[22] Equally important is the fact that mixed marriages with Russians are, as a rule, less stable than monoethnic marriages.[23]

Children of interethnic marriages are doomed to a marginal existence, particularly if the ethnocultural gap between groups is large. By assuming the nationality of the indigenous ethnos (in Tajik cities such choice is made by about 90 percent and in the cities of Tursunzade and Khorog by 99 percent of children of mixed marriages of Tajiks with Russian women) they identify themselves with the indigenous nationality. However, more often people marry within their own nationality: "An analysis of marriages of Tajik men and women with Russian women and men . . . shows that both spouses are marginals: their fathers are Tajik and the mothers are Russian."[24]

Interethnic marriages and mixed families have given rise to several problems in the republics of the former Soviet Union.

First, the excessive spread of interethnic marriages provokes accusations of assimilation and erosion of the very foundation of the existence of the ethnos. For instance, in Tatarstan the "Ittifak" radicals condemn fellow tribesmen who are allegedly destroying the gene pool of the nation.[25] (Incidentally, specialists in the field of population genetics fear that the genetic consequences of ethnic blending, that is, the outbreeding problem, can manifest themselves in the destruction of the adaptive complexes of genes, and retardation of recombinational stability.)[26] Such accusations are not groundless: in the republics of the European North, Volgo-Viatka, Volga, and Ural regions, more than a quarter of marriages

Table 11.1

Distribution of Married Couples of Titular Nationalities in Some Republics of Russia by Ethnic Homogeneity

Nationality	Percentage of married couples with spouses of given nationality	Percentage of mixed marriages involving Russians	Percentages of all marriages involving Russians
Karelians	17.1	80.2	66.5
Mordvinians	37.4	84.0	52.6
Komi	38.9	76.6	46.8
Udmurts	52.3	80.0	38.2
Mari	63.7	71.4	25.9
Tartars	58.0	60.6	25.5

Source: A.G. Volkov, "Etnicheski smeshannye sem'i i mezhnatsionalnye braki," *Sem'ia i semeinaia politika* (Moscow, 1991).

are of members of the indigenous population with Russians (in Karelia, two-thirds; see Table 11.1). Among Germans and Jews almost every second marriage is with Russians (48.6 and 36.0 percent, respectively). The share of such marriages is also large among Belarusians (31.5 percent) and Ukrainians (30.8 percent). It is hard to disagree with the assertion that "ethnic blending may, in certain conditions, engender a reaction in the form of xenophobia." [27]

Second, Russian women and their children in Central Asia, Transcaucasia, and Kazakhstan, due to the character of family-marital relations in these republics, find themselves hostages in their own households, with slim chances to dissolve the marriage and leave for Russia.

Third, spouses in mixed marriages not only experience additional psychological pressure in conditions of aggravated ethnic relations but may be the source of pressure themselves. According to a survey, 5 percent of women are involved in ethnic-conflict situations in their own families, while another 14 percent found it difficult to answer that question (38 percent of the women polled lived in mixed families).[28]

It is truly disturbing when ethnic conflicts affect families. A poll of refugees from Transcaucasia showed that a substantial percentage of their families—more than one-third—are founded on interethnic marriage.[29] The fate of Armenian-Azerbaijani families and their children is particularly unenviable. It is no wonder that the overwhelming majority of these mixed families thought it best to move to neutral territory, namely to Russia. It is not hard to predict that in the event of serious conflicts the overwhelming majority of mixed families in which at least one of the spouses is ethnically linked with a conflicting party will face two possible alternatives: disintegration of the family or forced resettlement to other regions where there are no conflict situations or where neither of the spouses belongs to the indigenous nation. Many mixed families may one day look upon the choice that was posed when the "punished" nations were exiled—either divorce or deportation—as a blessing.

Prospects for the Modification of Russians' Demographic Behavior in Different Republics: Ethnodemographic and Social Consequences

Russians in the republics have a hard life today; the sociopolitical situation in their places of residence has changed greatly compared with even the recent past. Everyone faces the same dilemma: either to adapt themselves to prevailing changes or be ready to leave.

The solution reached by the Russian communities of each republic will depend on a host of circumstances: the ethnocultural gap that must be overcome in the process of adaptation to the changing situation, the Russians' readiness to change (and distance themselves from the colonial mentality), the sociopolitical and economic situation in the republics, and many other factors. An important role will also be played by changes in the demographic behavior of Russians, changes that are already taking place and that could help worsen (or improve) the social situation and ethnic relations in the republics.

We are witnessing the modification of motives for Russians' migration. The rate of Russians migrating from their homeland has sharply declined, while the influx of Russians from outside Russia has grown.

Many migrants arriving in Russia explain their resettlement by the worsening of ethnic relations. According to a random survey carried out in September–October 1991 by the Russian State Committee for Statistics covering 23 territories (18,100 respondents), this motive was mentioned by a third of the migrants. The same reason was predominant among those who had arrived from Azerbaijan (cited by 70 percent of migrants from that republic), Tajikistan (64 percent), Georgia (63 percent), Lithuania (53 percent), Uzbekistan (51 percent), Armenia (50 percent), Kyrgyzstan (47 percent), Latvia (46 percent), Estonia (41 percent), and Moldova (36 percent). Two-thirds of those who left places of residence outside Russia were Russians.

However, the situation is still far from critical: the people who are leaving today made their decision under yesterday's conditions. So far there is no threat of a great resettlement of peoples. Russian communities in the republics are far from homogeneous. There are many with deep roots there owing to birthplace, length of residence, and knowledge of the local language, and these Russians will find it much easier to adapt. To all appearances this will be the case for a great number of Russians living in Ukraine, Belarus, Latvia, and Lithuania because many of them know the language of the indigenous nation or were born in mixed families. We must agree with V. Stashenko, director of the Department of Ethnic Relations of Latvia, who believes that a great number of Russians living

Table 11.2

Potential and Likely Russian Immigrants from the Territory of the Former USSR to Russia up to the Year 2000 (in millions)

Region	Potential immigration	Likely immigration up to the year 2000	Including the period before 1996
Baltic states	0.55	0.25	0.15
Ukraine and Belarus	1.5	0.3	0.18
Moldova	0.2	0.15	0.11
Transcaucasia	0.2	0.15	0.01
Central Asia	1.55	1.15	0.9
Kazakhstan	1.0	0.3	0.15
Total	5.0	2.3	1.5

in the republic will adapt themselves to the new sociopolitical conditions, and that potential migrants of Russian origin constitute 17 percent of the total number of Russians living there.[30]

An appraisal of the present-day situation in the republics that takes into account the degree of integration of Russian communities into the republics' social life, the level of ethnopolitical confrontation, history of past conflict, the economic situation, and other factors indicates that the total number of immigrants to Russia from the former union republics may reach 2.3 million people by the year 2000, with most immigrants expected from Central Asia (see Table 11.2).

Contrary to forecasts which connected inter-republican migration with the exacerbation of ethnic relations, in 1991 immigration to Russia from other republics of the former Union decreased by 60 percent from the previous year (from 11 to 7 people per 10,000). The same period saw a growing outflow from Russia to Ukraine: in the first nine months of the last year alone 60,000 people moved there. During the same period nearly 8,000 people left Russia for Belarus. The economic crisis gripping the entire territory of the former Soviet Union diminishes the probability of a large-scale influx of Russians from the republics to Russia, at least in the foreseeable future.

The situation may change if new hotbeds of ethnic conflict appear and escalate, or if social instability in the republics should increase, in which case we shall witness new flows of Russian refugees from the republics.

According to data from the Ministry of Internal Affairs, by the time of the disintegration of the Soviet Union there were 709,000 forced migrants (refugees) on its territory. However, the officially registered refugees are but a fraction of the total number of people who had to migrate for ethnic and political reasons; they amount to no less than 1.1–1.2 million people, depending on the specifics of their official status in the registration process.

According to the Ministry of Internal Affairs of the Russian Federation, there were more than 223,000 refugees on its territory at the start of 1992. Forced refugees fled primarily to the south of Russia: according to the Ministry of Internal Affairs of Russia, in October 1991, 44 percent of Russian refugees and 13 percent of refugees who are members of families of servicemen found refuge in the Krasnodar, Stavropol, and Rostov regions.

The large-scale influx of refugees to certain regions upsets the already unstable local social and production infrastructures. A poll of refugees shows that only 52 percent of those who have found refuge in Russia have permanent housing (only 0.2 percent in the Moscow region). Permanent jobs were held by 57 percent of the refugees, while in the Moscow region the figure was 3 percent.[31]

The sharp aggravation of food and housing problems and of the situation in the labor market result in the inevitable lowering of the living standards of permanent residents, a process that may drag on for years because of lack of sufficient investments and difficulties in their efficient and proper use. It is not difficult to imagine the sociopsychological climate in regions with a massive concentration of refugees if one takes into account mounting crime, deterioration of the epidemiological situation due to a lack of proper living conditions, growing environmental pollution and household wastes, and inefficient medical service. The refugees find themselves in a position where they have to compete with the permanent residents in virtually all spheres of life. Social outbursts are practically guaranteed, as in Dushanbe in 1990, when rumors that scarce housing would be allocated to refugees set off an explosion.

A comprehensive sociological survey carried out in the Russian Federation in 1991 showed that in various regions of Russia there are many people whose attitude to the arrival of Russian-speaking refugees from other regions of the former Soviet Union is negative. Their number is especially great in regions affected by the influx of refugees (30 percent of those polled in Moscow, 27 percent in North Ossetia, 22 percent in the Stavropol territory). A fair number of Russians (from 33 to 47 percent) are fairly indifferent to the fate of Russians in the republics, regarding them as competitors rather than needy compatriots.[32]

Excluded from their milieu living largely below the poverty level, refugees themselves are becoming a human time bomb. We witnessed this in Baku when refugees from Armenia initiated communal violence in January 1990.

In view of the fact that the majority of refugees prefer to stay in big cities (53 percent according to one survey),[33] they may provoke conflicts in multinational cities. In any case, this probability is not ruled out by 69 percent of those polled in North Ossetia, 45 percent in Stavropol territory, and 25 percent in Moscow.[34] Taking into account the strong tendency to be involved in conflicts on the side of one's own national group, a tendency in evidence everywhere, the consequences of such conflicts would be disastrous.[35]

Some of the refugees will live in the hope of returning home, as members of deported nations have lived for decades. It is not difficult to imagine that growing alienation, mounting conservatism, and the spread of religion among these increasingly lumpen-like refugees will inevitably result in the appearance of extremist organizations headed by fanatics whose aim is to repatriate the refugees at any cost. The experience of other countries shows that for some of the refugees the thirst for revenge, not excluding violence, becomes an *idée fixe*, shaping the way of life of the refugees and their descendants for decades to come.

Probably the most awful consequence of interethnic conflicts is the frightening destiny of children who have witnessed bloody events (6 percent of the Russian refugees who fled to Russia have experienced acts of violence and another 17 percent have testified to witnessing such acts against close relatives).[36] Indeed, the fanaticism of Irish, Tamil, or Palestinian militants may well pale before that of grown-up refugee children whose fathers and brothers were tortured and killed, whose mothers and sisters were raped and burned alive.

Changes in the migration motives of Russians living in the republics are also evident from the fact that many of them intend to emigrate from the former Soviet Union. The proportion of people wishing to leave the ex–USSR rather than flee to Russia is particularly large among Russians in the Baltic states (according to the Latvian Department of National Relations, about 50 percent of the 160,000 potential emigrants).[37]

As a matter of fact, Russians have made efficient use of the ethnic channel for emigration. According to estimates by the Israeli Ministry of Absorption, up to 30 percent of those arriving in Israel with Israeli visas are Russians. Taking into account the fact that 49 percent of Germans and 36 percent of Jews marry Russians (1985), one can estimate that the number of Russians who used this channel to leave the USSR in 1989–91 was 0.3 million.

Transformation of demographic behavior. Modification of demographic behavior also manifests itself in a sharp reduction in the number of interethnic marriages of Russians and changed reproductive behavior.

Reproductive behavior is strongly influenced as growing uncertainty persuades a woman (or family) to give up the idea of childbearing or to postpone having children. Uncertainty about one's future coupled with general socioeconomic instability will cause a further decline in the birthrate of Russians living in the republics, which will push them below the level that ensures the continuity of generations.

However, the possibility is not excluded that some groups of Russians living the republics (Cossacks, Old Believers, Dukhobors, etc.) will reactivate patriarchal family conjugal traditions, reorienting themselves toward large families.

The near future does not hold any promise of reversing the inexorable mortality of members of Russian communities in the republics. The socioeconomic situation is such that even keeping the age characteristics of mortality rates at a current level seems very difficult. The situation may sharply deteriorate with the appearance of new hotbeds of interethnic and social conflicts, which in turn could provoke extraordinary mortality rates.

The reference here is to higher mortality rates due primarily to armed clashes and acts of violence against the civilian population. Here are the facts: in 1990 a thousand people were killed and about four thousand wounded in interethnic conflicts,[38] a figure comparable to the average annual losses of the Soviet Army in Afghanistan. The same number of people were killed in Nagorno-Karabakh during the first three months of 1992. If the escalation of interethnic conflicts continues, tens of thousands of people may die in the near future.

In some areas the share of violent deaths is very high: in Nagorno-Karabakh, for instance, the number killed as a result of hostilities currently exceeds the number of those dying in their beds. Account should also be taken of those who die of wounds or have been reported missing. Indirect losses are at least comparable with military losses and murder. Finally, the hardships of refugees inevitably affect their health and result in higher mortality rates, especially for children and old people.

* * *

It seems that after the elimination of the rule of the central government, which pervaded all social institutions of the republics and which was involuntarily implemented by members of Russian communities, the 1990s signal the beginning of a catastrophic compression of the Russian nation within the borders of Russia. Russian communities outside Russia are doomed to a steady diminution of their role in the socioeconomic development of the republics, which will be accompanied by a reduction in the share of the Russian population (at least until Russian communities find their specific, complementary functions in the republics' life).

The future of Russian communities, apart from political, socioeconomic, and other factors, will be determined largely by the interethnic distance in the demographic behavior of their members and the indigenous population of the republics. Here an important role will also be played by the sober appraisal of the political consequences of certain decisions made by the Russian communities. For example, the construction of Cossack villages on the Kurile Islands and the subsequent settlement of Semireche Cossacks from Central Asia may complicate relations not only with Japan but also with the Central Asian republics, thereby aggravating the situation of Russian communities in these republics.

Much will depend on the balance of political forces and the policy which the governments of the republics will pursue with regard to the Russian population. Will they be interested in using the potential of the Russian communities whose members occupy their own niche in the employment sector and largely influence the local social and economic situation? Or, will they strive to oust Russians from all spheres of social life and in the end expel them from the republics? Yet another possibility is that the Russians may become hostages in the republics to be used as small change in political games, an intention openly stated by the opposition in Tajikistan during the events of May 1992. One cannot help but recall here the price set for each German or Jewish emigrant who was allowed to leave Romania or East Germany. The improvement of mutual understanding in all spheres, including the sphere of demographic behavior, which frequently gives rise to conflict situations and social tensions in the republics, can play a positive role in building a society in which the future of the Russian communities will be determined by a framework of civilized relations between nations.

Notes

1. *Mezhnatsional'nye otnosheniia v Rossiiskoi Federatsii. Informatsionnye materialy* (Moscow, 1991), p. 35; *Migratsionnye protsessy v Rossii i SSSR, vyp. 1, (Moscow, 1991), p. 111.*

2. K. Katus, "Migratsionnoe razvitie Estonii skvoz' prizmu migratsionnoi politiki," *Podkhody k upravleniiu migratsionnym razvitiem* (Tallinn: Valgus, 1989), p. 40.

3. V.C. Agadzhanian, "Armiano-azerbaidzhanskii konflikt," *Etnicheskie protsessy v SSSR* (Moscow, 1991), pp. 10–11.

4. V.B. Koltsov, "Sostsial'naia distantsiia v mezhnatsional'nom obshchenii: opyt postroeniia integral'nogo pokazatelia," *Sotsiologicheskie issledovaniia*, 1989, no. 2, p. 28.

5. V.N. Ivanov, "Mezhnatsional'nye konflikty," *Natsionalizm i mezhnatsional'nye konflikty. Informatsionnye materialy*, vyp. 1, (Moscow, 1991), p. 45; *Sotsial'no-politicheskie aspekty natsional'nogo soznaniia molodezhi* (Moscow, 1991), pp. 55–65; *Zhenshchiny i demokratizatsiia: obshchestvennoe mnenie zhenshchin po aktual'nym sotsial'no-politicheskim voprosam* (Moscow, 1991), p. 97.

6. *Sotsial'no-politicheskie aspekty natsional'nogo soznaniia molodezhi*, pp. 55–65.

7. *Narodnoe khoziaistvo Latvii 89* (Riga, 1990), p. 34.

8. L. Darskii and E. Andreev, "Vosproizvodstvo naseleniia otdel'nykh natsional'nostei v SSSR," *Vestnik statistiki*, 1991, no. 6, p. 5.

9. *Demograficheskii ezhegodnik 1989* (Moscow, 1990), pp. 91, 361.

10. *Chislennost', sostav i dvizhenie naseleniia v RSFSR* (Moscow, 1990), p. 166.

11. *Postfaktum*, 1991, no. 6 (April).

12. *Kommersant*, 1992, no. 27, p. 2.

13. *Demograficheskii ezhegodnik*, pp. 222–27.

14. Darskii and Andreev, "Vosproizvodstvo," p. 6.

15. A. Sadullaev, *Demograficheskoe razvitie Priaralia (Uzbekskaia chast')* (Moscow, 1991), p. 13.

16. *Chislennost', sostav i dvizhenie naseleniia v RSFSR*, pp. 183, 206, 207.

17. A.G. Volkov, "Etnicheski smeshannye sem'i i mezhnatsional'nye braki," *Sem'ia i semeinaia politika* (Moscow, 1991).

18. Ibid., p. 77.

19. K.P. Kalinovskaia, "Mezhetnicheskaia situatsia v Vostochnom Kazakhstane (po polevym materialam 1986–1989 godov)," *Etnicheskie konflikty v SSSR* (Moscow, 1991), p. 183.

20. Ibid., p. 25.

21. A.A. Susokolov, *Mezhnatsional'nye braki v SSSR* (Moscow, 1987), pp. 42–43.

22. *Sotsial'no-politicheskie aspekty natsional'nogo soznaniia molodezhi* (Moscow, 1991).

23. Susokolov, *Mezhnatsional'nye braki*, pp. 105–16.

24. L.F. Monogarova, "Proiavlenie etnicheskikh protsessov v semeino-brachnykh otnosheniiakh v gorodskoi sem'e tadzhikov," in O.A. Ganskaia and I.A. Grishaev, eds.,

Sem'ia: Traditsii i sovremennost' (Moscow: Institute of Ethnology and Anthropology, 1990), p. 185.

25. *Megapolis-Ekspress,* 1991, no. 33, p. 21.

26. O.L. Kurbatova, *Genetiko-demograficheskii analiz mezhetnicheskikh razlichii reproduktivnogo povedeniia: 4 Vsesoiuznaia shkola-seminar* (Ashkhabad, 1991), p. 4.

27. M.N. Rutkevich, "O demograficheskikh faktorakh integratsii," *Sotsiologicheskiie issledovaniia,* 1991, no. 1, p. 48.

28. *Zhenshchiny i democratizatsiia,* pp. 93, 97.

29. V. Cherviakov, V. Shapiro, and F. Sheregi, *Mezhnatsional'nye konflikty i problemy bezhentsev,* part 1 (Moscow, 1991), pp. 14, 22.

30. *Nezavisimaia gazeta,* January 22, 1992.

31. Cherviakov, et al., *Mezhnatsional'nye konflikty,* pp. 39–40.

32. Ivanov, "Mezhnatsional'nye konflikty," p. 75.

33. Cherviakov, et al., *Mezhnatsional'nye konflikty,* p. 29.

34. Ivanov, "Mezhnatsional'nye konflikty," p. 69.

35. Ibid., p. 44.

36. Cherviakov et al., *Mezhnatsional'nye konflikty,* pp. 24–25.

37. *Nezavisimaia gazeta,* January 22, 1992.

38. *Izvestiia,* May 11, 1991.

12

The Structure and Character of Migration of Russians from the Former Republics of the USSR

Lev Gudkov

The recent deterioration of interethnic relations which led to the collapse of the USSR and now threatens the integrity of the Russian Federation is a continuation of trends that began to appear in the latter half of the 1970s, when the ideological continuity of the communist regime was disrupted. The process of disintegration of the totalitarian system follows the same logic as its formation. Modernization and disintegration of the Soviet empire are thus two interdependent, albeit not uniform, processes.

Modernization, even in its socialist version (as opposed to the classical West European versions), led to a major change in the living conditions of many peoples on the territory of the USSR. This modernization was carried out bureaucratically ("from above") and was subordinated to the aims of forced industrialization and targeted urbanization, which first and foremost served the interests of a militarist state. The consequences of that process were different in the various regions of the country.

The spread of the modern urban standard of living, with improved health care, education, and overall living conditions, has combined with traditionalist orientations to produce a demographic explosion in the republics of Central Asia, Transcaucasia, and Kazakhstan. The indigenous population has doubled or even tripled during the last thirty years, a fact which in conditions of a one-crop, collective, and planned system of farming has brought about a profound agrarian overpopulation crisis. In the western republics of the USSR the population grew due mainly to the in-migration of Russian-speaking people, whereas in the republics of Central Asia it went up on account of the growth of the natural birthrate. Destruction of traditional economic structures, restriction of individual land plots, and the forced introduction of a settled way of life among Kazakhs,

Kyrgyz, Turkmen, and others caused massive agrarian overpopulation. Rural people were forced to move to cities populated largely by Russian-speaking people. The vast accumulation of social, cultural, and psychological tensions and frustrations brought about as a result of the disruption of former guidelines, authorities, and traditional notions is typical of the initial and intermediate stages of incomplete modernization often described in scientific literature.

Specific features of the socialist modernization stimulated and carried out by the state brought about an increased migration of Russians beyond the borders of Russia. Russians used to play a dual role in the republics and outlying national districts: in addition to being the bearers of the state system, agents of the central imperial administration and of a policy of Sovietization of non-Russian territories (in the Baltic region, Tuva, Moldova, and earlier in Central Asia and Transcaucasia), they were the bearers of a more developed culture. Russians proved to be not only intermediaries between the traditional cultures and the European enlightenment, but also educators, teachers, and models for the national intellectuals and the power elite. As in many other historically known cases, representatives of the center or mother country created in a colony conditions for a deformed yet intensive emergence of managerial and technical personnel as well as intelligentsia, and facilitated the development of national science and culture, thus initiating the growth of national consciousness. The influence of Russians on this process of modernization was very strong—one need only compare the living standards in Tajikistan with those of the neighboring and ethnically close Afghanistan. The role of Russians took various forms in different regions. In the Baltic region modernization processes started earlier and national formation had been completed by the beginning of the century, whereas in Central Asia or the Caucasus the same process took place only in the mid-1970s.

While outlying national regions such as Transcaucasia, the North Caucasus, and Central Asia produced some of the most active participants in business, the clandestine economy, trade, and so forth, Russia provided an influx of workers and specialists, builders with diverse qualifications and cultural levels.

Also contributing to the Russian diaspora were the placement of military bases and related enterprises in the Baltic region (which invariably attracted unskilled labor from the Russian non–Black Soil area), the development of the virgin lands in Kazakhstan, and the growth of heavy chemical and manufacturing industries in Central Asia and Kazakhstan. In many regions this only served the interests of local bureaucrats seeking to strengthen their position in the table of ranks. The national traditions and culture of the indigenous population were not taken into account, and this often necessitated the import of Russian-speaking workers and specialists (Ukrainians, Germans, Tatars, etc.) from other regions for work regarded by locals as lacking in prestige or below the standards of the traditional culture. Differences among the types of work led in turn to sharp constrasts in well-being, ways of life, types of consumption, and so on.

Members of the local population sought to occupy posts in the spheres of management, trade, law enforcement, culture, and so forth. There was a paradoxical situation in some spheres: despite an acute shortage of labor, the unemployment rate among the local population reached 40 percent of the able-bodied population, mainly young people. It was precisely the city-dwellers who considered themselves sufficiently educated not to have to do unskilled work. At the same time these people had certain aspirations and ambitions in life and under conditions of unemployment, lack of housing, and poor prospects for the future they formed an explosive milieu which generated an atmosphere conducive to massacres and pogroms in Fergana, Osh, Novyi Uzen, Sumgait, and other places. Even under incomplete conditions of modernization the empire has become a giant incubator of new nations. The policy of forming a layer of national personnel, intended to strengthen the basis of the regime, resulted in the emancipation of the local authorities from Moscow and the increasing ouster of Russians from key positions. During the last thirty years the share of Russians in Central Asia decreased 1.5–2 times. The weakening of the center which started in the late 1970s also signified the strengthening of powerful regional cliques and groupings that leaned on covert yet influential corrupted clan and tribal structures (not a factor, of course, in the Baltic republics, Ukraine, and some other republics) as well as on Soviet-type repressive and ideological bodies. A synthesis of these structures created parallel resources as well as management and coercive systems which made it possible to keep a distance from Moscow and gradually escape its pressure.

Disintegration of the central authorities intensified political struggle, giving rise to various social forces ranging from the national-democratic opposition to traditionalist and fundamentalist movements. However, the political structures in the republics did not in fact change, even when the personal composition of the higher governing bodies changed completely. The former administrative model was transposed to lower government levels—republican, regional, and so forth. The political parceling up of a single state organism which previously existed due only to a forced and mechanical integration of centralized management and planned distribution of the resources can be explained by the absence in the political realm of nonauthoritarian institutional alternatives and models of relations.

After the disintegration of the empire, Russians became only one of numerous national minorities. With their withdrawal from ideological and controlling bodies, the republican authorities lost much of the authority and stability they had enjoyed as deputies of the imperial center, a fact that entailed changes in the leadership in the republics in a sort of domino effect.

Seeking to stay in power, the communist functionaries in Central Asia, Azerbaijan, Tatarstan, and other autonomies (even if they changed their names) were forced to resort to national ideas advanced by the national intelligentsia which had developed during the modernization period. They did so in order to strengthen their own legitimate base and narrow the sphere of influence of the opposition. At the same time they could not help relying upon the Russian-speaking population, which to a large extent sustains economic life in the republics (especially in such spheres as transportation, communications, mechanical engineering, mining and manufacturing industries, health services, power engineering, and others). Russians were used by these functionaries as a support in their struggle against all kinds of anticommunist forces—from fundamentalists to national democrats who demanded the liquidation of the existing regime. This in turn strengthened the identification of Russians with conservative and repressive forces.

Since 1988, with the emergence of the prospect of secession of individual republics from the Soviet Union, the status of Russians living outside Russia has become the subject of frequent discourse in the mass media, the Russian parliament, and among members of the general public. Party bodies and the military and economic leadership tried to use Russians as hostages of the empire, as a force that could fetter the national-democratic movement. Russians living in the Baltic region (and to some extent in Russia itself) were threatened with the same sort of pogroms and massacres that occurred in the course of tribal conflicts in Central Asia (in the Fergana Valley, Novyi Uzen, etc.), Azerbaijan, and other regions. This kind of propaganda proved quite effective, especially as it was augmented by statements from leaders of radical nationalist parties and movements calling for the complete banishment of Russians from the republics, or at least the curtailment of their public and political influence. However, the overt use of force (the army and the KGB) for suppressing national movements and demonstrations in Vilnius, Tbilisi, Baku, Riga, and Erevan had the directly opposite effect. In the course of the Baltic referendums and elections to parliaments more than half of the Russians cast their votes for the complete sovereignty of their republics.

Nevertheless, as a political and ideological problem the situation of Russians in former union republics has remained the focus of attention of the press and politicians. This situation continues to be described in tragic colors, especially by those groups who sought to recreate the imperial character of the Union leadership in Russia's policy and thus put the brake on both economic and political reforms. Hence they estimated, on the basis of various analogous areas from Central Asia to Yugoslavia, the number of refugees and the scale of migration of Russians from various regions. Experts—including those who advised the members of the Commission on Refugees and Migration of the Supreme Soviet of Russia—predicted that the number of refugees would reach from three to five million, with eight to eleven million migrants in the next several years (including those from regions contaminated by the Chernobyl catastrophe and officers and men returning from Central and Eastern Europe).

It is obvious that even if the lowest estimates concerning the number of refugees and forced migrants from regions of interethnic conflicts should prove correct, the economy of Russia, already in the direst of straits, would collapse. The problem lies not so much in the absolute number of migrants as in the Soviet administrative-state system itself, with its forced registration of residence, absence of a labor market, lack of housing, extremely rigid institutions of social security and education, and underdeveloped infrastructure, all of which have rendered it unable to deal with such phenomena.

These circumstances also explain the absence of a law on refugees. Neither the Supreme Soviet of the USSR nor the Supreme Soviet of the Russian Federation succeeded in adopting such a law, for the state treasury is unable to make the necessary reparations to the victims and the respective government bodies cannot guarantee the refugees and the migrants who have been officially recognized as refugees the rights and opportunities due them in similar situations in accordance with international rules. For these reasons the authors of the official information as well as politicians and local administrative bodies issuing statements prefer not to use the term "refugees" with respect to Russians or Russian-speaking populations of former union and autonomous republics. The term is considered applicable only to two ethnic groups of victims—the refugees who fled the massacres in Baku and the Meskhet Turks exiled in Central Asia. Current are legally vague terms such as "migrants," "forced migrants," and settlers. This makes it possible for government agencies to shed responsibility for the fate of the people who left the regions of high interethnic tension and conflicts. But it is quite obvious that there is a great difference between migrants who left their former places of residence due to economic or personal reasons and people who fled pogroms and massacres.

The absence of legally correct definitions has had its negative effect on the statistical data that are unwillingly and irregularly supplied by the respective agencies of the Ministry of the Interior or the local governments. That is why the variability of the data on refugees that occasionally appear in the press and the contradictory data supplied by local government agencies raise considerable doubt as to their authenticity. The situation in Moscow is a vivid illustration of the actual state of affairs: the city, with a population of 13 million, has been unable for two years now to accommodate 30,000 refugees from Transcaucasia, although every year it hires 150,000 temporary industrial workers from other parts of the country.

Special research carried out by the Center for the Study of Public Opinion in the early 1990s confirms the more "moderate" forecasts concerning the scope of migration in the next few years.[1] If an expressed desire to leave a republic is conditionally taken as a real intention (which, needless to say, is not one and the same thing, but can be taken as the basis for estimates), the highest level of the Russian population migration from the republics may reach 3 million people before 1995 and some 1.5 million people of other nationalities.* (The year 1995 was set as the outside limit for possible forecasts because, as the experience of

---

*The difference in the likely numbers of migrants mentioned in the present article and in the article by Vladimir Mukomel can be explained by differences in research methods. —Eds.

the corresponding surveys showed, people do not make plans for more than two or three years ahead.) Simultaneously, some 3 to 3.5 million people would like to move from Russia to other republics.

The following estimates can be made with regard to individual republics. The numerically largest flows of migrants can be expected from Ukraine (some one million Russians), from Kazakhstan (about 500,000), and from Uzbekistan (nearly 400,000 people). Given the quiet nature of interethnic relations in Ukraine and even in Kazakhstan, as well as the more frequently cited motives for migration, a conclusion can be drawn that the migratory phenomena in these regions approximate models of "natural" exchange processes. A markedly different situation is observed in Uzbekistan, Central Asia as a whole, in the Caucasian regions, and elsewhere. In the rest of the republics—with the exception of the Baltic area and Tuva—the migration figures may range from 100,000 to 150,000 from each republic. The migration figures for the Baltic states and Tuva may run into tens of thousands.

A maximum influx of migrants—some two million—can be expected in Russia. A majority of them—about 1.5 million—intend to settle in Central Russian cities. Second to Russia itself as a new homeland for Russians from the former union republics is Ukraine, with some 200,000 Russians expected to settle there. Belarus can expect nearly as many migrants—some 180,000 people. Minimal flows of migrants—no more than 30,000 people—may move to Central Asia and Kazakhstan. Somewhat bigger numbers are expected in Moldova and Transcaucasia— 50,000–60,000—as well as in the Baltic area—nearly 120,000 people. In the latter case, however, the actual figure will be much lower due to restrictions imposed by the Baltic states' new governments.

Clearly, these estimates make it possible only to prognosticate the probable scope of migration. Enormous changes that have occurred in the political structures of the former Union since the opinion poll was conducted—namely, its total disintegration—will certainly affect Russians' migratory conduct in the future.

The above figures are based on data resulting from an expressed "firm" desire to leave one republic or another. However, on an average, 60 percent of the respondents who made this decision had difficulty specifying when they intend to carry it out. In other words, a majority of potential Russian migrants have not yet made a final decision.

Thus it turns out that the extensively debated threat of an influx of migrants to Russia is greatly overstated. For example, a desire to move to Russia in the foreseeable future (that is, within the next two years) was expressed by an average 23 percent of those polled, or some 500,000 Russian urban dwellers. A further 12 percent, nearly 250,000 people, would like to leave in the period from 1993–95. The overwhelming majority of the respondents in this group (62 percent) do not know exactly when they will leave.

The size of the above-mentioned groups differs greatly depending on the nature of the national, ethnic, or political conflicts and contradictions in a given republic or region.

The republics can be divided into four distinct groups with respect to respondents' specific plans for migration.

The percentage of respondents with plans for migration was smallest in the Baltic states, Ukraine, Kazakhstan, and Tatarstan (6–11 percent). More than half of those polled did not specify when they would like to leave their republic. By their basic characteristics, including value orientations, these respondents resemble the majority of Russians, that is, those who do not intend to move. The only thing that distinguishes them is a profound anxiety and uncertainty regarding the future (given the political changes of the past two years), which makes them give such indefinite answers.

Next comes a group of republics with an average degree of determination to migrate, in which the desire to leave was expressed by 20–30 percent of those polled. These include Yakutia (19 percent), Moldova (23 percent), Kyrgyzstan (24 percent), Azerbaijan (25 percent), Uzbekistan (25 percent), Turkmenistan (28 percent), and Tuva (27 percent). It was notable that a great uncertainty was expressed in these republics regarding the time of departure (which 40–54 percent of the respondents could not specify).

Considerable uncertainty with regard to a possible departure was registered in Central Asia, Moldova, Azerbaijan, Yakutia, and Tuva (41–54 percent).

Lastly, the greatest determination to depart was expressed by respondents in Tajikistan and Checheno-Ingushetia (36–37 percent). Furthermore, nearly a quarter of them are prepared to move in the near future because of the serious situation in these republics.

Reasons for intention to migrate may vary. A desire to move to a different region or republic may be conditioned by the labor-market situation, family and marriage circumstances, behavioral peculiarities of pensioners and aged people, a desire to receive an education or trade, living conditions, ecological problems, and so on. Some 40 percent of those polled intend to move for reasons of ethnic enmity, which certain political circles refer to as underlying reasons for Russians' migration. A "hostile attitude to the Russians" was cited more frequently by respondents from Moldova and Tuva (54–55 percent), Checheno-Ingushetia (52 percent), and Tajikistan (50 percent). Migratory pressure is the strongest in these republics.

The total number of migrants to Russia in the foreseeable future—until the year 1995—can be estimated, according to our calculations, at 160,000–200,000 (400,000, if all members of families are included). However, only 21 percent intend to move to Russia in the next one and a half or two years, evincing a real readiness to move. It can be surmised, then, that the level of migration caused by ethnic enmity or animosity toward Russians may reach 50,000–60,000 people a year should the situation become aggravated in these regions. It should be noted that these figures are close to those presently referred to by law-enforcement bodies (48,000–52,000).[2]

An absolute majority of the respondents, particularly in regions with a low level of interethnic conflict, are determined to retain their habitual mode of life and show no signs of panic. Few are prepared to make any kind of sacrifice for purely symbolic rewards such as the status of Soviet citizen or representative of the central administration beyond Russia's boundaries (unless it is connected with material advantages).

Another important reason for departure to Russia is the desire to reunite with relatives (expressed, on the average, by 28 percent of all those determined to move). This motive is referred to particularly often by respondents from Azerbaijan (39 percent)—more often, in fact, than ethnic animosity toward the Russians.

Other "natural" motives for departure (making it possible to assume a normal migration process associated with social mobility) include a desire to "improve material well-being" or "receive an education" (10 and 5 percent respectively). A greater-than-average desire to earn money or improve living conditions is voiced in Azerbaijan (14 percent), Kazakhstan (18 percent), Kyrgyzstan (13 percent), Checheno-Ingushetia (13 percent), and Yakutia (14 percent). More inclined to depart are, as a whole, younger, well-educated and unmarried people as well as respondents born outside a given republic who consequently have a shorter record of residence there.

A comparison of different groups of respondents leaving the republics with respect to occupation, social status, and the like reveals a disproportionate number of engineers, technicians and specialists in the humanities, as well as administrators.

Such an exodus of specialists (engineering and technical personnel, members of liberal-arts professions, doctors, lawyers, etc.), managers, and office workers can be observed in all the republics, with the exceptions of Ukraine and Estonia. By contrast, factory workers—regardless of their status and qualifications—are more inclined to stay in their republic indefinitely. In other words, people inclined to depart include those who were not merely "Sovietized," or put through a number of screenings and tests for ideological reliability, but also those who had to compete with the local personnel establishment or were ostensibly ousted on account of their ethnic origin. The transition of enterprises from Union to republican supervision, reorganization of the state apparatus, replacement of teachers and instructors in connection with a changed cultural policy—these and other factors deprive entire groups of high-ranking functionaries and specialists of prospects for the future or even jobs as such.

Although Russian college and school students are universally willing to leave their republics, their motives for departure differ greatly from those of specialists and civil servants. On the whole they are less ideologically influenced or pressured by daily concerns, family considerations, or career interests. Their motivation is in line with general paths of social mobility conditioned by urbanization. Their attraction toward bigger cities and capitals is explained by broader educational and career opportunities as well as by access to the values of modern urban life.

Thus, the pace and scope of migration from republics are determined by several circumstances, the most important being the material conditions of life at the place of residence and confidence in the ability of the institutional power structure to ensure a stable life and guarantee social order. A comparison of the replies given by respondents from different republics (including Russia) demonstrates that interethnic relations are not the main concern of the people polled.

The main concern for Russian minorities in the various republics (as well as for the population of Russia and the indigenous population in the republics) are problems of everyday life, that is, a shortage of goods and high prices. (It should be recalled that the poll was carried out long before the liberalization of prices, at a time when real cost-of-living growth far outstripped the growth of wages and other incomes.) The economic crisis is, in fact, pushing all other problems and fears into the background.

Food shortages rank second among respondents' most serious concerns (on the average 56 percent mentioned this problem).

Third among anxiety factors are worsening interethnic relations themselves (an average index is 42 percent, but it should be noted that specific evaluations of the situation vary greatly in different republics).

A fourth group of concerns has to do with processes of transformation of the state and political system in the country, which deeply affect the social status and self-consciousness of Russians outside Russia.

The disintegration of the USSR, which is the most significant manifestation of these processes, worries Russians in Moldova (44 percent) and in Azerbaijan (38 percent) most of all. The level of concern about these processes is rather high in the republics of Central Asia (50 percent in Turkmenistan, 33 percent in Tajikistan, 31 percent in Uzbekistan, 27 percent in Kyrgyzstan), as well as in Tuva (27 percent).

In the Baltic region fewer people express concern with regard to these problems (20–22 percent) compared with those more worried about worsening crime, unemployment, and ecological, cultural, and moral crises (26–33 percent).

Among social problems which cause anxiety only to an insignificant number of respondents are "the threat of dictatorship," "giving up the ideals of socialism" (3–5 percent on an average), and "weakness and helplessness of the Union authorities" (10 percent). More than in the other republics, the weakness of authorities is cause for concern in Moldova, Tuva, Checheno-Ingushetia—20, 15, and 11 percent respectively—and this, naturally, also reflects the instability of interethnic relations.

In short, the main sources of anxiety are problems of everyday life, while interethnic relations arouse concern mainly insofar as they pose a threat to the normal way of life, not in connection with the symbolism of belonging to an integral state and ideological whole.

Most Russians living in the republics generally consider their living conditions (compared with those in Russia or other regions of the former USSR) to be "far better" or at least "similar." This is a major indication of stability testifying to a very high level of adjustment on the part of the Russians and groups close to them culturally and socially (the so-called Russian-speaking people) in the heterogenous ethnic communities. Different replies are given by respondents from Yakutia, Tuva, and Tatarstan: most of them believe that "life in Russia is better" than in their republics. By contrast, among the respondents who stated their desire to leave a given republic, a majority—albeit a statistically insignificant one—feel that their living conditions are "worse than in Russia."

Although the Russians' trust in republican bodies of power is generally lower than that of the indigenous population, their attitude has changed considerably over the period under survey, with their trust in the bodies of power nearly doubling in Ukraine and the Baltic region. At the same time, it declined in the republics of Central Asia and the Caucasus, areas characterized by intensified interethnic tensions. There was a decline of confidence in the Union and Russian structures of power as well as in the army, law-enforcement agencies, and local authorities. Ratings of different parties, social movements, and organizations, including ethnic ones (both of the Russian and the indigenous population) are extremely low.

The last factor is extremely important for understanding the Russian milieu in these regions. Solidarity with the Union center and the central authorities plays a decisive role in the self-consciousness and identification structure of Russians. (Even half a year after the disintegration of the USSR nearly two-thirds of the respondents regretted the fact and would like to have it restored if possible.) The negative side of this identification is a dependence on paternalistic power and authority, transfer of personal responsibility onto "chiefs" and "managers," and an overall passivity and inability to take initiative and ensure autonomous existence.

In conditions of sharp political shifts or changes, this peculiarity of the political culture of Russians has meant a complete paralysis of social activity, boundless frustration, and lack of will to organize themselves and formulate their own national or group interests. In spite of what is going on in the republics, Russians simply do not see themselves as an ethnic minority and continue to place their hopes on patronage and protection from the leaders of Russia. (On the average 36 percent of respondents stated that the new Russian leaders "had left Russians in the republics to the mercy of fate," but in the regions of heightened interethnic conflicts these figures are higher—65 percent in Moldova, 50 percent in Tajikistan and Turkmenistan, 43 percent in Chechnia, 39 percent in Uzbekistan and Azerbaijan, 38 percent in Lithuania and Estonia.)

That is why a large number of Russians in the republics would welcome political and economic pressure from the former Union center or the new Russian government on the local authorities to protect the Russian and Russian-speaking population in these republics (on average, 41 percent of the respondents took such a stand, while in Moldova and Tuva it was 52 percent and in Chechnia 47 percent).

At the same time more than half the respondents resolutely opposed any attempts to use troops "for protection of Russians in the republics" (in the Baltic region and in Ukraine the share reached 67–70 percent). In places of inter-ethnic conflicts (e.g., in Kyrgyzstan, Chechnia, Azerbaijan, and Uzbekistan) the Russian-speaking population was more inclined to approve of such actions (42, 40, and 36 percent, respectively). In other republics this indicator is a little bit lower—from 26 to 30 percent.

On the whole, Russians cautiously or even negatively regard the idea of forming special Russian "detachments of self-defense" in the face of a sharp aggravation of the situation in the republics. Only 16 percent expressed readiness to participate in such detachments, and these were primarily young or unskilled workers living mainly in Moldova, Uzbekistan, Kyrgyzstan or Tajikistan.

The disintegration of the USSR and the collapse of Union power structures have altered the viewpoint and partially the character of identification of Russians outside Russia. The mythical image of Russians as bulwarks of power, statehood, and order, as well as the bearers of enlightenment, modern technology, and European culture, has been destroyed. These ideas, first called into question in the Baltic area, are now undergoing reappraisal in Central Asia as well. Russians living in the republics experienced greater shocks than those living in Russia itself, and they continue to live in a strained atmosphere. Consequently, Russians living outside Russia have proved to be more ardent advocates of the USSR's integrity than those within Russia itself. When asked which country they regarded as "theirs," 81 percent of the Russians in the republics answered "the USSR," not the republic where they live, or Russia. By the end of 1991, more than half of those polled expressed their desire to retain the citizenship of the USSR, not of a republic or the Russian Federation. It was only in the Baltic area that the number of Russians identifying themselves as citizens of Latvia, Lithuania, or Estonia constituted 24 to 31 percent of the Russian population. In various regions of Ukraine the figure ranged from 40 to 53 percent (in Central Asia, Kazakhstan and Transcaucasia this figure is from 20 to 35 percent; it is minimal in Chechnia, Tajikistan, and Kyrgyzstan—10 to 17 percent). Significantly, in the Baltic area and western Ukraine, where relaxed tensions have reduced the possibility of further conflicts, the vast majority of Russians are prepared to accept new role definitions and a new sociopolitical identification. By contrast, the situation in the North Caucasus, Central Asia, and Moldova is becoming ever more aggravated.

Russians as an ethnic group consider their status to be higher than that of indigenous residents in the republics of Central Asia, and similar or lower in the Baltic republics and parts of Transcaucasia. This reflects their overall professional qualifications and cultural and educational standards compared with those of the indigenous population. Furthermore, it fits in with contemporary concepts regarding the role Russians are supposed to play under such circumstances: the Baltic indigenous population is not regarded as an object of colonization or as a less civilized entity. In Russia itself, Estonians, Latvians, and Lithuanians are viewed as "close Europeans," well-nigh matching, by their value definitions, the image of a "real European" or Westerner—an Englishman, a German, or an American. This makes it easier for Russians to accept their altered status or even a subordinated position. On the other hand, Russians in Central Asia go through a role or status conflict. They see themselves as a more modernized group and therefore lay claim to administrative and other influential positions, refusing to acknowledge the legitimacy of new ethnic groupings that achieve or seek power, regarding such groupings as a mafia, national extremists, and so forth. Therefore, competition with the new ethnic political authorities strengthens opposition on their part, not to mention barely restrained currents of aggression, frustration, and fear.

The last three or four years in Russia itself have seen an extremely rapid process of disintegration of Great Power consciousness. The more routine forms of imperial consciousness are today preserved only in the ideological picture of reality common to lower strata of the population. As regards the majority, the previously held concepts of the USSR's or Russia's ideological and imperial role are currently expressed in a passive form, doggedly upholding the idea that Russia follows a "special path" among all other countries. It would be more correct to see this phenomenon as a holdover reflexive defense mechanism or "superghetto" complex rather than the means or symbols of a new national mobilization. In this sense I would prefer to speak of the end of the charismatic epoch in Russia.

The revival of the Great Power complex experienced by a particular category of Russians in the republics can be regarded as a typical exception, and with certain reservations at that. With new pressures affecting the Russians due to the loss of their previously held social positions, we see the resurgence of a socioideological and cultural type that used to be a prop of the communist system and that is indeed vanishing from Russia itself, where only a few radical groups uniting national patriots and stubborn communists can still uphold the relevant slogans and concepts. Election returns and surveys carried out by the Center for the Study of Public Opinion show that such groups in Russia are supported by people from older age groups, the provinces, and by less educated sections of the populace.

Notably, this type of people comprised the majority of those who expressed in our polls the desire to leave their respective republics, anxiety that the Russians might become "second-class citizens," the danger of pogroms and massacres, and the constant atmosphere of ethnic hostility and insults. The desire to flee the republics is not a concrete or pragmatic desire, but a confused disapproval of whatever is taking place in the republics now. Such massive responses can be viewed as a negative stand toward changes in the social situation in these regions and as evidence of anxiety and difficulty adapting to the situation. The results of the poll reveal regions with heightened tensions. Thus, replies to the question "Do you agree that Russians in the republic are subjected to oppression and discrimination?" were grouped as follows: an affirmative reply was given in Estonia (16 percent), Latvia (23 percent), Lithuania (22 percent), Ukraine (25 percent in the Western regions and 2 percent in the Eastern regions), Moldova (68 percent), Kyrgyzstan (56 percent), Chechnia (54 percent), Uzbekistan (46 percent), Tajikistan (44 percent), Tuva (36 percent), Azerbaijan (28 percent), Turkmenistan (26 percent), Kazakhstan (18 percent), Yakutia (7 percent), Tataria (6 percent), and the Crimea (4 percent).

In terms of motivation for migration, these people differ greatly from those who leave their republics with the aim of seeking a job, reuniting with relatives, receiving an education, and so on. This group is characterized by a comparatively small period of residence in a given place, an almost total lack of knowledge of the local language, culture, and traditions, as well as a considerable isolation in terms of information, occupation, and daily life. It includes far greater numbers of highly skilled specialists who used to work at Union- subordinated enterprises, as government officials, economic managers, party functionaries, intellectuals, servicemen, and members of law-enforcement agencies. People of this group are also characterized by a high educational level. Among them there are many young specialists and young people in general. In other words, we are talking about those groups of the Russian population who have suffered most from the policy of ousting Russians to promote members of native nationalities, and of changing the political elites. A gap between a high level of qualification, on the one hand, and actual opportunities, on the other, engenders frustration and latent aggressiveness toward new political forces.

Failure to understand the events taking place in the republics, combined with ever more stressful lives overall, makes this category of Russians exaggerate the feelings of ill will that they believe are aimed against them as an ethnic group, and in some instances provokes real aggression.

Ignorance of the native language can serve as grounds for feelings of superiority. If in the Baltic region more than a third of the respondents have a good knowledge of the native language, the figure in Central Asia does not exceed 8 percent, while the figure for Azerbaijan, Moldova, and Kazakhstan is around 16 percent. It should be emphasized that even a weak knowledge of the language helps reduce ethnic tensions by four or five times, thereby opening up chances for communication and mutual understanding. Thus, cultural and social isolation of Russians intensifies as one proceeds from west to east.

Transfer of some information media—television, newspapers, magazines—into republican hands has resulted in a sharp differentiation of spheres of information. The indigenous and Russian-speaking population are ending up with two different images of reality as well as divergent interests and preferences in getting information.

The marked ideological commitment and loyalty to the Soviet regime of these Russians makes them take a negative stand toward political and economic reforms such as privatization of state property, a market-oriented economy, and the like in their respective republics.

It will take a long time to consolidate Russians and involve them in new state and political structures that replace the disintegrated imperial ones. Migration flows should be accepted as inevitable due to the impossibility of attaining ethnic homogeneity no matter how the former USSR's political space is developed. However, these migration flows may intensify in the event of ethnic discrimination or blackmail, or, conversely, they may become more balanced and institutionally streamlined if the new authorities pursue a rational and balanced policy.

Notes

1. Questions concerning migration were posed in numerous polls and surveys of the All-Union Center for the Study of Public Opinion (called "All-Russian" since June 1992). But only in special surveys concerning the situation of Russians in the union and autonomous republics did these questions become the subject of detailed analysis. The pilot survey carried out in November 1990 covered 2,000 respondents from ten republics (Estonia, Latvia, Western Ukraine, Georgia, Azerbaijan, Kazakhstan, Kyrgyzstan, Tajikistan, Uzbekistan, Kabardino-Balkaria), including 1,000 Russian respondents and 1,000 from the indigenous population of the respective republics. In addition, a survey using similar methods was carried out in Tataria in December (1,045 persons, which is a representative sample for Tataria). On the basis of these surveys, a program and instruments for the survey of 1991 (July–September) were elaborated. The number of respondents reached 6,585 persons representing the Russian population of Azerbaijan, Kazakhstan, Kyrgyzstan, the Crimea, Latvia, Lithuania, Moldova, Tajikistan, Tataria, Turkmenistan, Tuva, Uzbekistan, Ukraine, Checheno-Ingushetia, Estonia, and Yakutia. A stable distribution of answers with regard to the most important parameters and questions made it possible to make a cautious comparison of data for the 1990–92 period.

2. These data of the Ministry of the Interior were published in a number of newspapers (*Izvestiia, Komsomol´skaia pravda*, etc.) on June 4, 1992, and announced on the television news programs "Vesti" (June 5, 1992) and "Novosti" (June 16, 1992). On the whole there are 222,000 officially registered refugees in Russia, among them 37 percent Ossetians, 20 percent Armenians, 20 percent Meskhet Turks, and 23 percent Russians.

13

Russian Refugees and Migrants in Russia

(Based on Ethnosociological Research in the Central Russian Countryside)

Aleksandr Susokolov

1. General Situation

While studying the processes of adaptation of Russian refugees and migrants it is necessary first of all to take into account the cultural heterogeneity of the Russian population. Russian settlers in former Union republics can be divided roughly into three main groups:

(1) local, predominantly rural, ethnic-religious groups (Molokans and Dukhobors in the Transcaucasus and Old Believers in Kazakhstan, Moldova, and Central Asia);

(2) Russian migrants from cities of other republics who migrated relatively recently and have maintained rather close ties with rural and urban populations in the territory of Russia (for such people it is easier to leave their present places of residence than for other groups of the Russian and Russian-speaking populations);

(3) indigenous urban Russians, who in some regions constitute from 30 to 70 percent of the population and have roots going back two or three generations. Some of these people have assimilated many features of the culture of the native population.

Moreover, a great part of "pure" Tatars, Jews, Armenians, Ukrainians, and others may be added to these. Together these peoples form huge strata within the urban population of former union republics and are today referred to as the "Russian-speaking population." The present-day migration situation is characterized by the newest tendency to separate Russians from the "Russian-speaking" people, and to provide them with different opportunities as far as their resettlement in Russia is concerned.

The forms and methods of the adaptation of these three groups of Russian migrants have their own specific features.

2. The Influx of Migrants and Refugees to Russia

According to certain estimates, today the scale of the migration of Russians to the central regions of Russia is almost catastrophic. For instance, in 1990 the aggregate growth of the population of Russia owing to migration amounted to 5,062,000 people, or three times the average rate for the preceding years. From 1989 to 1990 the balance of the interrepublican migration of Russian-speaking people to the Russian Federation grew by more than 200 percent—from 62,000 to 200,000 people, while the percentage of Russians among them increased from 38 to 59 percent.[1]

The sharp tilt in the balance of Russian migration was caused not only by an increased influx of Russians from the outskirts of the crumbled empire but also by a decreased emigration of Russians from the territory of Russia. However, the most serious social problems arise from the uneven character of the distribution of migrants and refugees throughout the territory of Russia and the fact that their social and occupational composition fails to correspond to the present-day requirements of the Russian economy.

The majority of the migrants in the last few years preferred to go to the southern regions of the European part of Russia such as the Krasnodar and Stavropol territories and the Rostov region, developed regional centers, and Russia's largest cities, most of all Moscow. The process of migration to the southern regions became especially marked within the last two years in the wake of the appearance of the new phenomenon of "refugees." It should be pointed out that the regions of Russia bordering the Caucasus are characterized first by a high rural population density and second by their unique status as the only part of Russia where the rural population has not declined but increased.

For instance, within the last several years at least three tendencies can be traced which support our conclusions concerning the trends in the development of migration in Russia. First, the number and percentage of migrants arriving from outside the Russian Federation grew at a steady rate; second, the number of people leaving the Krasnodar territory to go to other regions of Russia and elsewhere gradually decreased; third, although during these years the number of refugees arriving was less than the number of migrants of the "usual type," the difference was not so striking as in other regions, for instance, in the Smolensk region.

As can be seen from Table 13.1, most migrants, especially Russians, came from Central Asia, Kazakhstan, and the Transcaucasus. This tendency has been borne out by an analysis of the applications for resettlement submitted to the Voronezh Regional Employment Center in January–February 1992. The distribution of potential migrants to the Voronezh region according to the place of

Table 13.1

Migrants in the Krasnodar Territory

a. Arrivals and Departures, 1988–90 (in thousands)

Year	Russian Federation			Other republics		
	Arrived	Left	Balance	Arrived	Left	Balance
1988	89.6	76.0	13.6	75.6	58.5	17.1
1989	82.4	66.1	16.3	81.4	55.2	26.2
1990	77.0	49.6	27.4	82.3	48.3	34.0

b. Distribution of the Krasnodar Territory Migrants from Outside Russia According to Places of Their Arrival and Departure (percentage)

	All migrants		Russians	
	Arrived from	Left for	Arrived from	Left for
Ukraine, Belarus,* Moldova	26.8	34.2	25.7	40.1
Transcaucasia	25.5	13.0	21.5	4.9
Kazakhstan and Central Asia	25.8	9.6	30.0	14.6
Baltic states	1.5	1.0	2.1	1.7
Foreign countries**	20.5	42.2	20.4	38.7

Notes:

* *Postanovlenie SM SSSR i Rossii o bezhentsakh i migrantakh* (1973–90).

** Including long-term business trips, which involve the filling out of an address list and a coupon for the migration statistical register.

their present residence is as follows: national republics of the North Caucasus and Transcaucasus—25.8 percent; Central Asia and Kazakhstan—60.3 percent; other regions including Russia—14.9 percent.

The current population statistics, based on registration in places of residence, fail to provide a complete picture of the situation in the region. Important in this respect also are the data of the Russian Ministry of the Interior on the changes in the number and composition of refugees in various territories. As of January 15, 1992, 234,700 refugees have been registered. Of this number 39.5 percent were in the Rostov region and in the Krasnodar and Stavropol territories.

In nearly the entire period since early 1991 when the first statistical data concerning refugees became available, the percentage of refugees who settled in the North Caucasus continued to grow relative to other regions of the country. This was caused by two factors: first, the exodus of people from the regions of interethnic conflicts bordering the North Caucasus; and second, the probability

Table 13.2

**Distribution of Russian Refugees Throughout Regions
of the Russian Federation** (February 15, 1992; in thousands)

	Number	Percentage
North Caucasus	22.2	51.1
Central Black Soil zone and adjacent regions of non–Black Soil zone	6.0	13.8
Central and northwestern parts of the Russian Federation, including Moscow, St. Petersburg, and environs	8.7	19.9
Ural and Volga regions	3.6	8.4
Other regions	3.0	6.8

that many refugees who initially went farther north changed their minds and migrated to the south of the Russian Federation, or returned to their former places of residence. Twenty percent of the refugees were Russians. The Russian refugees settled more evenly than members of other nationalities. For instance, the concentration of Russians in the North Caucasus is much less than that of members of other nationalities (see Table 13.2).

An analysis of the statistical data on migration within recent years makes it possible to reveal the following migration trend: while in the late 1980s the distribution of migrants between towns and villages was still proportional to the urban and rural population of the regions to which they moved, since the early 1990s the additional influx of interrepublican migrants changed this ratio in favor of the countryside. This is even more true as far as refugees are concerned. The reason for this is that it is comparatively easier to procure a flat or a house and find a job in the countryside. This can also be explained by the policy of the Russian government.

Let us now discuss factors affecting the adaptation of migrants and refugees in the regions of Russia.

The importance of the normal adaptation of Russian migrants is self-evident.

(1) Spontaneous migration is dangerous, for it could lead to the revival of the administrative-distributive system. To all but deprive a great number of migrants and refugees of any rights and means of subsistence is to create a breeding ground for low labor productivity, social deviations, the destabilization of the family, and political extremism.

(2) Spontaneous migration can retard the normal development of economic relations. It may lead to a further surplus in the labor force; at some new stage of its development the Russian economy is bound to be faced with the phenomenon which hampered its development in the 1930s and the 1960s—surplus labor. In such a situation it is more profitable to employ ten unskilled workers than to introduce a single advanced technology. The fact that it is not yesterday's peas-

ants but yesterday's engineers who will find themselves unemployed only aggravates social tension.

(3) The migrants and refugees who fail to adapt create social tension in all spheres of public life. It is not by chance that the regions of highest concentration of migrants and refugees are alongside large cities, the places from which the greatest number of people go abroad. For instance, if in 1990 only 300 people went abroad from the Smolensk region, the number for the Krasnodar territory was twenty times greater, although the population of the latter is only 4.3 times that of the Smolensk region.

These current problems cannot be resolved without taking past experience into account, for, as has already been pointed out, the present migration situation is only a continuation of tendencies of the last ten or fifteen years—the same categories of the population migrate and they are faced with the same problems. The appropriate legal questions should be resolved first of all.

It is not easy to define the legal status of refugees and forced migrants within the territory of the former USSR, for it is not as yet clear whether those who resettle within the territories of independent states under the effect of either a potential or actual threat to their security should be considered refugees or displaced persons. The problems leading to their migration, and often the very act of migration, occurred from the legal point of view within the framework of one state, which means that forced migrants might be viewed only as displaced persons. However, after the official repudiation of the Union Treaty, they appeared to be refugees. As of May 1992 in Russia there were no legal norms for the definition of the status of a refugee or a displaced person. In recent years the government has adopted separate regulations aimed at somehow defining these notions, but they are hardly sufficient.

Up until 1990 there existed the category of "planned migrant," that is, a person who changes one place of permanent residence for another together with his or her family with the help of the state authorities. As a rule, the new residence was in a region with a shortage of labor. The destination was determined by Resolution No. 364 of the Council of Ministers of the USSR of May 31, 1973. The state guaranteed the new settlers rather significant privileges: free housing or interest-free loans for the purchase of housing; a large free advance grant which in the late 1980s amounted to three to five thousand rubles per family; and discounts for fuel, electric power, and scarce goods. That was how many Russian-speaking people migrated from Central Asia and other regions with a surplus of labor. The same is true of the resettlement of the Meskhet Turks in 1989. However, since the early 1990s this practice has been halted and the term "planned migrant" gave way to "forced migrant" in official terminology. The first document of this type was the resolution of the Council of Ministers of the USSR of April 7, 1990, "On Measures to Assist Citizens Forced to Leave the Azerbaijan and Armenian Republics." This resolution was connected with specific events and its provisions were not applicable to refugees and migrants from other regions. Moreover, since it was adopted by the all-Union government it envisioned financial assistance from the Union budget for refugees. As this budget is now practically nonexistent, it is not clear what should be used in its stead for the financing of the settlement of refugees in the territory of Russia.

At present (May 1992), an agreement with the republics, as members of the Commonwealth of Independent States, is being drafted according to which the states responsible for mass emigration of a population forced to leave their places of residence because of ethnic, religious, or social affiliation must, at least partially, finance their resettlement in new regions. In addition, two basic resolutions of the Council of Ministers on this question are in force in the territory of Russia: the Resolution of June 19, 1990, "On Additional Measures for Rendering Assistance in the Settlement of Refugees Arriving in the Russian Federation," and of November 22, 1990, "On Measures to Assist Refugees and Forced Migrants." Still, these two resolutions fail to clearly define the status and rights of refugees, and it remains the prerogative of the local bureaus of the Ministry of the Interior actually to confer refugee status. These bodies usually used as a criterion the very fact of the departure of a certain family from a region of interethnic conflicts. In principle, the resolutions guarantee a person the right not to be deported back to the place of former residence, the right to cash compensation for lost housing and personal property, the priority right to purchase scarce goods and housing, and the right to a job. However, in the present situation the guarantees of these rights, especially property rights, seem rather vague and will remain so until a respective agreement with the states is reached.

To ease the process of migration, it is necessary to provide migrants with proper economic and legal support not only at their destination, but also at their point of origin. This refers primarily to the right of ownership, both collective and personal, for it is precisely the violation of this right by government agencies of former union republics that makes this problem so intractable. In particular, an agreement should be reached with the republics on compensation not only for housing but also for collective—especially collective-farm—property. All-Union conventions and legal acts are required which would ensure the rights of all ethnic minorities living in the territory of former union republics to use their natives languages in educational, social and business intercourse, to form cultural societies, and observe national holidays—that is, acts and conventions precluding political and economic discrimination.

Two decades of experience in organizing interregional migration have demonstrated that the three different categories of Russian and Russian-speaking migrants formerly living among people of other nationalities (peasants, recent migrants who have preserved ties with Russia, and those who have virtually become part of the indigenous populations of Central Asia, Transcaucasus, the Baltic region, etc.) have adapted in quite different ways. Those from the third category encountered the most difficulties. Their percentage is especially great among the Russians of the Transcaucasus, a little bit less in Central Asia,

Table 13.3

Responses to the Question: "Do You Want to Leave the Village (Town) Where You Are Now Living?" (in %)

	Dukhobors	Refugee Meskhet Turks	Planned migrants	Unplanned migrants
Would like to leave:				
The town	0	34	28	12
The country	0	42	33	10
Have not decided yet	10	17	11	14
Don't want to leave	90	8	27	63

Kazakhstan, and Moldova, and the smallest in the Baltic cities. It was this category that tried to avail themselves of planned migration measures undertaken in the 1970s and 1980s. But those who have preserved personal ties with people in Russia preferred to migrate using their personal connections. So how did the adaptation proceed in the later period and by what factors was it influenced?

To supply an answer to this question a group headed by the author studied the process of adaptation of various categories of migrants in the villages and small towns of some regions of Central Russia (Tula, Smolensk, Ivanovo, Belgorod, Orel, Voronezh, Novgorod) and in the Amur region in the period from 1983 to 1991. For comparison, the data of the survey of the Meskhet Turks are given.

Among the main indicators of successful adaptation is a low migration outflow among the settlers. A rough conclusion can be drawn from the answers to the question on personal intentions which was studied in the course of an ethnic-sociological survey (see Table 13.3).

As can be seen from Table 13.3, the best adapted are the Dukhobors—Russian peasants from Georgia who in 1990 formed a compact settlement in the territory of the Tula region. Second place is occupied by those migrants who moved with the help of personal connections and who made preliminary arrangements before leaving. The last group consists of so-called "planned migrants" among whom the third category of the potential migrants prevailed—Russian-speaking people from Central Asia and Azerbaijan. The situation is the gravest in the case of the Meskhet Turks who were settled in central Russia after the tragic events of 1989 and almost all of whom would like to leave their present places of residence and settle in Georgia or elsewhere in a compact settlement. The survey data are borne out by the objective overall picture of adaptation: for planned migrants the countryside serves as a kind of a springboard on their way to a town. That is why 30 percent of them leave their new homes within the first two months after their arrival; 50–60 percent leave within a year. In two years not more than 15–20 percent of them remain. These data are similar in other regions of the non–Black

Table 13.4

**Correspondence of Present Living Conditions to Expectations
Among Various Categories of Migrants** (in %)

	Dukhobors	Planned migrants	Migrants upon agreement*	Unplanned migrants
Complete	27.9	21.1	36.8	32.3
Partial	55.8	15.8	42.1	52.3
None	16.3	63.2	21.1	15.4

* With a collective or state farm.

Soil zone and the Far East, where many migrants from Turkmenistan went. The lower estimation of living conditions by planned migrants compared to those who migrated on their own does not mean that the conditions in which the latter found themselves were much better; it only shows that the expectations of the former were much higher. Although those who migrated on their own accord did not enjoy all the privileges the planned migrants received from the state, their attitude toward their living conditions in new places of residence was more sober-minded (see Table 13.4).

What are the ethnic and social factors which brought about such different results from planned and unplanned migration? Why did those people on whose adaptation the state spent much less grow accustomed to their new way of life more successfully, compared with those who cost the state rather dearly? Those Russians who lived among people of other nationalities assimilated the culture and behavior patterns of the latter. For instance, the Russians who moved from Uzbekistan to the Ivanovo region appeared to be more hospitable, diplomatic, and easygoing. At the same time they were more shrewd and could better hide their true attitude, especially if it was unfavorable. When asked whether there is a difference between the Russians living in Uzbekistan and the rural Russian population of the non–Black Soil zone, 54 percent of the respondents from among the planned migrants said that there was a very great difference, 25 percent that the difference was slight. Seventy-five percent of those who noticed these differences had a negative attitude toward the local population, considering the Central Asian Russians more culturally developed and better behaved.

The realization of a gap in cultural levels did not result from language difficulties. All the migrants without exception—at least those who had become accustomed to their new places of residence—had a good command of the Russian language. For the majority of them it was their mother tongue.

In the opinion of the author, one of the main factors is the difference in the structure of personal ties and, consequently, the different social and psychological milieus in which migrants from different categories find themselves. All other conditions being equal, those who migrated as a member of a close-knit group managed to adapt more easily than those who found themselves in a strange social environment. One of the first successful experiments in this field was the organization of the "Tashkent" State Farm in the Novgorod region, which for many years succeeded in maintaining a level of population stability, even though its members were all Russian-speaking migrants from towns in Central Asia, making them the most unstable among potential migrants. The reason for its success lies in the fact that the members of the collective were selected through personal channels, from people who knew each other well. Indeed, success has been achieved despite the fact that the workers and employees of the "Tashkent" State Farm got no privileges as a consequence of planned migration.[2]

It is interesting to note that the principle of compact settlement was spontaneously used by migrants of the 1990s. For instance, by April 1992 among the applications for resettlement to the Voronezh region was one submitted by 161 families; 38 applications were from three to five families.

Another striking example of compact resettlement is the migration of Dukhobors. For thirty years now, Dukhobors and members of other ethnic-religious groups of Russians have gradually been leaving the Transcaucasus. The Dukhobors have succeeded in finding a place similar to the area where their group was formed in the late eighteenth–early nineteenth centuries, prior to their resettlement in the Transcaucasus. In this way they have managed to preserve their economy and the daily life they have been accustomed to for the last two centuries. In Georgia they lived in the mountains at an altitude of 2,000 meters where climatic conditions are more severe than in the Tula region where over a thousand Dukhobors are living (February 1991), now united into two economic units.

Soon, it seems, the organized migration of another ethnic-religious group from the Transcaucasus should be expected—the Molokans, who now number in the tens of thousands. In all, there are about half a million Russians belonging to stable ethnic-religious groups that may return to Russia—enough to organize successful agricultural production in five or even seven regions.

At present two types of organizations deal with the adaptation of migrants and refugees: (1) State establishments ("migration" committees, regional migration centers) that take the "charity" approach—gifts of money and housing, assistance in finding jobs, etc. At present some of the refugees live in young pioneers' camps, holiday hotels, and rest homes. They are given apartments on a priority basis. Still, such an approach can only slightly reduce the negative consequences of migration, and is on the whole ineffective, so the above-mentioned organizations are now looking for a new approach to the problem. (2) Independent organizations formed in various republics over the last two or three years. Currently there are about two dozen of them. They try to find housing for the migrants and reduce the flow of refugees. They attempt to operate on a commercial basis, establishing for this purpose a network of small businesses that engage not only in job placement, but also in setting up new production facilities and service establishments, using migrants as labor. They also search for jobs abroad. Among these organizations mention should be made of the Emigration Society in Tallinn, Migration Societies in Dushanbe and Baku, the Committee of Russian Refugees in Moscow, and others. Their work is hampered by the unpredictability of the economic situation in Russia.

Many migrants and refugees see the solution to their problems in the construction of their own compact settlements with diversified economies. There were several attempts of this kind, such as the one in the Kaluga region in the village of Bariatino. This one failed because the migrants considered the village to be too remote and because of the exorbitant prices of construction services and materials. The same causes underlie the failure of certain ministries and departments that have been eliminated (for instance, the USSR ministries of power engineering, hydraulic construction) to build settlements and relocate their former employees there. Others found themselves without any resources at all, which makes it virtually impossible for them to solve the problems of their employees working in the former republics of the USSR.

Success of adaptation depends largely on the migrants' professional profile. The fact that the majority of migrants are urban dwellers has been one source of social tension. Surveys of potential migrants to Russia showed that at least 70–80 percent of them planned to go to the cities. Now the situation has changed. According to data from the Employment Center of the Voronezh region, only 10 percent want to live and work in towns or cities, with the rest eager to engage in farming. However, the list of trades the future farmers possess is rather indicative: 14 percent are engineers, 12 percent are teachers, and 4 percent are members of intellectual trades who would have difficulty finding suitable employment in the countryside. Even such specialists as accountants, economists, machine tool operators, and electricians would have difficulty in finding jobs, for the supply is much higher than the demand in the countryside. Machine operators, construction workers, agricultural workers and specialists, and workers in the food and processing industries altogether constitute 30–35 percent of potential migrants. The same conclusions could be made after studying completed application forms at the Tallinn Labor Exchange (December 1990–May 1991). From among almost 300 families who wanted to move to Russia or Ukraine, 83.2 percent preferred to go into farming and only 16.8 percent asked for accommodations in a town. This means that potential migrants from outside Russia are now voluntarily agreeing to lose their qualifications partially or completely and to radically change their way of life. However, it should be kept in mind that for some of them, the countryside is only a stepping-stone.

The settlement of migrants in rural districts is bound to make the question of ownership of land even more urgent. As our surveys have demonstrated, the ratio between individual farmers and nearby collective farms will be a major factor on which the attractiveness of certain regions in European Russia for migrants depends. Different categories of migrants have varying attitudes toward the expediency of

Table 13.5

Attitudes of Locals and Two Types of Migrants to the Prospect of Setting Up a Private Farm (in %)

	Locals	"Dispersed" migrants	"Compact" migrants (Dukhobors)
Would like to	18	33	50
Would like to in general but prefer to wait a bit	3	4	12.5
Would not like to under present conditions	17	12	12.5
Resolutely against	36	20	12
Never thought about it	26	31	12

Source: Surveys conducted in the Smolensk, Tula, Ivanovo, Voronezh, and Belgorod regions; about 800 respondents altogether.

setting up a private farm. This is borne out by the data of the sociological survey.

As can be seen from Table 13.5, the local population, compared with migrants, is much less oriented toward establishing individual farms. This means that in some places migrants wishing to set up their own private farms would meet with the opposition of the local residents. One should also not rule out the possibility of competition over land between the local people and the migrants.

Finally, to determine the efficiency of organizational measures, it would be wise to know on whose help the migrants themselves rely. A survey conducted by *Literaturnaia gazeta* in October 1990, answered by over 220 people from various regions of ethnic conflicts in the USSR (95 percent of them Russians), yielded the following results. Of all the respondents 59.5 percent either did not answer this question or said that they could count only on themselves; 24.5 percent hoped various government organizations of Russia and the Soviet Union (which still existed at the time) would help them out; 11.2 percent relied on *Literaturnaia gazeta* and public organizations; 4.9 percent thought their ministry or department would help. According to the data of our 1991 survey, 79 percent of the respondents, both Russians and representatives of other nationalities, answered that they relied in their migration to Russia only on themselves or their relatives and friends; only 21 percent relied on state and local government agencies; and not a single person mentioned public organizations. When asked whom they would ask for help should the need to migrate arise again, only 12 percent of migrants and 13 percent of those who had received assistance from the state said that they would agree to that a second time. The overwhelming majority of both would have relied only on themselves.

Since the organizations now operating are highly inefficient, it is necessary to set up a Migration Investment Bank of Russia to issue credits on favorable terms, as well as commercial establishments that would provide migrants with housing and find jobs for them. This bank could also issue credits on favorable terms for the purchase of land for building settlements for migrants, or buy the land itself, for today such land is quickly sold out.

3. Conclusions

The following may be concluded:

(1) The departure of the Russian-speaking population from regions of inter-ethnic conflicts started long ago. It was done in part officially, by ministries and departments, and in part as "planned" migrations into the countryside of Russia. Although there are no "planned" migrants now, the phenomenon should be studied so as to better understand current problems.

(2) In order to determine the best organizational measures for proper adaptation, it is necessary to study the specifics of the various categories of migrants. Most difficult is the adaptation of Russian-speaking people who formed urban local subcultures of their own in various regions and who lost their Russian roots. In the view of the author, a successful adaptation strategy should be based on the following principles: economic expediency and a commercial approach; the creation, by employing the skills of the migrants, of advanced branches of the economy based on capital investment; a combination of state organization and personal initiative; a compact settlement in Russia and the formation of local subcultures; and maximum employment of migrant labor potential. However, it is obvious that it would be impossible to adhere strictly to these principles. The greatest damage would be done, and is already being done, to labor potential due to the inadequate use of highly skilled specialists.

(3) Analysis of the available data demonstrates that the structures now emerging, both state and independent, have a negligible effect on the solution of migration problems due to their economic insolvency.

(4) The destiny of the migrants will depend largely on the way economic relations develop in the territory of Russia.

Notes

1. Estimates have been made on the basis of current statistics, which are not completely reliable.
2. Their occupational composition did not meet the priorities of the Russian economy.

14

Religious Attitudes of Russian Minorities and National Identity

Natalia Dinello

One of the most disturbing findings obtained in surveys of Russian minorities is the predominance of Russians' negative perception of the social environment as conflict-ridden and insecure. An overwhelming majority of respondents in the Baltics and Central Asia (68.1 and 81.2 percent, respectively) acknowledged "national hostility toward Russians in the street, in transport, in queues, and in other places." "Recent negative changes in attitudes toward Russians" was indicated by 51.2 percent of respondents in the Baltics and 65.6 percent of respondents in Central Asia. The public notion of the illegitimacy and immorality of the new social order was evident in the prevailing view that the criminal mafia was the most influential political force.

Marked anxieties due to intolerance, animosity, and ambiguity of norms were exacerbated by the lack of confidence in new social institutions. In a survey conducted in August–September 1991 by the Center for the Study of Public Opinion, public distrust was directed not only at the discredited institutions of the fading Soviet Union but also at newly emerging democratic organizations. Although the evaluation of the "Movement for Democratic Reform" was significantly more positive in the Baltics than it was in Central Asia, "complete trust" of this movement in the Baltics was expressed by only 27.3 percent of Russians, and in Central Asia by only 18 percent. By comparison, confidence in the military in Central Asia was expressed by 35.1 percent of the respondents.

With the confidence vacuum in society, the only institution that inspired considerable trust among Russian minorities was the Russian Orthodox Church. On the eve of the collapse of the Soviet Union, "complete trust" in the Russian Orthodox Church was expressed by 45.3 percent of respondents in the Baltics, 44.4 percent in Ukraine, and 43.8 percent in Central Asia. In this respect, there are no significant variations among three designated regions of the former Soviet Union, although religions of titular majorities are different (the Baltics are domi-

Table 14.1

Religious Attitudes of Russian Minorities (percentage of all respondents)

	Baltics	Ukraine	Central Asia
Complete trust in Orthodox Church	45.3	44.4	43.8
No trust in Orthodox Church	6.1*†	7.7*	8.9
Acknowledge belonging to Russian Orthodoxy	36.1***	31.7***†	41.3***
Acknowledge non-religiousness	41.5***	54.7***	41.7***
Profess Orthodoxy as criterion of "Russianness"	5.9***†	2.6***†	11.6***†
Religiosity as a quality of Russians	5.5	7.7	7.3
Religiosity as a quality of titular majority	22.3***†	8.7***†	36.4***†

Notes:
* p ≤ .05, ** p ≤ .01, *** p ≤ .001;
† absolute value of standardized chi ^{2} residuals ≥ 2.0.

nated by Protestantism and Catholicism; in Ukraine, Uniate Catholicism and Russian Orthodoxy prevail; and all social life in Central Asia is permeated by Islam).

Public trust in the Russian Orthodox Church was also demonstrated by other surveys. A study of religious attitudes conducted in 1991 by the Russian Center for Public Opinion Studies on the territory of the Russian Federation (3,000 respondents) showed that 62.6 percent of participants in the survey either "entirely" or "in general" trusted the Russian Orthodox Church, while only 6.9 percent distrusted it. The Russians' present trust of this religious institution even surpasses the confidence in organized religion on the part of Americans, who are often considered by sociologists to be the most religious in the civilized world. According to NORC-ROPER social surveys, in 1991 36.8 percent of Americans indicated "a great deal of confidence" in organized religion; in 1988 this view was expressed by 20 percent, and in 1983–87 by 28 percent of Americans on the average.[1]

The dominant trust of the Russian Orthodox Church on the part of Russian minorities raises a question regarding the general religiosity of Russians in the former republics of the Soviet Union. As is evident from Table 14.1, religious attitudes revealed by the survey of Russian minorities contain contradictory messages.

"Religiosity" as a quality of Russians was designated by a small minority of respondents (no more than 7.7 percent); there are no significant variations among the three analyzed regions. "Professing Orthodoxy" as a criterion of "Russianness" was also indicated by a small number of respondents, although regional variations are significant in this case (Russians in Central Asia are twice as likely to choose this option than are Russians in the Baltics—11.6 and 5.9 percent, respectively). However, "belonging to Russian Orthodoxy" is acknowledged by a considerable portion of respondents (41.3 percent in Central Asia, 36.1 percent in the Baltics, and 31.7 percent in Ukraine).

Similar contradictory findings were obtained from the study "Soviet Man," conducted in 1989 by the aforementioned Center for the Study of Public Opinion, with more than 2,700 respondents from various republics of the Soviet Union, including 1,510 Russians. According to this survey, 34.6 percent of Russian respondents admitted that they "never thought about God," and 20.5 percent asserted that "God does not exist." At the same time, 35 percent of Russians identified themselves as Christian.

In a 1991 study of religious attitudes of Russians, 66.6 percent of the respondents revealed that they "never attend religious services," 71.2 percent confessed that they "never pray," and 86.5 percent indicated that they "did not obtain a religious education," or, in other words, were not socialized into religion. This pattern differs significantly from the American pattern of religious expression. According to the World Values Survey conducted during the 1980s, the rate of church attendance in the United States (percentage who attend religious services at least once a month) was 60 percent; 98 percent of Americans acknowledged their belief in God; 83 percent described themselves as "a religious person," and over 90 percent gave God high ranking from the point of view of importance in their lives.[2]

The disparity between Russians and Americans in regard to religious attitudes highlights two puzzles:

(1) A larger proportion of Russians (including those representing Russian minorities) than Americans acknowledge a "complete trust" of organized religion. However, the overwhelming majority of Russians neither attribute "religiosity" to their nation nor follow religious rituals and rules, while Americans both admit their religiosity and confirm it by religious practices.

(2) A significant segment of nonobservant Russians nevertheless claim that they "belong to Russian Orthodoxy."

The first enigma can be solved by reference to a gap in confidence in society, which was characteristic on the eve of the breakup of the Soviet Union and persists in the post-Soviet period. In an atmosphere of sharp criticism of, and public discontent with, both the Soviet past and current experiments in social transformation, the Russian Orthodox Church emerges as the only social institution that had no involvement in either the establishment of the Soviet regime or the mistakes and failures of perestroika. The swift onset of public disillusionment with modern social arrangements which followed the period of euphoria produced a drift of trust away from political institutions and toward organized religion. Hence, the trust of the Russian Orthodox Church is rooted in its relative political neutrality and in the prevailing public distrust of other social institutions, symbolizing not only a vote "in favor of," but also a vote "against."

The second enigma requires a more delicate inquiry into the nature of religiosity and the meaning of belonging to Russian Orthodoxy. Of course, it is impossible to embrace in this paper all facets of this vast and challenging theme, but several points are appropriate. First, religiosity cannot be confined to formal indicators of practicing religion. It was the early observation of Tocqueville that a certain number of Americans pursue a particular form of worship from habit more than from conviction. Theodor Adorno and his colleagues demonstrated that the traditional Christian values of tolerance, brotherhood, and equality are more firmly held by people who do not affiliate with any religious group.[3] According to the contemporary research of Ronald Inglehart and his colleagues, the question of how important God is in one's life constitutes a most sensitive indicator, explaining twice as much of the variance in acceptance or rejection of traditional Judeo-Christian norms as does church attendance.[4]

Therefore, internalization of religious values does not necessarily imply regular church attendance or membership in a particular religious denomination. Nonreligiosity in the sense of nonadherence to conventional patterns of religious practices does not signify a lack of spirituality.

Building on the first argument, it is important to understand the connotation of spirituality not supported by formal religiosity. Feodor Dostoevsky's maxim "He who is not Orthodox cannot be Russian" signifies an almost definitional link between religious and national identity in the Russian intellectual tradition. Both opposing streams in Russian thought—Slavophiles (who proclaimed an absolutely unique route for Russia) and Westernizers (who insisted on joining Western civilization)—claimed that Russian Orthodoxy is the foundation of the Russian spiritual type. In the contemporary debate on the means of de-Sovietization of Russia, Roman Szporluk designates the Orthodox Church as the only authentically Russian institution that represents a pre-Soviet Russia.[5]

Assessments based upon both Russian intellectual tradition and a Weberian sociological approach can be plausibly applied to the interpretation of the findings of the survey of Russian minorities. It can be argued that the relatively frequent indication of "belonging to Orthodoxy" on the part of Russian minorities does not specify the religious affiliation of respondents as much as it represents their cultural and national self-identification. Conversely, the "gaps" in internalization of religious values due to the fact that several generations of Soviet people were not socialized into religion are compensated by the emphasis upon secular cultural criteria of national identity. This provides cues to explaining the inconsistencies of religious attitudes among Russian minorities: self-identification as a Russian Orthodox is not always supported by self-perception as a religious person (Table 14.1); cultural criteria of Russian national identity prevail over purely religious criteria (Table 14.2).

As is evident from Table 14.2, participants in the survey of Russian minorities were more inclined to choose cultural criteria of Russian identity (language, traditions, belief in a great future for Russia, moral ideals) rather than "profess-

Table 14.2

Criteria of Russian National Identity (percentage of all respondents)

	Baltics	Ukraine	Central Asia
Professing Orthodoxy	5.9***†	2.6***†	11.6***†
Russian by descent	43.2***†	37.0***†	49.4***†
Consider self Russian	36.2	39.0	36.3
Russian according to passport	7.4***†	19.6***†	14.9***†
Russian as native language	34.5***†	20.2***†	28.4***
Maintaining Russian traditions	24.5***†	14.7***†	19.4***
Belief in a great Russian future	10.3*	4.6***†	10.7***
Sharing moral ideals of Russia	10.3*	9.7*	7.6*

Notes:
* p ≤ .05, ** p ≤ .01, *** p ≤ .001;
† absolute value of standardized chi ^{2} residuals ≥ 2.0.

ing Orthodoxy" as criteria of "Russianness," confirming tendencies registered during the 1970s and 1980s. This general trend did not overshadow regional variations in views. Respondents in the Baltics selected language and traditions as criteria of Russian identity relatively more often, while Russians in Central Asia were more likely to point to religious criteria. Analogously, there are more Russians in Central Asia who acknowledge their "belonging to Russian Orthodoxy" (41.3 percent) than in the Baltics (36.1 percent) or particularly in Ukraine (31.7 percent).

Interpreting regional variations in religious and national self-identification, it is relevant to imply that awareness of religious feeling depends upon the juxtaposition of the images "we" and "they." Since the nation asserts and maintains itself by constant self-definition in interaction with aliens, "mirror images" play an important role. The significance of mutual exchange of national stereotypes cannot be underestimated. The image of religious aliens is likely to encourage a stronger emphasis on one's own religious identity and influence the degree of importance attributed to Russian Orthodoxy. This is demonstrated by the dichotomy "Central Asia/Ukraine." Russians are more likely to define themselves in religious terms when surrounded by the Muslim ethnicities of Central Asia than by the Christian titular majorities of the Baltics or Ukraine. Russians are more likely to assert their belonging to Russian Orthodoxy and to select religious criteria of national identity if they perceive a titular majority as religious (Central Asia) rather than nonreligious (Ukraine).

In Central Asia "religiosity" as "a widespread quality of the titular majority" (see Table 14.1) was indicated by 36.4 percent of Russian respondents, while in Ukraine only 8.7 percent of Russian participants in the survey attributed this stereotypical feature to the titular majority. Correspondingly, in Central Asia, where Muslim doctrine is pervasive throughout secular life and Russians' aware-

Table 14.3

Religious and Cultural Criteria of "Russianness" as Predictors of Identity
(by logit regression)

	Effect on Odds			
	Russian identity		Soviet identity	
	"Russianness" as main value	Preference for Russian citizenship	Soviet Union as "our country"	Preference for Soviet citizenship
Orthodoxy as a criterion	1.80***	1.23	.78*	.68***
Cultural criteria	1.14*	1.41***	1.23**	1.13*

Models: Chi ^{2} = 26.69 Chi ^{2} = 26.29 Chi ^{2} = 12.76 Chi ^{2} = 21.15
    p = .000 p = .000 p = .002 p = .000

* p ≤ .05, ** p ≤ .01, *** p ≤ .001

ness of the "religiosity" of titular majorities is higher, the religious orientation of Russian minorities is also more pronounced. In Ukraine the similarity of the major Christian religions and the weak religious loyalties of Ukrainians as perceived by Russians partly explain their relative religious indifference and the emphasis on cultural criteria of Russian national identity. The survey of Russian minorities showed that the solution to the dilemma "broad cultural versus religious identity" does not follow any uniform rule. Variations in religious attitudes among Russian minorities in the Baltics, Ukraine, and Central Asia display different patterns of potential response to the universal necessity of negotiating a new place for Russians in their new minority position. In some cases the religious factor can eventually become a leading one; in other cases cultural values of spirituality apparently outweigh distinctly religious values.

A detailed analysis of public attitudes toward religious and cultural criteria of "Russianness" was performed using the technique of logit regression. The results provide evidence that professing Orthodoxy is a stronger and more reliable predictor of Russian identity versus Soviet identity than the combined cultural criteria (Table 14.3). According to the survey of Russian minorities, the choice of Orthodoxy as a criterion of "Russianness" increases the odds of agreeing with the rather strong statement "The fact that I am Russian is of main value to me!" by 80 percent, and the preference of Russian citizenship over Soviet citizenship by 23 percent.[6] Consistent with these findings, the indication of the same religious criteria of "Russianness" decreases the odds of selecting the Soviet Union as "our country" by 22 percent and the preference of Soviet citizenship by 32 percent.

In contrast with the religious criteria, the effect of cultural criteria upon na-

Table 14.4

Religious Self-Identification as a Predictor of Identity (by logit regression)

| | Effect on Odds | | | |
| | Russian identity | | Soviet identity | |
	"Russianness" as main value	Preference for Russian citizenship	Soviet Union as "our country"	Preference for Soviet citizenship
Belonging to Russian Orthodoxy	1.42***	1.06	.80**	.83**
Orthodoxy as a criterion	1.51**	1.29*	.83	.65

Models: $Chi^2 = 38.38$ $Chi^2 = 5.84$ $Chi^2 = 10.44$ $Chi^2 = 31.03$
$p = .000$ $p = .05$ $p = .005$ $p = .000$

* $p \leq .05$, ** $p \leq .01$, *** $p \leq .001$

tional identity is ambiguous. Their selection favors both Russian and Soviet identity. This finding is related to the fact that the development of the Russian cultural heritage was never before confined to the territory of the Russian Federation. The Soviet Union represented a universal cultural space in which Russian culture proliferated. The disintegration of the Soviet Union divides this all-encompassing cultural space and gives rise to Russians' regrets over cultural losses. In this context it is understandable why the emphasis on the cultural criteria of "Russianness" is connected with a now-obsolete Soviet identity.

The consistency of religious self-expression in promoting Russian identity is also demonstrated by the results of another regression model (Table 14.4). The acknowledgement of "belonging to Russian Orthodoxy" increases the odds of favoring strong Russian identity (an agreement with the statement "The fact that I am Russian is of main value to me!") by 42 percent, while decreasing the odds of identifying the Soviet Union as "our country" by 20 percent and indicating preference for Soviet citizenship by 17 percent. The choice of professing Orthodoxy as a criterion of "Russianness" displays a similar effect upon the odds of national self-identification, as in the regression model presented in Table 14.4: selection of religious criteria favors Russian identity and suppresses Soviet identity.

The above analysis of religious and cultural criteria of national identity gives clues to the interpretation of Russians' religious orientations and their relation to cultural priorities. Shedding light on the interconnectedness and mutual reinforcement of religious and cultural criteria of "Russianness," this analysis, however, reveals their specificity. The elaboration of the "religion and/or culture" theme also raises the question of national identity, examining "religious" versus "cultural" solutions to the problem of self-definition of Russian minorities.

The problem of national identity of Russians originates in the loss of identity of the Soviet social system. The whole set of values which constituted "the Soviet way of life" has been sharply criticized and all but repudiated. The ensuing dissolution of the Soviet Union signifies not only the collapse of social institutions but also a territorial split and the rupture of cultural tradition. For the first time in Russian history, Russian minorities are separated from the center. This results in a crisis of national identity. The sense of belonging is disturbed and confused, lacking firm ground for its reformulation. Soviet identity is outdated by the very fact of the breakup of the Union. Russian identity seems to be inherent to Russians by virtue of their descent. However, as is revealed by the survey of Russian minorities, self-evaluation as a Russian is not confined to a simple reference to descent; it involves contemplation of cultural foundations of national identity. Molding of republican identity also reflects a complicated pattern. The logit regression model demonstrates that public trust of political institutions and democratic movement in the republic significantly encourages republican identity of Russian minorities, while the assessment of social environment as hostile discourages it.

Soviet identity absolutely dominated in the minds of Russians in the Soviet period. On the average, 80 percent of Russians consistently considered the Soviet Union their motherland. This constituted a specific feature of Russians, distinguishing them from other nationalities of the USSR. Sociological surveys conducted during 1970s and until the middle of 1980s registered a conspicuous gap between Russians and non-Russians in their perception of their motherland. While an overwhelming majority of Russians associated themselves with the Soviet Union, the majority among titular nationalities in the areas where nationalistic feelings were pronounced (Estonia, Georgia) named a republic instead.[7]

In August–September 1991, Soviet identity still persisted among Russian minorities: 61.6 percent of Russians in the Baltics, 81.8 percent in Ukraine and 87.5 percent in Central Asia designated the Soviet Union as "our country." Russian identity was also strong: 47.7 percent of Russians in the Baltics, 40.9 percent in the Ukraine, and 53.6 percent in Central Asia agreed with the statement: "The fact that I am Russian is of main value to me!" However, more respondents in the Baltics expressed their preference for republican citizenship over Soviet or Russian citizenship (48.5 percent versus 9.5 and 21.9 percent), and 60.4 percent of Russian participants in the survey indicated their firm intention to remain in the republic (in comparison with 6.4 percent who planned to move away). The shift from Soviet to republican identity when practical decisions have to be made was also prominent in Ukraine: 73.1 percent of Russians intended to stay in the republic and 33.4 percent favored republican citizenship. In contrast, Russians in Central Asia were for the most part not willing to accept republican identity (only 18.2 percent were ready to become citizens of the republic, while 24 percent made a decision to move away from the republic).

The regression analysis provides evidence that cultural considerations of Russian minorities favor both Soviet and Russian identity, while religious orienta-

Table 14.5

Cultural and Economic Criteria of "Russianness" as Predictors of Identity
(by logit regression)

	Effect on Odds			
	Russian identity		Republican identity	
	"Russianness" as main value	Preference for republic citizenship	Republic as "our country"	Intention to stay in the republic
Economic criteria	.62**	3.71***	2.16**	5.64***
Cultural criteria	1.71**	.20***	.19***	.26***

Models: Chi ^{2} = 16.69 Chi^2 = 104.76 Chi^2 = 55.29 Chi^2 = 120.33
     p = .000 p = .000 p = .002 p = .000

* p ≤ .05, ** p ≤ .01, *** p ≤ .001

tions unequivocally encourage Russian identity. The question remains: what causes the drift from Soviet and Russian identity to republican identity when national self-definition is molded in pragmatic terms of citizenship and place of residence? How is this shift explained, while rather idealistic perceptions of self-association with a certain territory or nation support either Soviet or Russian identity? This question cannot be clarified entirely on the basis of cultural and religious foundations of identity, requiring an incorporation of the economic factor (Table 14.5).

In the regression model in Table 14.5, respondents' perception of living conditions in the republic as "better" compared to Russia are used as an economic criterion of the choice of national identity. Evaluation of Russians in the republic as "more educated and cultivated" than other nationalities serves as a broad cultural criterion. According to the results of logit regression, the cultural component of the model appears to be a good predictor of Russian identity, increasing the odds of favoring agreement with the statement "The fact that I am Russian is of main value to me!" by 71 percent. At the same time, the evaluation of Russians in the republic as "more educated and cultivated" than other nationalities discourages the development of republican identity in all its dimensions. In comparison with cultural criteria, the effect of the economic factor upon pragmatic choices of national identity is significantly stronger. The perception of conditions of life in the republic as "better" compared to Russia increases the odds of identifying the republic as "our country" 2.16 times, of preference of republican citizenship 3.71 times, and intention to stay in the republic 5.64 times. Therefore economic considerations of Russian minorities can impact crucially their acceptance of republican identity, particularly their decision to continue living in the republic.

Examination of potential options for and factors of identity-construction, of course, cannot overshadow the obvious fact that there exist limits of identity alterations. John Armstrong writes of "the strength of boundary mechanisms—semiotic or phenomenological 'border guards'—simultaneously reassuring the group member of his identity and deterring him from defection."[8] One's inclination to assume a new national identity can be severely constrained either by the lack of receptivity of conventional bearers of this identity or by the rejection of the change on the part of other members of the group.

The purpose of this paper is to discuss the grounds for national identity of Russian minorities in their own understanding. Of course, the development of republican identity can be seriously constrained by anti-Russian orientation of the titular majority and its discriminatory policy toward Russians. Of course, since the USSR no longer exists, self-identification with the Soviet Union is currently no more than an atavism, although self-identification with a new, succeeding totality is quite plausible. But before looking at the ultimate outcome of identity-negotiation it is necessary to study the initial preferences for national self-identification of Russians, and to compare religious, cultural, and economic criteria of their self-definition.

It was shown that economic criteria are particularly important for pragmatic decision making in regard to citizenship and place of residence, favoring republican identity if the conditions of life in the republic are evaluated as "better" than in Russia. On the contrary, religious and cultural orientations are instrumental for the preservation of idealistic ties with Russia in either their Russian or their broader "pseudo-Soviet" versions. Religious self-expressions unambiguously endorse Russian identity. These conclusions can be useful in dealing with the current crisis of identity of Russian minorities. Taking root in the fall of the Soviet Union and the dramatic rejection of the Soviet social system, this crisis is constantly exacerbated by the confidence gap, loss of meaning and purpose in life, and the deficit of legitimate national symbols and myths following renunciation of the previous myths. This destroys the sense of cohesion of Russian communities and complicates relationships with titular majorities, which have already been aggravated to the extreme. In this situation, penetrated by animosity and nihilism, religious aspirations of Russian minorities can be construed as a means toward the alleviation of anxiety and as an attempt to fill the spiritual and cultural vacuum.

The survey of Russian minorities, meanwhile, demonstrated that their religious attitudes are contradictory, revealing a lack of experience of socialization into religion. Cultural and economic factors play a no less important role in the construction of national identity than religious orientations do. While deeply interwoven into the cultural fabric of society, religious orientations are, however, less amorphous and less flexible than cultural priorities, displaying a stronger and more stable potential for the maintenance of Russian identity. The lack of feasible alternatives for withdrawal from the crisis of national identity can make a religious approach attractive, at least to those Russian minorities which perceive the titular majority as religious, relatively less cultivated, and less economically developed than Russians. This approach corresponds to the emphasis on Russian identity and the underdevelopment of a republican identity.

Notes

1. *General Social Surveys, 1972–1991: Cumulative Codebook*, NORC-ROPER, July 1991, pp. 198–200.

2. Ronald Inglehart, *Culture Shift in Advanced Industrial Society* (Princeton: Princeton University Press, 1990), pp. 187, 190, 200.

3. *The Authoritarian Personality* (New York: Harper & Brothers, 1950), pp. 219–20.

4. Inglehart, *Culture Shift in Advanced Industrial Society, p. 185.

5. Roman Szporluk, "The Imperial Legacy and the Soviet Nationalities Problem," in L. Hajda and M. Beissinger (eds.), *The Nationalities Factor in Soviet Politics and Society* (Boulder, San Francisco, & Oxford: Westview Press, 1990), p. 12.

6. Odds are the ratio of the probability an event will occur to the probability of nonevent.

7. L.M. Drobizheva, "Etnicheskoe i istoricheskoe samosoznanie narodov SSSR na rubezhe poslednego desiatiletiia XX veka," *Dukhovnaia kultura i etnicheskoe samosoznanie* (Moscow: Institut etnologii i antropologii, 1991), vyp. 2, pp. 75–76.

8. J.A. Armstrong, "The Autonomy of Ethnic Identity: Historic Cleavages and Nationality Relations in the USSR," *Thinking Theoretically About Soviet Nationalities* (New York: Columbia University Press, 1992), p. 26.

IV

Conclusion

15

The Future of Russians in the New States of the Former Soviet Union

Emil Payin

After the collapse of the Soviet Union, Russians in the former union republics were faced with three choices: to fight for the restoration of the Union and consequent preservation of their dominant role as imperial minority, to emigrate from the new states, or to adapt to new political conditions and reconcile themselves to their new status of ethnic minority.

The failure of the August 1991 coup in Moscow all but crushed the hopes of those who wished to remain an imperial minority. The political organizations and "intermovements" that supported the idea of restoring the empire were disbanded, and the centers that coordinated the activity of intermovements and other political forces aimed at the forced restoration of the imperial state ceased to exist (at least legally). Among the latter were the Communist Party of Russia, the "Soiuz" parliamentary group in the USSR Supreme Soviet, and, evidently, some of the departments of the KGB and other specialized services. But most important of all, Russia's foreign policy does not give grounds for illusions of renewed empire, at least in the foreseeable future.

According to the estimates of demographers, including contributors to this volume, the number of immigrants to Russia from former union republics could reach from 2.3 to 5 million by the year 2000. Thus, even according to the most pessimistic forecasts, the number of Russian migrants would not reach more than 20 percent of all the Russians now living in the new independent states of the former Soviet Union, which means that the majority of them will have to adapt to the way of life of an ethnic minority in new sovereign states.

It is no simple matter to sort out the factors promoting and impeding the adaptation of Russians in the republics of the former Soviet Union. For instance, while political and legal conditions such as language and civil rights laws are less favorable for Russians in Estonia and Latvia than in the states of Central

Asia, the exodus of Russians from the Baltic states is much less intensive than from the southern states.

However, it is possible to distinguish certain historically stable signs of favorable or unfavorable conditions for the adaptation of Russians in other ethnic areas.

Since the 1960s, when the system of state regulation of migration flows became less rigid, the Eurocentrist tendency among Russian migrants became more pronounced. Since then and up to 1991 the percentage of Russians in the population of the European republics steadily grew. At the same time their percentage of the population in the Transcaucasian and Central Asian republics and Kazakhstan began to decrease (in the latter case, since the 1970s).

Among the most sensitive indicators of the real state of interethnic relations is the number of ethnically mixed marriages. During the entire Soviet period the number of such marriages (where one of the spouses was Russian by nationality) was highest in Ukraine and Belarus, rather high in other European republics, and the lowest in the republics of Central Asia and Kazakhstan.

If we factor in Russians' level of knowledge of the language of the titular nation we can develop a provisional scale of the regional conditions most favorable for the adaptation of Russian minorities.

These parameters indicate that Russians, as might be expected, adapt best in Ukraine and Belarus. There they enter into marriages with members of the titular nations almost as frequently as with the people of their own nationality. Naturally, Russians, Ukrainians, and Belarusians easily understand each other's language. The outflow of Russians from these republics is still less than the inflow, so there is no question of an "exodus" of Russians from East Slavic republics. But it must be kept in mind that although the historic kinship of peoples is an extremely important factor for the adaptation of people in a foreign ethnic milieu, the example of Serbs and Croats shows that in a certain political situation such tolerance can give way to prolonged interethnic hostility. More often than not such a radical change in the character of interethnic relations results from unilateral changes in the national structure or territorial claims. Neither of these factors has as yet violated the mutual ethnic and cultural affinities of Russians and Belarusians. Russian-Ukrainian relations have deteriorated due to disputes over the Crimea, the Black Sea fleet, and other issues, but as yet there have been no fundamental changes in the mutually tolerant type of these relations.

In descending order, most favorable conditions in European Russia for the adaptation of Russians are found in the Baltic states, Georgia, Armenia, and Moldova.

No matter how vocal the national radicals of the Baltic states are about "migrant-invader" Russians and no matter how hysterical the Russian national-patriots are about the "genocide" of Russians in the Baltic region, there basically remains a high degree of cultural compatibility between the Russian minorities and the majority of the populations in these states. According to the surveys of the Center for the Study of Public Opinion, only certain social groups of Russians experience extreme psychological discomfort in the Baltic states. As a rule these people have lived there only for a short period of time, do not know the language of the titular nation at all, and are isolated from the local population informationally, politically, and in everyday life. They are mostly workers of enterprises formerly of Union provenance, officials of Soviet, economic, and party bodies, and the military—in other words, those categories of the Russian population that were personally affected by the national-state transformations in the Baltic states. At the same time, it should be pointed out that openly discriminatory laws on language and citizenship adopted in Latvia and Estonia have had a pronounced detrimental effect on Russians' adaptation in the Baltic region.

The percentage of Russians in Georgia and Armenia was the lowest among the republics of the former Soviet Union. At the same time, almost half of the Russians living there were born there and about a quarter had roots stretching back several generations. This testified to a high degree of adaptibility of the Russian minorities in both republics. Up until recently relations between Russians, on the one hand, and Armenians and Georgians, on the other, did not give grounds for concern. Moreover, in the percentage of mixed marriages with Russians, Armenians were surpassed only by members of East Slavic peoples. Today, however, both republics are involved in acute interethnic conflicts and, although Russians are not party to them, these conflicts indirectly aggravate the position of Russians.

According to sociological surveys and statistical data, Moldova has the worst conditions for adaptation of Russians of all the European regions. The reason for the strained relationships between Russians and Moldavians lies in the situation in the Dniester region, among other circumstances. Nevertheless, Moldova ranks somewhere in the lower middle with respect to conditions for the adaptation of Russians.

The most unfavorable conditions for Russian minorities are in the Caspian region, which includes Azerbaijan, Chechnia, Dagestan, and the republics of Central Asia. This region accounts for 80 percent of all the Russian immigrants entering the Russian Federation. For instance, in one year (1991) over 90,000 Russians left Tajikistan alone. Obviously, a sharp increase in the migration of Russians from this region was caused by interethnic and internal political conflicts. However, Russians began to leave the cities of this region even before the flare-up of acute interethnic conflicts, so that the ratio between the inflow and outflow of Russians began to change in favor of the latter back in the 1970s. Thus, migration of Russians from this region had already become a trend. This region is also characterized by the lowest percentage of Russians with good command of the language of the titular nation and of mixed marriages. Moreover, the existence of a social distance between Russians and members of the titular nations is borne out by the fact that the majority of Russians are urban citizens, while the local population are mostly rural dwellers.

There is no doubt that the majority of Russian migrants come from Central Asia. Social and political instability verging on complete political chaos and an armed conflict in Tajikistan unparalleled in the number of its victims forced the majority of Russians and Russian-speaking people to leave this republic. Next on the scale of adverse conditions is Kyrgyzstan, where interethnic relations unfavorable to Russians have taken shape despite the liberal-democratic course of President Askar Akayev and his personal tolerance for various ethnicities. Russians are orientated toward migration in the rest of the Central Asian republics as well.

In the period of communist construction projects, forced industrialization, and accelerated urbanization the state could ignore ethnic distances between peoples, sending alien parties of workers to various regions with unfavorable conditions for adaptation. But life takes its own course and sooner or later the structure of the ethnic settlement should have reverted to its natural proportions, with Russians returning to Europe. It is quite another matter that these natural restoration processes are developing in troubled times and assuming the distorted forms of forced migration and refugees.

To some extent the process of adaptation of Russians is also hampered by such consequences of imperial mentality as the lack of desire to learn the language of the titular nation and insufficient tolerance of the Russian minorities toward national culture and the way of life of the ethnic groups on whose territory they live. But the authors in this book have proved that there is a tendency toward a radical change in conservative imperial attitudes. The number of Russians who have mastered the second language is steadily growing. The children of those who arrived in union republics comparatively recently have a better command of the local language than their parents do. In almost every republic the percentage of Russians who support its independence has significantly increased.

Almost everywhere Russians in the republics have been turning into special distinct ethoses with special interests and values and unique ways of life that differ not only from those of the ethnic majority but also from those Russians living in Russia.

The political self-consciousness of these Russians is evolving and they are developing cultural and political centers in the newly independent states. These institutions are not only the means of ethnic self-preservation of Russians and their political self-defense; they also play an important part in the system of Russians' political communication. Russians use their parties, movements, and representatives in the parliament for constructive cooperation with the government, the ethnic majority, and other ethnic minorities.

Unfortunately, the political self-consciousness of Russians is still not sufficiently developed and the majority of them act as an amorphous mass with no positive objectives, increasingly suspicious and predisposed to nonconstructive actions.

At the same time, it seems that the main factor retarding the process of adaption of Russians today is not so much their own mentality as the radical-nationalistic position of the government in many republics.

In many of the new independent states the ethnic majority has not yet overcome the ethnic minority complex from which it suffered during the imperial period. That is why many laws adopted in some of these states are not so much acts of ethnic self-defense as instruments of aggression against national minorities, primarily Russians, who are still considered to be the fifth column of the metropolitan state. Such discrimination makes Russians more suspicious and politically active. Global experience proves that segregation promotes interethnic discord and leads to acute interethnic conflicts. Such a policy is suicidal for small states, especially those as weak both ecologically and politically as the former Soviet republics. It is in their interests to involve the ethnic minorities into the life of the new states as quickly and as fully as possible, to make maximum use of their intellectual and labor potential, and to guide them toward the achievement of common civil objectives. Naturally, this requires real equality of rights for all citizens irrespective of nationality and broad representation of all ethnic communities in power structures. In other words, what is needed is a policy of ethnic cooperation, not hostility.

Index